FANTASTIC INVASION

ALSO BY PATRICK MARNHAM

ROAD TO KATMANDU

FANTASTIC INVASION

NOTES ON CONTEMPORARY AFRICA

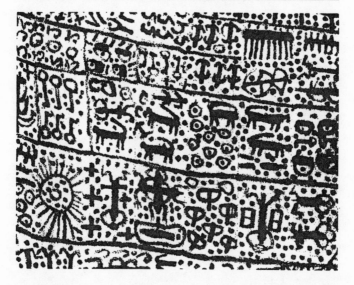

PATRICK MARNHAM

HARCOURT BRACE JOVANOVICH
NEW YORK AND LONDON

Requests for permission to make copies of any part of the work should be mailed to: Permissions, Harcourt Brace Jovanovich, Inc., 757 Third Avenue, New York, N.Y. 10017.

The author wishes to thank the following publishers for permission to quote from the sources listed:

Andre Deutsch Ltd.: *In a Free State* by V. S. Naipaul. Copyright © 1971 by V. S. Naipaul. Published in the United States by Alfred A. Knopf, Inc. Reprinted by permission of the publishers.

Doubleday & Co., Inc.: *God's Bits of Wood* by Sembene Ousmane. Translated by Francis Price. Copyright © 1962, 1970 by Doubleday & Company, Inc. Reprinted by permission of the publisher.

Faber & Faber, Ltd.: *Africa Dances* by Geoffrey Gorer. Copyright © 1935 by Geoffrey Gorer. Published in the United States by W. W. Norton & Co. Reprinted by permission of the publishers.

Indiana University Press: "Africa's Plea" by Roland Tombekai from *Poems from Black Africa*, edited by Langston Hughes. Copyright © 1963 by Langston Hughes. Reprinted by permission of Indiana University Press.

Set in Linotype Caslon

Printed in the United States of America

Library of Congress Cataloging in Publication Data

Marnham, Patrick.
  Fantastic invasion.

  Includes bibliographical references.
  1. Africa, Sub-Saharan—Description and travel. 2. Africa, Sub-Saharan—Politics and government. 3. Africa, Sub-Saharan—Social conditions. I. Title.
DT352.M38   967   79-2763
ISBN 0-15-130301-0

FIRST EDITION

B C D E

HBJ

CONTENTS

To C. S. C.

The high stillness (*of the forest*) confronted these two figures with its ominous patience, waiting for the passing away of a fantastic invasion.

Joseph Conrad, *Heart of Darkness*

INTRODUCTION

This book is concerned with some of the independent
states of Africa, the countries south of the Sahara and
north of the Zambezi, which took self-government a generation ago. Here one can see the fate of Africa after
the colonial era, and here one may even find the beginning of understanding.

For the outsider who enters Africa, the governing
dream has always been to change the place. The models
for such change have been drawn from "the North"—
that is, from the nations of Europe, Asia, and America
that lie between the thirty-fifth and sixtieth parallels—
where the corn comes from.

I have divided this account of the relationship between
the North and Africa into three parts. "East Africa"
describes the newest recruits to the fantastic Northern
pageant which continues to cross the African landscape.
"West Africa" displays the phenomenon of Northern
aid and development as a form of warfare. "Parallel
Africa" examines the often secret resistance put up by
the new countries of the entire continent to this implac-
able process of interference.

As the North has penetrated Africa, it has proved less
and less capable of learning from the experience; we can
only instruct. Even the anthropologists, who originally
approached their subject in the spirit of pure inquiry, are
increasingly willing to place their knowledge at the disposal of governments or international companies whose
objectives are less than detached. The North justifies its
pedagogy by characterizing the African as ignorant, un-

educated, or impoverished. At the same time it has found in Africa "a refuge from the intellect" or an invitation to indulge in stupidity and dishonesty on its own account. It becomes increasingly difficult for us to explain the prolonged frustration of Northern plans in terms of "backwardness" or "isolation." Much of Africa has had close contact with the North for six hundred years and the African characteristics that have survived such long exposure are not going to be eliminated now.

African resistance to the North takes many forms. But its constant purpose is surely to reject the alien uniformity which the North strives to impose on the unnerving variety of African life. The North finds this variety unnerving because it challenges the necessity for the progress, control, authority, and research with which we order our lives. We fear Africa because when we leave it alone, it works.

PART 1

EAST
AFRICA

THE FANTASTIC INVASION

The realisation that he is white in a black country, and respected for it, is the turning-point in the expatriate's career. He can either forget it, or capitalise on it. Most choose the latter.

Paul Theroux, "Tarzan Is an Expatriate,"
Transition 32

CHAPTER 1

COUNTING
ALL THE ELEPHANTS

I saw a gigantic beast called the karkadan, or rhinoceros, which grazes in the fields like a cow or a buffalo. Taller than a camel, it has a single horn in the middle of its forehead, and upon this horn Nature has carved the likeness of a man. The karkadan attacks the elephant and, impaling it upon its horn, carries it aloft from place to place until its victim dies. Before long, however, the elephant's fat melts in the heat of the sun and, dripping down into the karkadan's eyes, puts out its sight; so that the beast blunders helplessly along and finally drops dead. Then the roc swoops down upon both animals and carries them off to its nest in the high mountains.

The Second Voyage of Sindbad the Sailor

The most famous wild elephant in the world lived in the mountain forest of Marsabit and was called Ahmed. He was remarkable for the beauty of his tusks. They descended almost to the ground in a graceful curve, and their slender points were sharp at the tip and slightly raised. Ahmed was protected from danger by special presidential decree. He was a symbol of all the remaining animals running wild in Kenya, and as such he was of some importance to both the science and the business of supervising elephants. It would have been a very serious matter if the president's wishes had been ignored and Ahmed had been poached. Everywhere he went through the forest of Marsabit he was followed by two armed forest rangers. When he left the safety of the mountain reserve and wandered off into the surrounding desolation, which was divided up into hunting blocks, his guards went too. Because of this, his position was always known to the local authorities, and he became accustomed to people. He was very easy to photograph, and every tourist who came to Marsabit wanted to see him. Thousands of visitors even made the uncomfortable trek hundreds of miles away from their usual haunts in order to view this singular beast.

But one night Ahmed died. The rangers who watched him said that he had been looking unwell for several days, although to most people he looked normal. On his last evening Ahmed and two younger bull elephants, his "acolytes," left the grassy slopes where they had been grazing in full view of the tourists and disappeared into the forest for the night. The rangers disappeared after them, on foot. The only description of Ahmed's last hours was supplied by one of these rangers. He said that during the night Ahmed grew weak. At one point he staggered, and to save him from falling the two bulls supported him until they reached a group of large trees. Ahmed rested against these trees for six hours at an angle of forty-five degrees. Then his acolytes departed. In the morning Ahmed, still at an angle of forty-five degrees, was examined and found to be dead. Later the ranger who produced this description admitted that he had made it all up. He had not actually seen Ahmed during the night because he had been at home in bed.

As soon as Ahmed's body was found, the alarm was raised, and a party of elephant experts was flown up from Nairobi. These included a professional hunter, the head of the department of national parks, and several game wardens and conservationists. Since Ahmed had died deep within the forest, a special road had to be cut through the trees for several miles, and after walking along this, the official party eventually reached a clearing where no fewer than twenty-five rangers were gathered around a fire.

At the edge of the clearing was Ahmed. There was a

septic wound in his side, but the experts were not sure
whether or not he had been poached. For the time being
they were unable to decide how he had died, and so, after
a brief discussion, all but one of the party set off again
for their airplanes, guided through the forest by a child
who was wearing a T-shirt with a slogan on it that read
"Support your local animal." Almost as soon as they left,
the cool glade began to fill with flies and blood and the
smell of an elephant carcass. For the man left behind
was Wolfgang, Nairobi's leading taxidermist, and he had
started skinning. There had been another presidential
decree. Ahmed was going to be stuffed.

Nobody has ever counted all the elephants in Africa.[1]
Despite the concern about their declining numbers, they
still inhabit regions so vast and remote, and travel such
distances, that the task is impossible. And when approximations are made, the sense of concern about the elephant's survival is not always reinforced. A continental
survey carried out in 1977 discovered a population of
81,000 elephants living in an enormous park in southern
Tanzania which was found to have been omitted from all
previous estimates.[2] Nor, if the objective is to obtain exact
information rather than to increase the sense of concern,
is counting elephants any more rewarding. In 1966 a plan
to shoot 2,700 elephants in Tsavo National Park (in
order to gain more information about the effects of over-
crowding, which could presumably be used to assist the
survivors to avoid being shot in another such experiment)
was abandoned in the face of public disapproval. Five
years later a drought in the same park caused the death
of about 6,000 elephants from among the overcrowded
population. So one of the classic battles of the elephant
industry developed: the biologists declared that the
subsequent die-off in the drought had vindicated their
"heartless" demands for a control operation, and the
conservationists argued that it was a mistake to interfere

in the natural process and that to shoot 2,700 elephants that were within the protection of a game reserve was grotesque. Perhaps both sides were right, and both sides were ridiculous. One year after the drought the population of elephants within the park had restored itself to its previous level, a mystery that has never been explained.

But although the African elephant cannot be numbered, it can be profitably managed, or farmed, and the profession of elephant farmer already has several branches. It is, like all modern farming, both a science and a business, but the first elephant farmers were neither scientific nor very businesslike. They were the first white hunters who put their skill out to rent and who invented the elephant as an object of value beyond the natural value of its meat or tusks. For them the elephant was a beautiful and dangerous trophy which their clients could pursue and destroy, though never to the point of the extinction of the species. Reflecting on this problem in 1903, Captain Richard Meinertzhagen noted the activities of an African hunting tribe in his *Kenya Diary*. "My tent was pitched close to a deserted Dorobo encampment. These people live by hunting, and it was clear that they had had good sport in the neighbourhood. The ground was strewn with the heads of rhino, in all twenty five skulls, impala, zebra and bushbuck. . . . It convinced me of the amount of harm these people must do to game, but they are fast dying out, which is a blessing."[3] "It is a pity," he noted later, "that an intelligent creature like the elephant should be shot in order that creatures not much more intelligent may play billiards with balls made from its teeth."

Meinertzhagen, dining off a wild duck he had shot and roasted, found that he had slaked his own bloodlust and decided that others, too, should be prevented from killing, so he proposed the first game reserve, where the animals would be protected from the attentions of unlicensed hunters. Sportsmen might still enter the reserve and kill regulated numbers of game, but uncontrolled killing must cease. And so the interests of the native and the expatriate hunter were instantly opposed. A new principle, that of regulated slaughter unrelated to need, was imported, the offense of elephant poaching was invented, and the second class of elephant farmer was conjured into existence, the game warden.

The theoretical basis of elephant farming rests on the belief that the species is in danger of extinction. The controlled reserve, the earliest form of elephant farm, is presented as an institution for preserving the existence of creatures in their wild state. The paradoxical nature of this proposition is effectively disguised by the atmosphere of crisis which is essential to the well-being of the farm. Nobody actually knows how close the extinction of the elephant may be because it is impossible to discover the number of animals alive today, let alone compare it with the number that existed in the past. So, in the absence of knowledge, approximations have to serve. Since no one disputes that the total number of elephants in Africa is diminishing, the approximations are increasingly pessimistic. And as their numbers shrink, the remaining animals acquire a new importance; and as their value rises, so does the number of people who are able to make a living out of them, the elephant farmers. It should even be possible today to produce a completely new elephant number, the *optimum* number of elephants in Africa; that is, the lowest number of elephants commensurate with both the continued survival of the species and the employment of the highest number of elephant farmers. The fewer animals that are left, and the greater the sense of crisis, the more people around the world there will be to take an interest in the problem and the more there will be employed in supervising and stimulating that interest. If, by some terrible calamity, elephant numbers were to be reestablished on their old flourishing level, elephant farming would immediately collapse.

But this is unlikely to happen soon. At present the

elephant is being drawn into greater competition with man for the use of land. It is losing this competition partly because of its inability to hide. And if its numbers are not to diminish even faster, it must be assisted. The African elephant's chief competitor is the African cultivator, and insofar as the elephant industry exists to defend the elephant from the penalties of losing this competition, the expatriate elephant farmers are themselves in competition with the African crop farmers for the use of African land.

A properly constituted convention of elephant farmers would include specialists from every branch. At the bottom of the table would sit the original member, the unevolved figure of the professional hunter, now holding the humblest status in the elephant-farming world. The hunters like to kill elephants. Sometimes the elephants kill them. This is not the latest approach, but the primitive and universal excitement of the hunt is still an important part of the elephant's value. Even the most sentimental tourist is partly attracted to wild animals, from the supposed safety of his bus, because they are dangerous. And even the most exsiccated biologists exchange stories of the risks they run in their unarmed quest for information.

On almost as low a level as the professional hunters are the game wardens, disarmed hunters in spirit, many of whom spent much of their earlier lives hunting and whose duties include hunting even today. Next are the conservationists, whose essential task is to raise funds by publicizing the most tenuous possibilities of animal extinction. Their motto, that man the conservationist "holds the fate of all creatures in the palms of his uncertain hands,"[4] is a little embarrassing to their more sophisticated colleagues; but it is good for public relations, and from the industry's point of view, the conservationists have one irreplaceable quality: their activities in the interests of wildlife cause as many problems as they solve and so ensure a steady flow of new work all around. Above the conservationists are the ecologists, a surprising number of whom now represent private commercial interests. They differ from conservationists in that while the latter wish to preserve wilderness, the ecologists are more concerned with the most efficient way of managing wildlife; they can be quite scornful, for instance, of the idea of a crude game reserve. At the top of the table sit the biologists, usually the ecologists of the future who have not yet fallen because they are still able to obtain funds from university departments. Their first task is to guarantee the scientific purity and high seriousness of what might otherwise appear to be a gathering of boy scouts and fire chasers.

The meeting would be chaired by the wildlife administrators—that is, by the only people who are native to the country in which it takes place. Their governments own the elephants, and if they merely responded to popular opinion, they would have been unlikely ever to have set up a single game park. The game park is not an African notion. The parks have always been unpopular with the people of Africa, and the governments of Africa are sufficiently responsive to popular feeling to avoid such disruptions where possible. It is likely that given free expression, African opinion would be hostile to every assumption that united the other interests present. But a convention of elephant farmers is hardly a forum for the free expression of African opinion, the most eloquent record of which is to be found in the annual poaching figures.

For the elephant farmers, as for most Northerners in Africa, human life is an obvious threat to wildlife. The only relationship the two can enjoy is one of fierce competition. Everything in the Northern experience teaches this. If wildlife is to survive in close proximity to humanity, there must be rigorous supervision and expert control. If necessary, the people and the animals must be prized apart physically, and if the animals are to be destroyed, this must be done in a duly authorized manner and to the enrichment of the industry. Nor is the destruction of wildlife in this rational fashion ever referred to as killing. The appropriate word is *control*.[5] But control (a euphemism in the finest Northern tradition, as expressive as the old-fashioned hunters' term for wildlife, *game*) is in itself a threat to the survival of the elephants. For instance, the official figures for Kenya show that in 1960, 329 elephants were "controlled": shot on the orders of the game authorities. But by 1971, at which time the elephant population was said to have been enormously reduced by poaching, the number of elephants that died from "control" had risen to 448.[6]

To achieve the required degree of "control," enormous areas of Africa, particularly in Kenya and Tanzania, have been set aside as game reserves. The Tsavo National Park in Kenya, only one of a dozen, is the size of Wales or Massachusetts; the Selous Game Reserve in Tanzania is twice that size. And in the interests of elephants, it has even been suggested that much larger areas will soon be needed. It used to be thought that an elephant population might range over anything between 20 and 1,500 square miles, depending on the amount of food the land contained. Among elephant farmers, that passed as a respectable approximation, and such assumptions determined the existing size of the African game reserves. But more recently the ecologists have suggested that elephants extend their range over a period of several hundred years through an area so vast that none of the present national boundaries of Africa could contain it. In other words, an elephant game park, if it were not to imprison its inhabitants within crippling bounds, would have to be capable of containing a species whose behavior apparently rivals that of humans in its scope and complexity—a prospect to daunt the most ambitious park planner. For a start, the suggestion that game reserves might have to be extended across international borders poses serious political problems for African governments which are finding the burden of the existing conservation schemes too heavy to bear. It is already apparent that in imposing the present plans, they are not responding to any indigenous demand. And they are aware of the suggestion that game reserves are no more than an attempt to rearrange Africa along lines that are preferable only to expatriates.

The natural state of humans and wild animals everywhere is a chaotic jumble.[7] In Africa this state of chaos is still visible. The creatures tend to mingle with the people, living each off the other, coming and going, their numbers fluctuating in an undisciplined fashion; so before the animals can be controlled, they must be separated and placed in an area from which the human inhabitants have been removed. Then the people can be directed to take the place vacated by the animals. Such interference in human freedom clearly demands another neutral technical term, in this case *translocation*.

Some animals that carry a greater value because of their supposed rarity are "translocated" over exceptional distances. In the 1960s there was a general feeling that the scarce white rhinoceros was a threatened species, and so two thousand white rhinos were hoisted into aircraft and flown from South Africa, the country in which they had until then survived, to the supposed safety of game parks farther north.[8] The process by which an unsuspecting rhinoceros can be interrupted in its daily habits, attacked in the center of the territory which it has painstakingly marked out with a trail of urine and feces, rendered unconscious, bound, and then airlifted to a distant wilderness—there to be released and encouraged to resume the daily grind—is swift, extremely expensive, and as unmarred by self-criticism as the building of the Ark. But it has very little to do with preserving a species from extinction; rather is it a simple assertion of human authority. Translocation tidies the shelf and displays the conservationist's collection to greater advantage, and with the translocation of elephants it reaches its greatest heights of extravagance. Here is a species that is still too numerous to count; nonetheless, whole herds of elephants have been translocated around Africa, regaining their freedom in an area of forest superficially identical to the one in which they were anesthetized, but this time, if only they knew it, enjoying the benevolent protection of, perhaps, President Mobutu of Zaire.

When it is too difficult to translocate animals, it is usually possible to do it to humans instead. Many of the game reserves were originally cleared in this way. The misery that resulted is long forgotten, but the recent experience of the Ik people of Uganda is a reminder. In 1958 farsighted men working for the colonial administration declared a remote part of northern Uganda to be a game reserve. The country already had two large reserves, but the new site was chosen to complement them and to provide a balanced sample of "the extraordinary diversity of the country as a whole." The valley of Kidepo was described as a place of "wild, thirsty plains scored by waterless sand rivers and fringed by wooded hills, arid for the most part but relieved by stretches of pleasant savanna in favoured areas." Kidepo was consequently ruled off, the animals were protected from human pursuit by armed rangers, and a lodge was erected for tourists. What the farsighted men had ignored was that these wild, thirsty plains were the hunting grounds, or meat larder, of the people of Kidepo, the Ik. Now, with their unrivaled view over the pleasant savanna from their "primitive settlements on the fringe of wooded hills," the Ik were in a unique position to count the seventy-odd mammals and two-hundred-odd bird species known to occur on the plain, while they starved to death.

The anthropologist Colin Turnbull, who described this

event in his book *The Mountain People,* concluded that
the only hope of saving the two thousand remaining
members of the Ik tribe was to retranslocate them all in
trucks to southern Uganda, where they could be re-
educated as farmers. (In the event, the Ugandan authorities did not adopt this suggestion, and the Ik remained
on their hillside—still undernourished, their numbers
declining, and their behavior toward one another de-
teriorating from its former standards, but refusing to
leave their own country, even in that extremity.) In the
absence of any action the predicament of the Ik can be
expected to continue, and that corner of the African
shelf, if untidy, is at least still occupied, however pain-
fully. "Luckily the Ik are not numerous . . . so I am
hopeful that their isolation will remain as complete as
in the past until they die out completely," wrote Turnbull in 1972, unconsciously echoing the words of Meinertzhagen, on the Ndorobo in 1903: "The amount of
harm these people must do to game, but they are fast
dying out, which is a blessing." Turnbull, the moralist,
viewed the possibility of the Ik's extinction as fortunate
in view of the evil nature of the society that they had
developed in response to their crisis. Meinertzhagen, the
adventurer, was merely concerned for the future of
the animals. But from the point of view of the Ik and the
Ndorobo their predicament was the same. Both tribes
were identified as a threat to wildlife, although the people
of both tribes depended for their whole existence on the
survival of wildlife. Both were consigned by conservationists to possible extinction. Both illustrate the penalties of separating people from wildlife and of believing
that it is in the best interests of the latter that it should
be controlled.

In fact, the practice of conservation through game
reserves is largely irrelevant to animal survival. Even
today the greater part of Africa's wildlife survives outside the reserves, and the reserves have played no

significant part at all in averting the threat of extinction for any save a very small number of genuinely threatened species.

There is one group of people whose activities evoke the disapproval of both conservationists and African governments and whose rights can therefore be violated without causing any political problems. They are the nomadic pastoralists, such as the Masai; to deal with them, a different solution has been found. Since nomads are in a continual state of "self-translocation," the way to control them is to restrict their movement rather than to increase it, and in Tanzania a refinement has been added to the usual conservationist armory. Whereas game reserves exclude only certain human activities, such as unlicensed hunting, and national parks exclude most activities essential to intelligent life, the Ngorongoro conservation unit is a flexible mixture, avoiding an unacceptable degree of exclusion but permitting a complete degree of control in specified areas. The unit takes in the Ngorongoro Crater in northern Tanzania, an extinct volcano that has evolved into a refuge for wildlife and stretches for more than one hundred miles of grassland as far as the Serengeti National Park. These three districts—the crater, the conservation unit, and the park —cut right across the essential migration routes of the Masai pastoralists. At first the Masai were excluded from all three, but this proved impossible to enforce since the Masai are not a weak tribe as are the Ik. So a "conservation unit" was created between the crater and the park in which they were once again permitted to graze, although, to save official face, the grazing is supposedly supervised by conservation officers. But when the Masai get to the lip of the crater, and can see the grassland which they traditionally reserved for use toward the end of the dry season when the surrounding food supply was exhausted, they are forbidden to go any farther.

Instead, they are permitted and encouraged to station their children as an attraction for the tourist buses at the point where the track (which their own herds made) plunges down to the abundance below.

The Ngorongoro Crater, with its lakes and plains and streams and woods, certainly supports an unusual variety of creatures, and until recently these included man, in the form of pastoralists. But it is now such a highly controlled area that no one may enter it except by a government bus. Such strict entry regulations would be impossible to enforce in most parks because they are far too big to fence. But Ngorongoro needs no fence. There are only two tracks into it, both spattered with boulders and easily supervised. So man can be totally excluded except on license.

The African crater came to an end when the Masai, who had enriched its life, were banished from it. Now that has been succeeded by the European crater, empty of man as an inhabitant, but seething with man as a day tripper. Even the light aircraft that deliver the tourists are forbidden to fly around the crater lest they disturb the natural environment, but nothing could be more forced than the pretense that Ngorongoro is in some way preserved from human influence. The magnificent display of unspoiled nature is as artificial as a safari park in the grounds of an English stately house, because without man as pastoralist or hunter there is nothing "natural" about the balance that is so painstakingly conserved.

The people who created Ngorongoro, insofar as anyone created it, did not do so by admiring the landscape or by understanding the effects of their actions. They did it by experiencing nature and, where necessary, submitting to it. The Masai without the grass of the game reserves will eventually be reduced to the level of the Ik, snatching the food from the mouths of their own children. The life of the crater, bereft of the impact of man pursuing his own survival, is also threatened. The conservationist who banishes man from the Ngorongoro landscape is as adept at reproducing a real landscape as a painter who paints only in sunlight. Without rain the painter's trees will eventually fall down, and then, if the illusion of summer is to be preserved, they must be propped up again, their bark retouched, and their dead leaves glued on and sprayed a lifelike shade of green.

Time and again in African parks steps have had to be taken to prop up the trees, to redress the crisis that has arisen as a result of isolating an area from African influence in an attempt to preserve it. In an isolated game reserve such as Ngorongoro human intervention is considered necessary when animal numbers, through lack of competition, rise to the point where the balance will shortly redress itself in the form of mass starvation. At that point the conservationist acts. He has long out-lawed tribal hunters and trophy hunters. Now he offers his own solution, the control hunter: himself. For the banished Masai, who lives off his cattle and never hunts even for food,[9] the spectacle of the control shoot in Ngorongoro or Serengeti or Mara national parks must be confirmation of the dim-sightedness of the game con-servers, the foreign men who spend their lives gazing in rapture across the land and seeing nothing at all.

Whereas the conservationists demand bigger and bigger game reserves, the ecologists are beginning to oppose the idea of game reserves altogether. They do so, however, with a very different end in view from that foreseen by the Masai. The ecologists have discovered that the natural range of elephants is governed by rainfall and may follow regular cycles and that their movements in search of food across known vegetation patterns in themselves have a significant effect on the spread of vegetation. Therefore, they argue that it is not helpful to cage elephants within a reserve without understanding the factors governing their range and without appreciating how the balance of vegetation in the areas they inhabit, or are prevented from inhabiting, will be affected. Their proposal is to remix the game and agriculture together in an entirely new form, the game ranch. This suggestion fills the conservationist with an instinctive sense of horror. It is industrialization by sleight of hand, the tame death of wildlife. If the farmer is taught how to live with the game, how long will it be before he insists on entering the game reserve? Unfortunately for the conservationists, the ecologists are supported by the high priests of the profession, the biologists. Wild buck convert pasture into protein more efficiently than cattle. And the more species that are allowed to use a pasture, the more efficiently that pasture is used. The utilization of vegetation by wild animals is always more efficient than the most intensive form of beef ranching. The "best" meat herds are herds of wild buck. To the biologist the conservationist's beloved Eden, the game reserve, is a much-admired but unused protein plant. The game ranch is also potentially lucrative, not a point to escape the ecologist with his professional interest in the least detail of the organic experience, any more than it would be overlooked by the African administrator. And the industry's constant element, control, would also, of course, be present. The entire savanna, with its mixture of cattle and game, would be as closely controlled as a fattening station, and it is late in the day for the conservationists to object that such a degree of supervision over African grassland is alien and possibly destructive.

But what would happen, on a game ranch, to the experience of communing with nature in a wilderness, to that "spirit which lives in the wilds," the search for which has always been the true motivation of the conservationist? If wildernesses can no longer be justified as places where animals can be protected, how long will they survive as areas where the conservationist can resort to refresh his battered soul?[10] How much official

cooperation for that private purpose can the conservationist expect? Even for the conservationist to ask for it
is to reveal himself in his true colors, as a man not
concerned to protect the diversity of species so much
as one concerned to defend the individuality of himself
and as someone so ill attuned to the world he shares
that he wishes to refashion it in a shape from which
everyone else is excluded.

Now and again the elephant farmers have to pay a fee
for the license they have been granted to manage one of
Africa's most valuable resources. It is part of the agreement they have struck with the national governments
that they should never be seen to be in charge of wildlife, and, to assist this part of the deal, it is sometimes
politic that they should clearly be seen to be under orders.
So the elephant farmers will offer up a scapegoat from
among their number, and this role invariably falls to the
junior branch of the industry, the professional hunters.
The hunters are well suited to this task. Their pursuit is
widely unpopular among the tourists, who provide so
much of the industry's revenue, and they are also unpopular among the African officials because in the course
of their work they are always stumbling on evidence of
poaching, which is frequently organized by the officials
themselves. Finally, the hunters' business is a shambles.
In the old days, in colonial times, the whole country was
divided into hunting blocks, which had to be booked by
the hunters for a particular client. Once this was done,
all others were excluded, and the hunters could feel
confident of being able to offer their clients "a decent
trophy," some remnant of the carcass that would be
accepted as decorative when hung on a wall. But today
the booking system has broken down, and hunters frequently arrive on their allotted block to find it crowded
with other people, all bearing an identical and exclusive
permit. Many of these interlopers are what the profes-

sional hunters term "residents"—that is, Africans—rather than visitors. In fact, there are about 2,500 "resident hunters" in Kenya, and only about 100 professionals. And most of the residents are after elephant because the cost of the hunting permit, though high, is far less than the value of the ivory that can be obtained from the hunt.

Nor do these resident hunters always favor the classical technique of safari hunting: the slow stalk upwind; the silent final approach; the single shot from a sporting weapon, which has to be placed exactly if it is to kill the elephant rather than enrage it to charge. Some of these present-day residents are quite capable of driving around in a truck and opening up with a machine gun. Faced with this behavior, and aware of the growing clamor of the men who say that hunting is the natural right of the Kenyan citizen (and who mean that they, too, wish to obtain a little ivory), the professional hunters have suggested that certain areas of the country be set aside for the residents to exercise their ancestral rights and that others be set aside for sport hunting. But since no one is prepared to admit officially that the behavior and motives of the resident hunters are just as the professional hunters describe them, this proposal is unacceptable. And despite all protests, despite the agreed fact that the number of elephants killed by professional hunters is small and well regulated and that the male elephants being hunted for trophies are invariably past forty—the limit of the age of reproduction—and that the fees paid for hunting licenses pay for most of the country's conservation program, a ban on professional hunting, the only form of hunting that does nothing at all to threaten elephant survival, is usually in force. And the hunter, like the pastoralist, is banned from Eden.

Such stratagems clear the way for the senior levels of the industry to carry on. And this they do, sometimes in the least predictable fashion. Which hairy-chested white hunter could have foreseen that his place in the bush might one day be taken by a bespectacled biologist, exercising fieldcraft in the pursuit of big game in order to calculate the relationship between fecal weight and body size? The size of elephants can be related to their age. If, after due comparison of bolus circumference and diameter, the relationship between the size of an elephant and the size and frequency of its motions were to be established, the biologists could, instead of counting elephants, just count their droppings—a more precise and less hazardous undertaking.

It is in the collection of such statistics that much of the elephant industry justifies its existence. The biologist, like the dung beetle, busies himself with his ball of animal droppings and eventually emerges from it triumphantly clutching a mouthful of facts. For what the elephant farmers fail to consider as they compile their records and measurements and deductions is that the uninstructed African, in his profound ignorance of the average circumference and density of elephant droppings, and laboring under the delusion that the stars are God's cattle, has achieved a way of living with elephants and with all the other wild species that has resulted in the survival of those creatures to this day, so rendering scientific stratagems redundant. The African who fashioned the habitat that the Northerner so much admires did this not because he yearned for its beauty but because he yearned for its food. The conservationist, loving the appearance of this landscape, took possession of it in the only way he could, as a beautiful luxury, a playground. But for the African the land was a necessity. He had to live off it, and to do so, he did not try to control it; he sought to survive in it, and if necessary, he was prepared to rearrange himself. At this he was an expert. The idea of improving his condition by the imposition of radical modifications was baffling to a man whose concept of an ideal condition was the success he enjoyed not at deliberately modifying nature, but at surviving within it. But the conservationist has never been able to come to terms with the possibility that it is not man who threatens the "untouched" landscape he so admires, just Northern man who does so. Rather than admit this, which would imply that modern methods of land use should cease, he asserts that all human activity threatens it and takes steps to isolate the land from human activity. By doing this, he is obscuring the real choice between the old life, which resulted in the creation of such natural wealth, and the new one, which is intended to create material wealth.

The conservationist wants his African landscape to resemble the world he found when he arrived; his guilt at the destruction that Northern activities entail can be soothed, so long as this ornamental scene exists, undisfigured, as he supposes, by use. To the Northerner the unspoiled African landscape presented a visual harmony which delighted him, but which demanded that he, too, should submit to the land if he were to live on it without destroying it. But submission did not come easily to the Northerner in Africa.

The African by contrast had never consciously chosen to submit; it was simply that all experience of survival in Africa taught him that a degree of submission to nature was the key. Those who failed to realize this did not usually survive in Africa for very long. And it may be this reflection that explains the habitual passivity of the presiding officials at the convention of the elephant industry.

For a period of time this passivity will continue. But eventually the pressure on the empty land will grow to an uncontainable degree.[11] And when it does, the destruction of wildlife may be very much greater than if the conservation movement had never been started. By setting up reserves in which men who trespass can be shot, conservationists are intensifying the struggle between wild animals and men.[12] There are a limited num-

ber of duties that one mortal individual can discharge to
the advantage of other creatures, and each increase in
the total of rights demanded on behalf of animals entails
a diminishment in the number of rights enjoyed by
humans. Sometimes, as in the case of the Ik or the
Ndorobo, human rights are ignored in the interests of
conserving wildlife. But almost every game reserve in-
volves some interference in the rights of some local
population. The Kamba have been dispossessed by Tsavo,
the Masai by Nairobi National Park and by the reserves
at Amboseli, Tsavo, Masai Mara, Serengeti, Ngorongoro, and Lake Manyara.

From the point of view of the Kamba who cluster
around the eastern edge of Tsavo in shantytowns, lacking both jobs and land, the colonial governments have
gone, but the colonial game reserves remain, dividing the
land and its life. If it should occur to them that the
quickest solution would be to kill all the animals that
could not be caged or driven away, then the conservationist Noah will not only have built an unseaworthy Ark
but will have been responsible for opening the flood-
gates as well.

It took four days to skin Ahmed. Because the whole
elephant was to be mounted in the National Museum as
a monument to Kenyan conservation, the skin had to be
very carefully removed and immediately salted. It also
had to be kept damp. Then the ribs, limb bones, and
skull had to be cut out with tusks intact. Wolfgang,
Nairobi's leading taxidermist, spent most of that time
inside the rib cage. He was dressed in short trousers and
gum boots, and he tied a handkerchief around his face
to keep out some of the flies and the smell. On the fourth
day the eggs that the flies had laid in the intestines as
soon as the stomach was opened hatched out. Opening
the stomach was a difficult operation. It was full of wind,
and as decay set in, it swelled up even more. There was

COUNTING ALL THE ELEPHANTS

clearly the risk of a fairly sizable explosion, and neither
Wolfgang nor the forest rangers wanted to be too close
when it happened. The rangers kept well clear, but Wolfgang had to lead the operation. "Nobody is pushing,
except me," he shouted, and his voice echoed oddly from
somewhere within the carcass. "I have too much salt and
not enough skinners." Now and again he emerged and
stood on a log and harangued the rangers, in English
but with a strong German accent, about the need for
speed and the penalties that would ensue if the president's
wishes were disappointed. Few of the rangers understood
English at the best of times, and this had little effect.
"He is *your* president, not mine," shouted Wolfgang,
dripping with sweat and waving his knife, so that drops
of blood flew all over the clearing. "If I don't get the
skin off tomorrow, it will be too late to stuff him.
Harambee!" But not even the slogan of national unity
could rouse the rangers, who sat around in their neat,
cool uniforms, feeding a smoky and aromatic fire to discourage the flies and chewing a relaxing cud. As soon as
Wolfgang stepped back into the elephant, they lay back
again, and nothing disturbed the profound silence of the
forest except their hacking and sneezing and coughing
and spitting and the occasional muffled cursing from
within the shuddering carcass. The rangers seemed relieved by the death of Ahmed and by the termination of
their impossible duty to follow this elephant everywhere.
Much of the time of the entire Marsabit game department had been devoted to this one task. The one calamity
they all had feared was that some casual poacher would
shoot Ahmed without realizing who he was.

At night, when it was too dark to work, Wolfgang
would leave Ahmed in the care of the rangers, who built
up the fires to keep lions off the carcass, and return to
the tourist camp in Marsabit, where he was closely ques-
tioned by an attentive committee. There was the district
officer who had been charged with making sure that all

necessary assistance was given for the great enterprise, and there was the game warden who was always interested to hear theories about the cause of death. As Wolfgang continued his dissection, he threw out new pieces of information. The great explosion had never occurred because his stomach had been empty. "Ah," said the game warden. "Just as I thought. He died of starvation like all old elephants. His teeth wore out."

"No," said Wolfgang, "his teeth were in good shape, but something must have upset his digestion."

There was a brief sensation when Wolfgang discovered two bullets at the base of the tusks, but then he said that they might have been there for years. Perhaps they had given Ahmed a toothache so that he could not eat. Or was it the wound in his side that had upset him? The game warden looked modestly around, always prepared to defer to anyone else's opinion. A party of conservationists from the National Audubon Society of America was staying at the camp and wanted to see the carcass. The warden arranged this with Wolfgang, who was quenching his thirst, while the delegates, in their paramilitary jungle shirts and Audubon shoulder patches, watched from a respectful distance. Wolfgang was certainly very interesting; but he was probably tired, and also, well . . . of course, he had taken a shower, but . . . wasn't there a rather peculiar smell from his direction?

The district officer was very worried about a £20 million ($38.4 million) loan made by the World Bank for a tourist circuit in northern Kenya. Without Ahmed, Marsabit might not have much to offer. Perhaps they could keep him in a local museum, rather than send him down to Nairobi? Wolfgang was scornful. "Why am I stuffing this elephant?" he demanded. "He is not even very big. His tusks weigh one hundred pounds below the record. He is only ten feet at the shoulder. Do you know what the record is?" Nobody did. "Thirteen feet!" Wolfgang was stuffing a dwarf.

By the end of the week the district officer had departed for his next outlying station and Ahmed had been flown down to Nairobi. Wolfgang was still uncertain about the cause of death. He knew only what the elephant had not died of. The wound in the side had not looked very serious. It certainly wasn't starvation. It was hard to say. The most closely observed wild elephant in the world had died suddenly, and despite its bodyguards and the immediate inspection by a party of experts and the total dismemberment of the carcass, the cause of death remained a mystery. For all that could be said, Ahmed might as well have been impaled upon the karkadan. It was not only the elephant who was well and truly stuffed.

NOTES

1. An attempt to do just this which was announced in 1977 was abandoned within eighteen months by researchers working for the World Wildlife Fund.

2. A similar predicament was faced by an ecologist who was commissioned by an international body to report on the threat to leopards in Kenya. Because leopards were seen less frequently, it was naturally assumed that they were dying out. The ecologist discovered, over a period of two years, that the reason why leopards were less frequently seen was that they had more reason to conceal themselves and were extremely adept at doing so. They had become suburban scavengers and flourished in large numbers among the trees that adorned the gardens of some of the very people who had instituted the research. The leopards were growing fat on the pet dogs and cats of the altruists who were so concerned for their survival. The ecologist was severely tempted to suppress his report.

3. The Ndorobo still number 21,034, according to the latest census.
4. *Uganda National Parks Handbook, 1971.*
5. That it is not the killing of animals in a game park which distresses conservationists is shown by the following quote from the *Uganda National Parks Handbook*: "Poaching in a National Park is intolerable not so much because animals suffer and lose their lives, as because there is no control over which animals die." The warden's job is no less than to control these animals in their wildness, and it is the poacher's arbitrary interference in his arrangements that he finds truly intolerable.
6. The figure for "controlled" buffalo killings had also risen, from 399 to 500. And between 1967 and 1977, during which time the Kenyan game department estimated that rhinoceros numbers had fallen from 5,000 to a few hundred in one park alone as a result of the activities of poachers, 3,000 rhinos were shot in the interests of official "control."
7. It might be thought that there are some areas of intensive human activity that wild animals would naturally avoid. If so, they are not always the obvious ones. "People seem to think," said the Kenyan minister of tourism in 1975, "that when they step off their jet at Nairobi Airport they will see lions. They know nothing of our modern city." Nine months after the minister's statement a Boeing 747 struck a hyena on the main runway during takeoff.
8. Several white rhino families were deposited in Uganda, for instance. Others went to Kenya, where two were poached in 1977 in the Meru National Park.
9. The Masai's skill as a game preserver was understood and admired by Meinertzhagen in 1903.
10. The very success of game parks all over the world has recently forced the conservationist movement into an embarrassing admission. In the future it is hoped that such parks will contain "wilderness areas" which people can enter only on horseback or on foot. In other words, most people will not be able to enter them at all. This policy is thought to be the most important step forward taken by the conservation movement since the first wildlife reserves were established in 1933. The reserves set up then have become so popular that they must now be denied to most of the people who wish to visit them, lest those few visitors who do get in have to look at each other and realize where they are.

11. There are signs that in Tanzania this process has already started. In January 1978 "elephant meat at bargain prices" was put on sale as an innovation in the effort to ease meat shortages. The meat was obtained from animals that had been shot under a "control" program. In the same month the United States government, at the request of conservationists, was preparing to declare the African elephant an endangered species.

12. The law allows poachers to be shot in Kenyan national parks if they resist arrest. Reports of such shootings occur regularly, and one of the advantages of the periodic hunting bans, according to the game authorities, is that all armed men in the bush can be treated as poachers. In 1973 poachers speared to death a rhinoceros in Amboseli National Park which turned out to be "Pixie," a conservationist symbol. Photographs of this animal were displayed in the papers in order to alert animal lovers to the event. Subsequently an enthusiastic letter from "one of Amboseli's friends" urged that in the future the law should authorize the authorities to shoot anyone in a game reserve who failed to stop when challenged and that no inquests should be held on such deaths to save the time of game department staff.

CHAPTER 2

A MANHUNT
IN THE GAME PARK

Nothing creates a greater surprise among the Negroes on
the sea coast, than the eagerness displayed by the European
traders to procure elephants' teeth; it being exceedingly
difficult to make them comprehend to what use it is
applied.

Mungo Park, *Travels in Africa,* 1799

The magnificent game parks which once attracted thousands of tourists each year now belong only to the animals.

Newspaper report from Uganda, 1976

As the African state and its game parks become more
independent, they fall to pieces. In the seventy-odd years
since Meinertzhagen first cast his critical eye upon the
Ndorobo, neither the Northern nor the African attitude
to game has essentially changed. And once the Northern hold on the game park slackens, the African attitude
begins to reemerge, and the balance of life, the potential
regulator of life in Africa, is reestablished.

The first change that occurs in the African game park
is frequently in the name. And with that everything can
change. The few African syllables which succeed the
name of a European explorer erase the European certainties that rested on the familiar sound, and the place
itself as an area of unique interest attracting unwelcome
attention recedes into the indistinct generality from which
its naming had rescued it. But even before the change of
name, even before the expatriate presence has departed,

fundamental changes can occur unless daily supervision takes place. The Kenyan national parks are among the most admired in the world. But already some of them have, under independent administration, been altered beyond recognition. In one of the smaller parks near Nairobi the process was well under way. The new warden of this park was an able and quick-witted man who had once been a zealous official. But then he suffered the ill luck to catch a poacher, a former Mau Mau general.[1] The warden's prosecution of this influential potentate failed; he himself was subsequently demoted. The rules of the game had changed, and until the warden discovered what the new ones were, he was disinclined to take any more risks. His period of disgrace gave him sufficient time for reflection, and by the time a new appointment came, he had decided on his new policy.

At first it seemed to add to his difficulties that this new appointment was to a park that was in the tribal land of his own people. In the event, this suited his plans perfectly. It was, in a way, his official cue. One of the justifications of conservation in Kenya is the enormous revenue it is supposed to bring to the country. But this money seldom reaches the people whose land has been taken for the parks. The warden decided that in his park at least this matter would be put right. As compensation for losing the park the people would be allowed to seek a direct revenue from within it. He appointed men of his own tribe to the staff, and he allowed their wives to come into the park and sit by the road selling souvenirs for tourists. Instead of the district's people being the chief enemies of the park, they became its chief dependents. Gradually more and more of them found a use for it, working in the administration, working at the hotel, or— poaching. The rangers kept their cousins, the local poachers, informed of any movements of game and of any new security plans. The warden turned a blind eye and, by doing so, behaved in a highly moral fashion by the standards of his own people: he provided for them.

At the same time other official functions were simplified. The drivers of the tourist buses, for instance, changed their methods completely. Instead of driving around on the tracks at 10 mph, allowing their passengers to see whatever they could, they set out in fast convoys and then left the track in a line abreast and just roamed about the park, looking for the only animal most of the tourists wanted to see—lions. The park was crisscrossed with tire tracks, much of its smaller vegetation had been broken down, and not all the animals were able to ignore this disturbance. On one occasion the park received the rare pleasure of a visit from a pair of cheetahs. The cheetah hunts by stalking game and then breaking cover at a distance and running its quarry down at great speed. This tactic requires that the game be undisturbed over a wide area. Everywhere the cheetahs went they were followed by the tourist vans, crammed with photographers. When they rested, they were surrounded by vehicles. When they moved, the vans started up and competed for the closest position. After two hungry days one of the cheetahs left the park and found sanctuary in the unsupervised country outside it, while the other, confused by the vans, remained behind. For several hours it trotted up and down a ridge, letting out a melancholy birdlike call, the tourists continuing to follow it around until dark.

Among those who were infuriated by this state of affairs was a party of zoologists who had come out from England on a professional survey of the animals. They were camped around a ruined house at some distance from the tourists, but they still found that the number of animals had diminished so much, and the remaining ones were so disturbed, that their program had to be abandoned. The only animals they could still watch were zebras. By a complicated system involving a plumb line, a spirit level, a watch, and a compass they hoped to be able to establish whether at midday the zebra herds changed their angle of feeding vis-à-vis the sun. It was some time before they discovered that at midday most zebras were not feeding in the sun but resting in the shade.[2]

For those zoologists who could not occupy themselves with zebras there were the tourist buses; they spent the day following the tourists and "monitoring" their behavior. The scientific method at least has this advantage, that if zoology proves impractical, sociology is frequently at hand. Eventually the park authorities did intervene, but only to prevent the zoologists from following the tourists. The constant scrutiny and taking of notes were disturbing the tourists in their hunt for lions.

While this park was disintegrating under the untroubled eye of the national parks administration, the warden of another Kenyan park was subject to constant official scrutiny. David Sheldrick was one of the last European wardens, widely renowned for his uncompromising attitude to poachers, and he consequently felt a growing sense of insecurity about his position. His game park, Tsavo East, was enormous, and most of it was sealed off from the public. To reach the prohibited area, one had to pass a control post and ford a river and cross a low line of hills. There was no one around. No one was allowed to live in the reserve, although its borders were crowded with the people who had formerly inhabited the land. And the tourists who provided the park's entire revenue were restricted to a corner of it. This arrangement had been made by the warden in the interest of both wildlife and good management. For the park was particularly noted for its elephants, and he and his patrol of armed rangers were the only people who legally entered the restricted area. Anyone else found there was presumed to be poaching.

And so, for a brief period, Victorian Africa was re-created with its wealth of game and hostile natives and the European's private army. Under the previous colonial administration Warden Sheldrick's independence would have been constantly supervised; shortly his job would be "Africanized" (he already had an African assistant, deferential, watchful, ambitious). But for these few years he could exercise his own will on the park. He could manage the animals and its people, enjoying the first and hunting the second, and no one interfered or even noticed.

To reach the warden's "field headquarters," one sought special permission and then drove for several hours through the deserted bush, until the track reached the place where his men were camped beneath a cliff, on ground that sloped gently down to a lake about a mile to the west. In the heat of the evening this lake shim-mered blue, distorting the tiny profiles of the animals occasionally gathered around it. But its water was bitter and polluted; all drinking water had to be brought for miles by truck. The rangers had erected a wireless hut, and beside it they had laid out an airstrip for the warden to use on his daily visits. At night, camped under a giant baobab tree, one could hear leopards among the rocks of the nearby cliff, and sometimes a hyena. But although this camp was in the deepest part of a game reserve, days might pass before any quantity of animals became visible through the haze surrounding the tents. Africa, in this area of carefully maintained emptiness, without roads or settlements, seemed once again enormous, too great to be mapped. The sense of solitude was deceptive. On the horizon beyond the lake there was the outline of a dark plateau where the poachers hid in caves and tried to oversee the movements of the camp.

The rangers' day began with a parade. There were thirty of them at the camp, and they paraded in field uniform, ready for the hunt. One man paraded in a cotton towel, saying that he should be excused work on the grounds that he had nearly died the day before. He was a member of a section of five who were skillful trackers and who knew the country; but in the heat of a chase after poachers they had tried to cross the central expanse of the park, which was waterless, and they had exhausted their small supply of water. After a day and a night had passed, the warden flew around looking for them and eventually saw them sitting under a tree, completely exhausted. Their quarry had escaped by bicycle.

Early in the morning, before the heat, a convoy of trucks, keeping well apart to avoid each other's dust, carried the rangers up onto the plateau. Periodically they stopped to put down a section of rangers, who immediately disappeared into the thick scrub through which the vehicles had to force a passage. Each man carried a rifle and a small water bottle, and each section had a radio. In appearance they bore a close resemblance to an anti–Mau Mau patrol, and the day's objective, to hunt Africans under European direction, was nearly identical—although the rangers were not supposed to kill the poachers they caught, unless in self-defense. Nothing could be seen or heard when the men had disappeared. The silence was disturbed only once, when a lion suddenly sprang from the top of the rock.

Then, when the last of the trucks had completed a semicircle, it was time to descend. The various sections would now in theory be converging on the edge of the plateau, thereby trapping any poachers who were between them and the lip of the cliff. Overhead there was the occasional buzzing of the warden's plane, flying back and forth across the plateau, trying to spot poachers, occasionally diving down to indicate the position of a dead elephant. The patrol formed into single file and set out, in good order, through the thornbushes, confident that in the matter of hunting men through a reserve of wild animals, it could have no better guide.

The poaching of elephants in Africa reached a periodic

peak in 1973.[3] At that time the world price for ivory
was £9 ($18) a pound, and the eventual value of the
tusks of an average elephant might be £200 ($400). Even
the low price which the elephant poacher obtained from
his local ivory dealer made the elephant by far his most
valuable quarry. One walk through the game reserve
might enable him to set himself up in business, or buy
a smallholding, or pay for the education of his children,
or simply feed himself and his family for a very long
time.

In this reserve, poaching was taking place on a daily
basis, and even this small force of rangers was catching
three or four poachers a week; the warden estimated
that in the course of a year, from his reserve alone, one
thousand elephants had been poached. Not that he ever
used the word *reserve* when talking about the game park;
as far as he was concerned, the "reserve" was the area
outside the park where the natives lived. He had been
brought up in a wild country where man made no impression, where one could look out a hundred miles over
land that held nothing but game, and he now believed
that he would see the time when the elephant would become extinct from the activities of poachers alone. Not
everyone shared this opinion. Many experts disagreed
with the warden, believing that the chief reason there
were fewer elephants was that there were more people
and that this principle should even be applied to his game
reserve, from which the people had been excluded. Here
the struggle between man and elephant appeared to be
a hunt for ivory rather than a competition for land. But
to what extent was the need for ivory stimulated by the
loss of the land, and was the game park itself, the elephant sanctuary, the greatest threat to the elephant?
The ultimate effect of setting up an elephant sanctuary,
the population of which was continually expanding and
contracting (either from culling or natural causes) and
then being restocked from the diminishing number of

elephants outside the sanctuary, might be to suck all the elephants in Africa into such parks, thereby draining their numbers faster than would otherwise be the case. But the warden did not consider possibilities that brought into question the wisdom of having a reserve.

Away from the truck, having passed through the first barrier of thorns, the country opened out, and it was possible to see a gentle rise toward the highest part of the plateau. The first impression that Africa made on the popular imagination of Europe and Asia was as a place of monsters. It was not only the people of temperate northern climates who were appalled by the extravagant fertility of Africa. Even the dhow sailors of the Arabian Gulf (where the heat is greater than on the east coast of Africa) returned home with legends of a place where the sun was so hot that it could melt the flesh of an elephant. Something about Africa caused the Arab sailors to exaggerate, and so legends grew of a place where there were birds so large that they could blacken the sky and lift the impaled carcasses of a rhinoceros and an elephant. Even today there is enough of this Africa left for the newly arrived traveler to experience a shiver of excitement and horror and to see monsters where an African would see only food.

The rangers then came upon a rhinoceros. For most of the party the first warning was given when the feet of the man in front suddenly stopped. The leading ranger had halted and was looking intently to his left. A complete silence had fallen among his companions. Then, without a word, the experienced leader turned on his heel and started to run very fast to his right. Immediately his well-disciplined and heavily armed formation was dispersed. Everyone ran as fast as he could, though where to or what from nobody could have said. After the first panic and with nothing apparently behind them, they stopped and looked back, hoping to see what it was that had caused this sudden rush. The leading ranger had paused by this time and was pointing his rifle toward a bush from which there slowly emerged a snout with a horn on it. The ranger fired into the ground, raising a little puff of dust in front of the snout, a warning shot. At once the rhinoceros started to trot toward him. The ranger fired again, this time to kill. The only effect was to make the rhinoceros run faster. The ranger dropped his rifle and also ran. Everyone ran. For five minutes the rhinoceros chased eight men and one woman around its territory. Equipment was dropped, rifles, notebooks, a box of dates, a canvas bucket, some fresh figs, items of clothing. Even the shortwave radio was dropped, crackling and spluttering, into a bush. The rhinoceros cantered between the column of scattered rangers as though it were running a gauntlet, the men on either side dodging from its path and firing toward it, and each other, as it passed. There was little noise. The popping of the guns, the crackling of the radio, occasional sharp explosions as twigs snapped beneath shoes, none of these broke the silence of concentration. It was the rhinoceros that was concentrating harder and harder, and closer and closer came the loudest sound, its chuffling breath and thumping feet. From behind a small thornbush it was possible after some time to look back and see the line of men stretching away across the land into the haze, some armed, some disarmed, some just out for the day, and to watch the rhinoceros running toward the center of the line. Then to see it turn and work its way up the line toward that very thornbush, drawn to the refuge as though by magnetism, the frequent shots not slowing it for a moment; then to decide that contrary to reports, its eyesight was clearly quite capable of penetrating the bush; then to wait till the last moment and dodge around the far side of the thicket and run once more, this time flat out, and, in glancing back, to see the gray shape, by now apparently twice the size of any known rhinoceros, turn with great nimbleness directly behind; then to trip headlong right in front of it and fall hard enough to lose one's breath, keeping just enough sense in one's head to decide that one wouldn't feel a thing. And not to feel a thing except the thorns in one's skin, the rhinoceros having decided to trample on somebody else and having at long last and a few yards away been shot to its knees before it could do so.

"Hello. Come in, come in. . . . Are you there, Corporal? Corporal? What the hell is going on? . . . Absolute shambles. . . . Come in, Section Two." The voice of Warden Sheldrick was crackling across Africa; from five hundred feet above ground all he could see was a group of little figures being driven back and forth by a rhinoceros. Section Two picked up its bucket and hats and guns and shot the rhinoceros twice more just in case. Then they cut the horns out of its face, surprisingly easily, with a pocketknife. Then the majority of the party, the warden having sent the woman home, proceeded onto the plateau. Back at the truck its driver, the senior sergeant, was dozing. He had heard the gunfire and presumed that the rangers had been ambushed by poachers. With a calm assumption of calamity he lifted his head to inquire, "How many dead?" On learning that only one rhinoceros had perished, he instructed a junior ranger to find his binoculars, then to find his binocular case, then to place the one in the other and arrange them beneath his head. Finally, he lay back and closed his eyes, resigned to the day's efforts for animal conservation passing without him.

For the rest of the day Section Two hunted poachers. Directed by the warden from his plane, the rangers tramped across the plateau, seldom resting, once running for half an hour through the rasping heat to form an ambush for a party of armed men who had been seen from the air but who never turned up. Four times they came across a freshly killed elephant carcass, the first sign of which, the smell, once experienced, is never forgotten. Most poachers kill elephants by the cheapest and surest means. They buy poison, apply it to an arrow in a sticky black tar, and then approach close enough to an elephant to plant the arrow anywhere in its body. Time will do the rest. The poison disrupts the nerves that govern the action of the heart. The poachers just follow the elephant for a few hours until it collapses. Each of the carcasses found on the plateau that day had been killed by poison, but the tusks had not always been removed. Eventually Section Two came to a carcass that had been dead for only a few hours. There was the usual arrow wound in its side, and beneath one ear a second wound; the poachers had been cutting meat and had been disturbed by the rangers' approach. The hunt was getting closer. The poachers were so cautious that even when they cut meat from the carcass, they did it in such a way that they could conceal the cut if they heard a plane approaching. That way there would be nothing to distinguish the carcass from the air as a fresh one. As the rangers examined the wound, the plane flew low overhead, and the warden dropped a hand ax. One of the rangers started to chop at the roots of the tusks; two others disappeared on the trail of the poachers. They would follow the tracks as far as they could before night fell.

In the pleasant warmth of the evening all returned to the truck, water bottles empty, bearing the day's haul of recovered tusks. The rangers still carried most of their water, believing that the more one drank, the thirstier one became. There were no more animals to be seen, although the warden, who had landed his plane, said that from the air it was clear that they'd been passing between many elephants and rhinoceroses. He had forgiven everyone for the earlier shambles and flew off into the sunset toward his whiskey and his wife.

But the field force had not finished. There were sections scattered all across the park, and it was the clear duty of the senior sergeant to drive around in the night and find them. His eyes were bloodshot after his day's sleep, and he had some difficulty in operating the radio. But he could remember how to drive the truck and did so very fast toward a deserted tourist lodge which still held a reserve of beer. By the time he had quenched his thirst it was late; he drove even faster across the plateau and down onto the plain, where, somewhere in the night, by the side of the track, the various sections were waiting. To pass the time as the truck lurched and rattled from one identical clump of thorns to the next, he named all the animals seen that day: hyena and ostrich and elephant and giraffe and impala and gerenuk, a rhino, a lioness and wild dogs and porcupine, a kudu, a zebra, a buffalo, a jackal, a snake, a heron, a barbet, an eagle and doves and a quail. Once, as he recited the list, a leopard showed up in the headlights. And once a dik-dik blundered into the truck's wheels, and once a genet. And the journey was punctuated by the noise of insects slapping against the windshield and sometimes the louder thump of a nightjar rising from the dust in front of the truck and being bowled over.

During the next two days the rangers hunted and caught six men. They all carried poisoned arrows and tusks. The poachers habitually treated the arrows rather casually. They not infrequently managed to poison themselves, the substance, which comes from a tree bark, being able to enter the bloodstream through the tiniest cut. It is known to be an unusually painful death. In this knowledge the loosely wrapped arrowheads, with their sticky black tips, exercised a terrible allure. One had to make an effort of will not to stretch out one's hand and touch them.

Most of the fugitives tried to escape by running into the waterless bush, usually being caught when they tripped. One had run into a tree. Another had fallen over a cliff, broken his leg, and inflicted a deep cut in his head. The three who had been disturbed eating the elephant on the plateau were caught just after dawn on the following day when they were actually in ambush by a water hole. Five minutes after they were disarmed, a large bull elephant came down to drink and, despite the excited group of men, approached to within twenty yards before it became alarmed, demonstrating how little skill is needed to stalk an elephant. The skill of the poachers and the trackers was used entirely in pursuing or evading each other, but once the poachers were caught, there was little sustained hostility between them and their guards. There was a formal lecture, some finger wagging, and a few blows to encourage the poachers to give up the names of their dealers.

But once back at camp, capturers and captives, all expert trackers and hunters, seemed to have as much in common as not. Corporal Dube, who went hunting in rubber wellington boots, bore the same grave and diffident appearance as Mwanzi, the man he captured, an old man for a poacher, who had already sent most of his ivory out of the park. Mwanzi had been caught poaching once before, five years earlier, when he had been sentenced to two months. From that time to this he had been working as a skinner for a firm of white professional hunters, but the government ban on all forms of elephant hunting had cost him his job. He had no money, so he had turned to poaching again; his home was on the edge of the reserve. He said that all his family were coming into the reserve to poach "except when it was raining." He respected the warden, whom he called the *bwana,* his friend. And he realized how difficult it was for the *bwana* with all this poaching and how hard he tried to stop it.

But Mwanzi and his family would continue to come in to poach. The dealers supplied them with poison and gave them a price which was one-sixteenth of the ultimate value of the tusks. It was too high a price for them to be able to refuse.

Occasionally the routine was interrupted by an unexpected incident. Once Section Three found the mangled remains of a poacher who had been killed by an elephant. His companion was arrested and said that as the two of them had approached this elephant, it had seen them and had charged. Each had run away, and his friend had climbed a small tree. As the elephant passed him, this man had descended the tree and shouted, "Where are you going?" The elephant heard him and charged again. This time the man took refuge in a pig hole, but the elephant pulled him out with its trunk and speared him with its tusks and then trampled him. "As soon as he shouted," said the survivor, "I knew he should never have said that thing to that elephant."

After a few days, when there was a full load, a truck set off from the field headquarters for the local courthouse. There the poachers faced sentences of a few months in prison or a light fine because the local magistrate said that they were small men and the real culprits were the bigger men who organized the business. This was a prudent policy: many of these men were much bigger than the magistrate. At the same time the warden passed on all the information about the ivory dealers to the local police, but no arrests were made. The police were as cautious as the magistrate. Outside the reserve the warden had no jurisdiction. The poachers knew this very well. Sometimes, as they crossed the boundary, they would write derisory messages in the dust for the men who were tracking them, such as "We got three. . . ." It was here in the dust that the warden's private vision faded into the African reality. The chase was over; his troops were just park rangers; the fugitives were private fellow citizens of an independent country. There was no room for wardens.

He used to talk of needing "just a little more time" to train his successor and apparently hoped that eventually a more honest administration would stop the "big fish." But the warden died before either had been achieved. Before his death his patience and hope became exhausted, and the battle in the prohibited area became more and more violent. The ivory store in his park eventually contained 300,000 pounds of tusks in excellent condition, the result of his work over many years, which he was always careful to keep under his own supervision. But he knew that one day it would all be transferred to "government care" in Nairobi.

In some game parks it is now possible to see the process of evolution carried still further. All the apprehension of the European wardens has been justified, and their African successors have indeed proved incapable, but not because the park has been handed over to them too soon. The extra time the wardens wanted was for themselves, not for training their successors.

One significant change that may overtake the renamed African park is its known locality, the certainty as to where, if at all, it is. The most fundamental aspect of a game park is its boundary, as often as not a straight line, unknown in nature, which runs, to the perplexity of the people of the area, across rivers and hills and forests and tracks as though these did not exist or as though the men who drew the boundary were only sometimes blessed with a dim sight which enabled them to distinguish a wide river or great lake sufficiently well to abandon their own unreasonable notions.

The line is of great importance to the local people because human behavior on either side of it has to be ordered so differently: on the one side normality is permissible; on the other lies a madhouse, where the lighting of a fire, the pissing of a dog, the cutting of grass, even the squashing of a beetle[4] could lead to punishment of a severity historically reserved for cases of criminal behavior.

To alter the line, the pressing need of the people living outside it and wishing to graze their cattle, would clearly cause problems. Maps travel. If the African authorities were to alter the line on the map and diminish the size of the park, this could provoke feelings of disappointment and severe criticism from those who had first imposed that line and who, although they were no longer present in the flesh, still maintained an imperfect and haphazard spiritual (and financial) influence over the game department. The line, therefore, had to remain exactly as before, but since for the most part it existed only on a map, it would remain unaltered only on a map. Its physical manifestations—the entrance gate, the signboard, perhaps the elephant ditch—would also stay as before, but the people might cross it and enter the park and settle within its edges and use its land.

There would be a new line, as invisible as the first; indeed, since it appeared on no map, more so. Its course would be established by discussion between the gatekeeper and his neighbors, thereby returning to each the dignity associated with independent judgment. This was the situation that greeted the inspector of parks, an occasional visitor from Europe, who, as he approached Kabalega Park in Uganda in his official capacity, was faced with the problem of where it was. Was he in the park, which had been called Murchison Falls when he last saw it? In which case, what were these cattle doing grazing beside what appeared to be huts inhabited by people? Or was he outside the park? In which case, why had the authorities moved the signboard down the road to enclose this village? Could it be that under the new Ugandan regime the area of the national parks was being expanded? This possibility, not one that could rest unpursued, was to be raised during an opaque discussion with the new warden.

The park was centered on an old tourist lodge, beside which the warden lived. The lodge occupied a magnificent position above the Nile River valley. During the heat of the day there was little to see, but in the evening the river came to life. Flocks of bats poured out of the hotel's deserted rooms and made for the valley below. To reach it, they had to pass a tall tree from which a bat hawk launched itself in attack as each flight passed. The hawk strained up in the gloom after the bats, which dodged it by twisting abruptly like falling leaves while the hawk gained and lost momentum; one attack after another failed until at last the hawk twisted as fast as one of the bats and struck it, causing it to shoot upward like the solid dead object it had instantly become, and the bat hawk turned in a leisurely curve, caught the bat before it hit the ground, and carried it back to the tree. Beneath all this the Nile glowed softly, its banks speckled with the animals that had come to drink. The hippos emerged from a day spent beneath the surface and prepared themselves for the serious browsing of the night. Once they were out of the water their characteristic sound, which had echoed up and down the bank, ceased. It was a noise which suggested that they spent the tedious underwater hours repeating jokes, at which they chuckled in appreciation, slowly and coarsely and one by one, the final pause frequently being followed by the sound of a final hippo, laughing uncomprehendingly and much too late.

That night at the lodge the inspector was able to entertain the warden and to inquire about his problems. A curious conversation was struck up between them, each knowledgeable on what should have been the same subject, but with almost no knowledge shared. If anyone wanted to know the possibilities of seeing a particular bird in the park, he would have to address the question to the inspector, who was an ornithologist. The warden would require notice of that question and would then have to spend considerable time consulting whatever reference books were still around. But if one were wondering about the state of the elephant population, it would be more sensible to ask the warden. This the inspector did. Were there any problems of overcompression? Five years previously there had been so many elephants in the park that several thousand had been culled; the inspector was most anxious to find out if the problem had recurred. He could always arrange for experienced game con-

sultants to be flown in if a further cull were needed. The
warden thought probably not. There had been such extensive poaching that the elephant population, in his
opinion, would require no other form of control for some
time. The poaching was being done by troops from the
nearby barracks. They had shot so many animals that
they had been unable to collect all the ivory, and he had
been instructed to pick up the rest and send it on, as he
had done. He was, however, confident that the poaching
would now stop—for a time at least. Under a new ordi-
nance the penalty for poaching in Uganda was death. He
was also confident that elephant numbers were now at a
satisfactory level. The inspector wondered what method
he had used to count the elephants. An aerial survey
would have been best, but the inspector imagined that the
warden had been unable to keep his plane. Not at all,
said the warden. He had the plane, and he had the fuel.
It was just that he was terrified of flying, so he had not
used an aerial survey. The inspector began to wonder if
the warden had persuaded the army to stop poaching elephants on condition that he did it for them.

As the inspector's questions grew more pointed, the
conversation was interrupted by the sound of drums.
Then there danced onto the floor of the dining room a
group of one dozen half-naked women of striking size.
For the rest of the evening the conversation had to be
carried on above the noise of the drumming and in competition with the distractions of the dance. It was a dance
especially for the inspector, in his honor. On the matter
of the park boundary the warden assured the inspector,
at the top of his voice, that there had been no alterations.
He suggested that the inspector read his monthly reports,
which were kept absolutely up to date with all significant
developments. Sure enough, the reports disclosed no information about the park boundary. A crocodile had been
found with its jaws bound with wire; the warden knew
where the animal was and intended to cut the wire off at

some convenient moment, certainly before the crocodile starved to death. Murids (rats) had been observed in the staff lines. There were fifteen thousand elephants present. The hippopotamus named Mr. Henry had badly slashed an intruding hippopotamus which challenged its own exclusive use of the hotel trash cans. It was all in the report, which could just be made out in the flickering candlelight. At the end of the evening, as the exhausted party of women, together with the warden, made their departure, the inspector put his final question: "Who are these girls?"

"They are the wives of the men who work here," replied the warden.

"Most accommodating of them," murmured the inspector, and he climbed the stairs to a baffled night's rest, like an ambassador who has been courteously rebuffed.

Before they parted company, the inspector asked the warden if there was anything he needed. The warden had one request. Owing to the disintegration of the post office and government spending cuts, he had been unable to renew his subscription to his favorite wildlife magazine. He just needed to be put on the list of complimentary copies. It was not simply that conversations with visiting inspectors would be so much easier if he could receive this magazine. It was as though without it, lacking even that one slight link with the old order, the park's new invisible border might also cease to exist, and the land would revert to its unconserved state.

The purpose of the inspector's visit had been to decide whether or not to recommend that a grant should be paid toward the support of this park from an international foundation. But as he drove away in the government car at the end of his visit, he had no idea what to do. On the one hand, the park was clearly in need of money, and the warden in his growing isolation was in need of more than that. On the other hand, the possibility could hardly be ignored that the park no longer existed in any form that he would recognize. Was there a park left at all? Certainly it was full of animals, but it also seemed to be tolerably stocked with people. Was there extensive poaching, and if so, was the warden himself directing it? The truth was too obscure; the facts had been Africanized with the park and had withdrawn into an impenetrable thicket which obscured the clear certainties of the conservationist. The warden had been reassuring in his confidence and sincerity, but there had been no *feeling* in his descriptions of the game. It was this that the inspector missed most, a sense of excitement when glimpsing the shoe-billed stork. In the African park, in which life is reunited after the divisions imposed by control, there is no thrill at the sight of a rare bird, no urgency about the task of preserving a dwindling species. Either the warden was indifferent to the familiarities of his environment or he refused to acknowledge the idea of global death which is at the basis of conservation. Perhaps he just found it difficult to put his heart into numbering the animals because he did not believe that a deluge was on the way.

The figures herding cattle within the park waved cheerfully at the inspector as he drove away. Unlike the tribespeople in Kenya who had lost their pastures, they had no need to squat in the dust, offering wooden dolls to Europeans. The inspectors with their strange rules had passed on, and the land could be rearranged as it had been before their invasion. Years before, the colonial authorities had cleared everyone out of Kabalega because of the ravages of sleeping sickness borne by the tsetse fly. The herds of antelope which carried this infection were themselves resistant to it, so the area had been a natural game sanctuary free from human interference. Then the fly had been eradicated, and the official reserve had been imposed as an artificial haven. Now the reserve was dissolving, and the people could return. Eventually, as the insect-control program broke down, the tsetse fly could be expected to reappear. Until then the people would at least be free of the conservationists' manhunts.

The last that the inspector saw of the park was from the rough-hewn terrace of a new hotel. The site had been carefully chosen for its romantic view, and the building designed to be unobtrusive, but the care was wasted on this place; the developer, an Asian, had been deported, and the project had been forgotten. It was an uncharacteristically dull day, and in that light the gentle hills on each side of the Nile assumed a desolate air. The monotony of land and water was accentuated, and their hazards were emphasized by the reeds which clustered on the riverbank and disguised the meeting place of the two. Harriers tossed and called on sheets of wind above the shivering reeds, failing to impress even their quick life on the unapproachable slab of water, which moved thickly between two nameless lakes, overlooked by nothing save the abandoned building, where the mirth of the hippos rang with a mocking note.

NOTES

1. The Mau Mau have had a long association with elephant poaching. Shortly after Kenyan independence they were granted special "collectors' permits" which entitled them to possess ivory they had supposedly discovered in the Aberdare Forest during the Emergency. In effect the permits made it impossible to prosecute them for possessing tusks. They looked on this as one of the fruits of victory.

2. Zoologists frequently find wildlife unexpectedly difficult to manage. In 1975 a wild cheetah turned up at a tourist lodge near the Serengeti National Park in Tanzania. It was nearly dead from starvation and was wearing a radio collar. Once fed, the cheetah refused to depart. The animal had been captured, domesticated, and then supposedly "rehabilitated" by

researchers stationed in the Serengeti. It was not, however, sufficiently rehabilitated to be able to feed itself in the wild. And despite its radio collar, it had apparently been abandoned to its fate.

3. By 1977, when poaching was thought to be less widespread, figures presented to the World Wilderness Congress in Johannesburg suggested that between 100,000 and 400,000 African elephants were poached each year, out of an estimated total population of 1.3 million. The value of the ivory has also risen enormously.

4. "Insects are accorded the same protection in the National Parks as the large mammals." Ugandan Parks Regulation No. 14.

CHAPTER 3

A TOUR OF INSPECTION

It is, of course, as difficult to judge what is going on in the Upper Nile as it is to judge what is going on on the other side of the moon.

Lord Salisbury, 1897

As the game parks degenerate, those who have used the parks' solitude for purposes of spiritual refreshment have to find somewhere else. In some cases it is a matter of urgent necessity that they should be successful in this search.

Ned was a retired game warden who had fallen in love with lions. Searching in his old age for an occupation that would allow him to relieve this passion, he discovered that the game parks of Europe and America which went in for lions very quickly became overstocked. Ned decided that rather than have the unwanted animals shot, they should be returned to the bush, and he volunteered to reinstill in them that fear of man which, when allied to hunger, would reawaken their hunting ability.

His first attempts were carried out in a special enclosure on the edge of a national park. All went well until one of his newly released lions, sufficiently frightened of man to attack, but insufficiently frightened to need a reason for doing so, carried off one of the park ranger's children and consumed it. This was particularly disappointing since the lion in question had been operated on for a broken leg and had several times been flown around in an airplane. When it repeated the attack, this time on the small son of the park's European warden, it was agreed that something would have to be done. The old warden's theories were clearly still in an experimental stage. The question of Ned's lions was decided eventually by the director of national parks himself, on the principle that there was no problem with the lions; "the problem was with Ned." So Ned and his enclosure were moved hundreds of miles north, away from the park, to an area notorious for its game poaching. Unfortunately his technique was still not perfect. Under the new arrangement he was, in effect, living in the cage while the lions roamed around outside, recovering from their agoraphobia. But after a while Ned hired an assistant. One day this young man ventured out of the cage, and he too was severely mauled. At first it was thought that this attack was carried out by a wild lion which had joined the camp, but later Ned discovered that it was another of his former pupils, returned after a bad week's hunting for easy pickings, only to be shot just as if it had never been shipped back from Bedfordshire. "The problem with Ned" was made no easier by the activities of his wife, who spent much of her time searching the bush for "orphan" lion cubs, which she domesticated and then disposed of, usually to European game parks. It seemed that eventually it would be Ned, rather than the lions, who needed rehabilitation.

Ned's need for a sanctuary was identical with the public's need for peace of mind, but there are other cases of merely private need. Fortunately there is still one remote territory that is large enough to accommodate them.

The Northern Frontier District of Kenya is one of the ungoverned parts of the world. With Equatoria and the Upper Nile it forms a solitude eight hundred miles long which is nominally administered by the governments of Kenya, Uganda, the Sudan, Ethiopia, and Somalia. But between these governments and their various subjects there is a continuing struggle. Before Kenya became independent, there was a plan to turn most of the area into a game reserve which would have occupied twelve thousand square miles, all the way from Lake Rudolf to the Somali and Ethiopian borders, an area so remote that it seemed inconceivable that any conflict with human interests could arise.

Instead, such a conflict arose at once. Somalia laid claim to most of the land in question, and bands of Somali irregulars, known as *shiftas,* made the place unsafe for anyone not carrying arms. Under these circumstances the Kenyan district commissioners (who were unlike their colonial predecessors in being gregarious and ambitious) made little impression. They lacked the resources and the unbidden impulse to take day-to-day decisions, and the frontier began to resemble its precolonial state. It is inhabited by nomadic tribesmen, who live by raising cattle and raiding each other's herds. There are no paved roads, and the half-mapped tracks that do exist are subject to flash floods that wash them away, drowning travelers and their vehicles. The scattered police forces cannot be relied on to defend even their own barracks, and little of what happens in the region is recorded. Since Lord Salisbury's comment, the other side of the moon has come under hourly observation, but the Upper Nile and the Northern Frontier remain much as they were. Any tour of the district today will be punctuated by the abrupt emergence at infrequent intervals of various solitary eccentrics who have been attracted to this wasteland as to a pleasure garden and who, viewed as a company, resemble the exhausted rear guard of a fantastic and defeated invasion.

Driving north, one reaches Maralal, the last place at which there is a reliable gasoline supply. It has the proper air of a frontier town. It was once noted for its forest and its elephants; but both have dwindled, and its only current attraction is a game lodge, which is run by an animal trapper. Now, where the animals once crowded between the trees, there is a well-planned clearing with watering points and a salt lick and a viewing balcony to ensure that such examples as remain will at least be seen. This sense of prearrangement does not extend to the town itself. Up and down its stunted avenues stroll or sprawl the tribesmen who have been attracted to this metropolis, more for its novelty than for any hope of wealth. Here one sees the Turkana at the southernmost extent of their range, stocky, unsmiling men with feathers inserted into the mud cakes on their heads and spear shafts sticking out from beneath the hems of their cloaks. Despite having been ordered north by the administration, which is hoping to reduce tribal warfare, thirty-five thousand Turkana are believed to remain in the neighborhood of Maralal, causing particular resentment among the Samburu people, whose traditional land it is. There is no telephone line to the town, but there is a radio link, which is used by the police to organize their occasional forays into the hinterland to intervene in tribal battles. It is also used to organize Maralal's chief industry, which, apart from the game lodge, is elephant poaching. Although the local herds are all but extinguished, Maralal remains the center for the northern ivory trade. It is the place where the "big fish" from Nairobi meet their local agents and arrange to receive loads of tusks from as far away as Moyale or Wajir. In Maralal people are sometimes quite open about the ivory trade. "Only Europeans make all this fuss about elephants," said one Asian dealer. "Why? There are too many elephants in Africa. They are a pest because they destroy the crops. We have to shoot them out. But don't worry. There are thousands of them out there. Breeding away like rabbits. There will always be enough for the zoo." And he continued cleaning his guns and arranging for his next hunting expedition, confident that he was in tune with his times, which have substituted a salt lick and a gasoline station for a forest full of elephants.

North of Maralal the beef ranches peter out. The fences and ditches that still cut across the cattle trails are sturdier, giving an impression of fortification; this is the verge of the true wilderness and the scene of occasional and confused meetings between the two worlds. At the time of Kenyan independence in 1963 an anthropologist[1] studying nomadic people could conclude that their traditional warrior caste, the *morani,* no longer had any warlike function. It was believed that after forty years of imposed peace they must have acquired a merely symbolic status.

Nobody would take that view now. Cattle raiding, which had nearly died out, has been restored to its former importance. A succession of dry years has resulted in increasingly fierce competition for animals and for land. The people of the extreme north have been driven farther and farther south in their search for grazing. In and out of the Rift Valley, from the Ethiopian border to the edge of the deeded land, tribes such as the Suk, the Samburu, and the Boran struggle for the advantage. But exact news of these encounters is infrequent, and driving across the country, one can see why. On a ridge, as one looks fifty miles over to the next hillside, none of the intervening settlements is distinguishable in the haze. Nothing moves on the pitted land except its blanket of air, and that is never still. Even if a battle were to occur a few miles out on the plain, from a vantage point in the hills above, it would never take place at all.

The descent from the hills north of Maralal is by a track which limps out from among the boulders and is soon lost to view. The whole dusty expanse is overlooked by Mount Nyiru, the mountain venerated by the Samburu, once the focal point of their territory but now, under the pressure of Turkana expansion, standing too

far north for most of them to see at all. At each settlement there is a police station, a mission, a dispensary,
and a school. These settlements seem to lead lives of
marked independence from each other, barely connected
by the unpaved track through the dry thorn scrub which
divides them. The police, it is true, have the radio, but
they seldom have anything to say which demands such
swift means of contact. Sometimes they set out in convoys of trucks on some official pretext, such as the need
to give evidence at a trial. When they leave, they seem
to take everything with them: most of the garrison, its
vehicles, guns, beer, beds, and girls. All are heaped into
the trucks and disappear in a happy and melodious cloud
of dust, sometimes for weeks at a time. When this
happens, the settlers show no signs of unease, perhaps
because they feel no sense of security when the police
are there. There seems little enough to defend. Life goes
forward with a certain inconsequentiality, a lack of steady
purpose.

Up and down the single street the Somali traders sit
outside their shacks, puffed with the importance of their
possessions. Each shack contains a few shelves of tea or
sugar, some handkerchiefs and rolls of cotton print, a
can of corned beef, a carton of matches—little enough
wealth but all that there is to be had for several days'
journey in any direction. In Baragoi the Somalis spat into
the dirt and fiddled with their enormous padlocks and
seemed to do no business, but there were few people in
town who did not owe them money. One shack remained
heavily barred and shuttered, a flapping sign outside
marking it as the local headquarters of KANU, the
country's only political party. Backward and forward in
front of the shuttered office wandered the *wananchi*,
KANU's beloved people, groups of women and young
girls, Samburu or Turkana, passing separately by the
notice board, illiterate and uncaring, their presence in
the settlement rather than out in the scrub with their

flocks apparently a matter of chance. "KANU and the People," the sign said, "Building the new Kenya."

The only evidence of communal life was provided by the arrival of an elderly white woman in a floppy hat who sat herself in a deck chair under a thorn tree. Around her a small crowd of tribeswomen gathered together, sitting in the dust with their legs straight out before them, keeping one eye on their camels, dove gray or brown with black manes, which they left nearby in the charge of children; it had rained two weeks earlier, and the animals were able to graze. Beside the deck chair, a paper chart pinned to a portable easel was covered with brightly colored drawings. There was a tiger being speared in the eye by a devil with green horns, a tortoise surrounded by a golden radiance, a disembodied white face floating between two thick books. The old lady gave out a radiance of her own, a feeling of placid authority, as she beamed at the naked females stretched out before her, but she said nothing and seemed untroubled by their wandering attention. A Luo woman, her burly black shape in sharp contrast with the delicate brown tones of the Samburu, stood in the sun beside the blackboard, wearing a blue wool dress and cardigan and a pink headscarf, and harangued this polyglot audience in one language, sometimes gesturing toward the chart. The religion being imparted bore no similarity to any of the great world systems, and its symbolism must have baffled the congregation, since neither the tiger, nor the tortoise, nor, indeed, the thick bound book is to be found on the Northern Frontier. But it was an appropriate religion in the circumstances: a baffling religion for a baffled place.

The public meeting caused no stir of interest in the nearby police compound, whose occupants gave the impression that they reacted to nothing short of gunfire. In order to avoid tribal favoritism and to reduce bribery, the Kenyan police are posted to areas where they are

strangers to the inhabitants. For most of their professional lives they have very little to do, and they are
absurdly overmanned. Then suddenly there will be trouble
with cattle raiders or an attack by Somali irregulars, and
they will be hopelessly outnumbered; this combination of
stupefying boredom and paralyzing fear often overwhelms all initiative.

Past the deserted guardhouse and across the extensive
parade ground was a small hut marked "Reports and
Enquiries" and then, lower down, "Signal Room. No
Admittance." From this hut four sleepy policemen dressed
in immaculate white underwear emerged and talked. The
police barracks was the only place that might stock beer.
Did they have a surplus? "Yes," said their leader. "We
have beer. We have all the beer for all the policemen
in the north. This is the depot. We have even five thousand bottles." Negotiations took some time; but eventually six bottles changed hands for a fifth more than the
official price, and the officer in charge, who was "hailing
from the coast of the Indian Ocean," tried to buy the
basket that contained the empties. Then he felt the need
to explain himself, the world. "I am here," he said, "to
defend these people"—and he waved his arm around his
head to enclose every corner of the land—"against . . .
each other. We have thirty riding camels here. You
should have been here this morning. You could have
taken my picture as I rode my camel. Now it is too late."
And he bade good-bye regretfully, a martial figure in his
underpants, having issued careful directions to proceed
by a particular road, which three hours and seventy miles
later stopped dead in the middle of the bush. There were
only three ways out of that settlement, but the officer
was not familiar with them all.

It is not difficult to get lost in the Northern Frontier
District—that is partly what the place is for—but it is

better to do so with most of the day still to come. So
camp was made some distance from where the road
ended, on a salt flat beneath a bleak volcanic escarp-
ment. The wind got up almost at once, blowing sand
into the food and the tents and deadening one's sense
of any nearby sounds. Eventually a full moon rose and
revealed half a mile away on the salt a single hyena,
sloping off the desert and toward the slag hill and paus-
ing for a moment to look at the camp as though surprised to see one in that place. This impression of
familiarity with its surroundings was reassuring. Later
in the night lions started up a great noise nearby, and
in the morning a diversion was made to look for them.
Almost at once the idea began to lose its appeal. Off
the flats the bushes grew thicker and reached up to the
roof of the truck, and after an hour of searching all
that had been found were some old prints. By this time
the tangle had grown so thick that it would have been
impossible to see a lion unless one were on top of it.
The only remaining landmark visible above the thorns
was a hill that was known to be on the far side of the
road; but after an hour of slow progress the very foot
of this hill had been reached, yet no road had been
crossed.

By this stage the bushes had grown so thick that it
was impossible to proceed forward at all. The road had
completely disappeared, two hours' gas had been wasted,
and there was complete disagreement about which way
to proceed. On all sides there was only silence and the
identical thorns and the misleading outlines of the distant
hills. Occasionally a partridge or a swallow passed
overhead, and once a crow emerged from beneath a
bush and strutted around with its beak ajar; but the
bird's evident confidence, unlike the hyena's, was merely
frustrating. Eventually a frail reasoning suggested that
the road must have been crossed unawares, though this
hardly seemed possible.

The truck was reversed back along its own tracks, and after a very long time there emerged the faintest outline of other tire marks at an angle to its route. This was the road. Although not difficult to follow when one was on it, it became almost invisible if approached at even a narrow angle. Up and down its length, the thorns pressed in no less closely than elsewhere, the road twisting between them rather than shouldering them aside. The tire tracks in the sand were all it amounted to. If a week had passed without a vehicle, the only road on the map would have had to be made all over again.

The next figure to emerge during this tour of inspection was yet another warden, perhaps the strangest one of all. At midday he approached around a bend in the road at the head of a small convoy of vehicles, a large, elderly man dressed in khaki shorts that reached below his knees, long khaki socks, and roomy army boots. He sprang out awkwardly from behind his dust cloud, weighed down with two bandoliers, a knife, a rifle, and a pistol at his waist, and asked to see permits. He was, he explained, "on patrol," accompanied by seventeen uniformed rangers, each carrying approximately the same weight of arms. One man at least had not given up the idea of the Lake Rudolf[2] National Park.

The reason for his patrol, he said, was tribal fighting. The Gabbra had attacked the Shangila. They had penetrated to the north of the lake, killed fifteen men, and emasculated two more. Then the Shangila had replied in force and driven the Gabbra 150 miles right out across the Chalbi Desert as far south as Marsabit Forest. Many Gabbra had taken refuge in his camp, and in order to protect them, he had armed his men.

The warden did not like the Shangila. They had settled on an island in what he considered the national park and had eaten some birds' eggs. He had expelled them from the entire area of his jurisdiction and had been gratified to notice that the birdlife had considerably increased. The possibility that his own efforts had initiated a tribal war was not mentioned, though it seemed far from unlikely. To declare a new national park over an area where resources were so scarce was almost bound to result in increased and violent tribal competition.[3] The tranquillity that the warden created was illusory, brought about at the price of emasculation or death for the people who, before his arrival, had looked on his sanctuary as their home.

Perhaps it was an illusion that he too had difficulty in sustaining, for he hurried off again, back to his birds, as though disturbed by the presence in his world of anyone capable of conducting a rational conversation. The land he looked out on had to remain empty. His park would never be so beautiful as now, when it existed only in his own imagination. Visible figures spoiled the view.

The next morning, at an oasis, in the still dawn, when there was no heat to mask the colors of the trees and the pool and the plovers and geese that flocked near it, two figures with a camel stopped at a distance on seeing the truck, seeming ready to fly at the least alarm. When reassured, the taller figure, a woman, led her camel and the boy with her to a safe position on the opposite side of the water, then slowly approached to speak. She stepped lightly and was dressed in a faded muslin wrap with a black scarf around her head, and she wore eight thick silver chains around her neck and more silver at her wrists and elbows. In greeting she raised both her hands above her head and touched them, then lowered them to her waist in two graceful arcs. But she spoke only Gabbra, and it was impossible to discover why she had been afraid at the sight of Europeans in a truck.

One characteristic of the people who have found a way to survive in the Northern Frontier District is that they regard each other with the gravest suspicion. They possess an exaggerated critical distance, the personal aura which they feel impelled to defend if it is penetrated. But the potential need to draw on each other's resources in an emergency (a broken leg, an exhausted stock of tea) prevents them from indulging it very frequently. It does, however, remain a point of pride with them not to admit to their interdependency.

On the edge of the ranching country, George, an American anthropologist, had set up a camp to complete the fieldwork for his thesis on the Samburu. He had used the usual inducements to gain the confidence of the local clans, making himself useful or interesting to them in a small way and thereby encouraging them to tolerate his questions. And he had succeeded in making them his friends, to the extent that he had long outstayed the period of eighteen months originally allotted for his fieldwork. His camp was set up about a mile off the road and was impossible to find without a guide. He had a trailer and several spacious tents and even a shower from a perforated bucket. He was going to build a wooden house and had already started on the foundations. He preferred a tent, but his wife insisted on the house. It would be safer for the children at night. In the evening when the family sat around the fire and the children stopped fighting and the stars shone through the trees, they made a romantic group, reminiscent of their great-grandfather's generation in the American West.

There was no question about the sincerity of George's admiration for the Samburu, which was based on four years of patient observation. If he ever published the results of his work, it would be a considerable addition to the understanding of pastoralism. Nor did he seem to feel any strain in respecting the object of his inquiry. He never, for instance, betrayed the astonished triumph of the anthropologist who meets a "primitive herdsman" and discovers that he possesses a degree in anthro-

pology, such an encounter apparently providing a life-
giving confirmation of the anthropologist's respect for
the unevolved values of his specimens. This myth of the
graduate herdsman now occupies a position of equal importance to the earlier African myths of ferociously
savage behavior, and it plays an equivalent role in justifying interference in the affairs of a less powerful and
disturbingly strange people.

But there were barriers nonetheless between George
and the Samburu. Some of the openness that had once
existed between them had gone. Perhaps it was because
of their natural suspicion of men who turned in reports
to the government, of scientists as spies, that this had
happened. Or perhaps it was because George had stayed
so much longer than they expected and had begun to discover more than they wished to reveal. Or perhaps it was
merely an unacknowledged limitation in the scientific
technique that had caused this opacity to form. It was as
though the attempt to record an oral culture were in itself
a destructive process, as though the very precision necessary for scientific description were a misrepresentation
of imprecise and previously unrecorded truth, and as
though the fact of recording preference or custom encouraged those under study to alter both, to change
their behavior in order to defend their freedom to make
such changes.

Squarely in the foreground of these distant and
shadowy possibilities, George faced another problem:
his wife. The second of their two children had been born
at the camp; but during the birth complications had
arisen, and she had nearly died before they could get
her back to Nairobi. Now she was pregnant again. This
time her husband had rigged up a land line to the nearest
radio telephone, a friend's plane was standing by to fetch
her, and their truck was kept in an unusually good state
of repair. All this had to be paid for, as did the camp. If

George had been prepared to abandon both his role of observer and his family, he might have managed to live among the Samburu without his long-expired grant.

But he would not, so he sold the only thing he had to sell: his knowledge of the tribe and his relationship with its members. He set up another camp some distance away from his own and invited tourists to stay there and imitate the life he led. Parties of visitors moved off each morning with a tribesman as guide and toured the several villages. George gave lectures in the evening on various aspects of tribal life. Whatever game might be in the area could also be viewed. "Only the specialists meet people," he said. "I wouldn't want to put them on view, like the animals." But in practice everyone who wanted to do so met the tribesmen.

Although George's experiment had long since been completed, the scientist could not bear to leave his laboratory, and so he had become a tourist guide, and the people who were originally the object of strictly scientific inquiry were now on show to any idle passerby who could afford his fee. He who had set out among these uninstructed people as their patron had lingered on until his resources were exhausted; in becoming dependent on their complaisance for his livelihood, a protégé of theirs, he confirmed the superiority of their "primitive" habit. Though it was, for George, an unexpected reversal of roles, it was not inconsistent; what better basis for "respect of the savage" could there be than dependency on him? The only drawback was that the respect should be so one-sided. For the pastoralists had little use, beyond the gratification of curiosity, for George's knowledge. Thus, they reduced George to the status of camp manager; their disuse for his science compromised his status as scientist.

In the light of all this, the group around the fire in the evening lost some of its warmth. George's wife

worried about the children locked into the caravan behind her and the problems that might arise with her
next baby. That week a pack of wild dogs had run right
through the camp, and a jackal had taken one of her
ducks. The tribesmen who spent day after day lounging
around her tents were beginning to get on her nerves.
Sometimes, without thinking, they cut the land line to
the radio transmitter. She looked out into the dark, with
its rustling shadows, and shivered.

The anthropologist was not the only scientist who suffered
from the lack of popular interest in his work. Of all the
figures in the long procession of Northern scholarship
which winds across the African scene, few can be stranger
than the hominid paleontologist with his improbable belief that man existed in Africa more than three million
years ago and that the evidence of this is still lying
around on the surface of the land. For the pursuit of
this quest the Northern Frontier District provides the
perfect setting. Here on the eastern shore of Lake
Rudolf, six hundred miles from Nairobi, is the emptiest
mirror of all, where man can gaze at nothing but the
traces of his own presence three million years before.
   The study of prehistory is an expensive discipline
which has to be pursued for a lifetime in places whose
inaccessibility can price a season's work at £100,000
($200,000). Since paleontology is of no practical use, its
students are denied ready access to official funds, and
their only alternative sponsors are the public. The sole
aspect of paleontology in which the public takes a con-
sistent interest is the "missing link," the direct evidence
that man and animals have a common ancestry. This
results in a conflict for the paleontologist between scientific standards of proof and the demands of publicity. In
managing this balancing act there must be occasional
stumbles, and in disguising these from the international

spotlight the remoteness of the Northern Frontier District comes into its own.

The degree of "control" demanded by the hominid paleontologist exceeds even that of the conservationist at his most ambitious. At Koobi Fora there has been established a lakeside camp which is surrounded by five hundred square miles of "protected area," in which it is forbidden to lift or disturb a single stone. The reason is that all the fossils coming from this site have been found scattered on the ground, and this rule, which is naturally impossible to enforce, enables the director, Richard Leakey, to warn off anyone who approaches the camp without his permission. The staff has even been instructed to obtain the director's authority to fill the water bottles of any travelers who may apply for assistance.

The drawback of this exclusiveness is that while it is no doubt ideal for purposes of academic reflection, it is fatal to public interest. To this problem an ingenious solution has been found. Since there was no well of public patronage to be drawn from in Africa, the search has been carried farther afield. The director's father, the late L. S. B. Leakey, managed to interest the National Geographic Society of America in his work, and he led the society's members in a lively dance up and down the Rift Valley in their search for the fossilized remains of prehistoric man. Since the patrons were so far away, they could inspect the sites only occasionally, and when they came, they all came together as a learned package tour and with mobile canteens, to enjoy a private view.

This, the sponsors' official inspection, is a particularly difficult moment for the hominid paleontologist. Much of the work on the site has to do with the whole range of fossilized life—giraffe's teeth, a porcupine jaw, the teeth of a hyena, the teeth and limb bones of assorted bovids, the teeth of an elephant, the whole collection of fauna. Then there are the stones, axheads, skinning knives, and curious smooth pebbles whose probable use, if any, is completely unknown. But the sponsors cannot be told more than once or twice that no one knows the answers to their interminable questions. It calls the whole expensive business into question. L. S. B. Leakey had a brisk solution: he invented imaginative theories. The pebbles were *bolas*; prehistoric ape-man fastened them to vegetable cords and whirled them around and around his head. He, L. S. B. Leakey, linguist, anthropologist, archaeologist, polymath, made such a rope and repeated the trick in front of a camera, roaring with laughter. But time has passed, and Leakey's laughter has been echoed less generously and for too long, in the laboratories of his rivals, and his widow, Dr. Mary Leakey, an expert on stone tools, now describes the *bolas* theory as "ridiculous."

Then there were the fossilized footprints. These curious marks in the stone of Olduvai Gorge, the Leakeys' other camp, eight hundred miles to the south in Tanzania, do bear some resemblance to the print of a naked human foot. At one time they were described as "the first evidence of the nature of the soft tissue anatomy of early man." But that sort of comment, while fine for the National Geographic Society's research committee, does not go down so well at other levels. So when the society members passed by the footprints on their last visit, they were not invited to inspect them. Sadly, the human footprints theory is also "no longer mentioned."[4]

Saddest of all is the fate of Leakey's most celebrated discovery, "Nutcracker Man," the skull which in 1959 received worldwide publicity as the "missing link" and was the starting point for the association between the National Geographic Society and the Leakeys. A small museum still stands at Olduvai, perched above the gorge, to explain the significance of this find, the best-known fossil since Piltdown Man. Outside the museum there is a prominent notice board stating that since "Nutcracker

Man" emerged, the work at Olduvai has been sponsored by the National Geographic Society of America. The implication is clear: a unique discovery resulted in a generous subsidy. Without the discovery there would be no money; without the money, no more discoveries. But the notice board is out of date, and the museum has become an exhibition of abandoned hypotheses. Everything first claimed for "Nutcracker Man" by L. S. B. Leakey has since been retracted. The massive skull was supposed to be that of the earliest human ancestor, a member of the genus *Homo* directly in line with *Homo sapiens*. Now it is agreed by the majority of learned opinion that *Australopithecus boisei*, to give Nutcracker its scientific name, is not a human ancestor, nor is it a representative of a genus within the hominid family, nor is it a representative of a new genus, and so not even an original discovery of the most commonplace sort. Instead, it is merely another specimen of the established genus *Australopithecus*, an apelike creature of minimal intelligence first discovered by Leakey's great rival, Professor Raymond Dart, in South Africa in 1924. In serious conversation the name "Nutcracker Man" is also "no longer mentioned."

But the research committee, which on the last visit included President Johnson's widow, Lady Bird, did not have to go away entirely disappointed. If they could not yet be sure of the human family tree, they could at least catch a glimpse of the excitement which overwhelms the most rigorous paleontologists on the conviction that they are looking at a stone that has been molded over millions of years from a bone in the body of some human ancestor. Just as the committee arrived to view the routine excavations, one of the excavators began to unearth a skull. Eventually this was classified as that of a prehistoric baboon, but for a few moments the irrational fascination of hominids had been visible for all to see. Or nearly all; one of Lady Bird's Secret Service men described the whole incident as " a stunt."

As the party proceeded with its inspection, each elderly member sensibly fitted out in sun hat and safari suit, it was watched by a group of Masai, some of whom occasionally assist the excavation by bringing in the stones which their eyes can pick out so much more quickly, although the significance of these finds bypasses their comprehension and interest. Before the gorge was discovered for Europeans, by an entomologist pursuing a butterfly through the thorn scrub at its lip, it was known for time beyond memory to the Masai; they valued the medicinal properties of the shriveled *olduvai* shrub which grew there and after which they named it.

In one part of the gorge, where there is a curious pattern of stones, the Masai had made a ceremonial place for their *morani*. Acting on the theory that this place is a repository of very unusual tools, the excavators erected a secure shelter over it, and the Masai are now forbidden to use it. Here is a further paradox of control. In order to develop an understanding of how the gorge was once used by man, the men who still find a use for it are expelled. What may be the only continuing human link with prehistory is snapped so that the site may be preserved. But the site would not even exist if the use which the Masai found for it had not preserved it. Was it coincidence that they selected a prehistoric reliquary for their own ceremonies? In any event, as soon as the intervention had taken place and the control reassuringly imposed, the site was damaged. The *morani*, irritated by this interference with their traditions, vandalized the shelter and destroyed some of the relics.

There is no danger of an equivalent problem arising at the other Leakey camp at Koobi Fora. There the only possible threat has been removed with the disappearance of the Shangila people. There are now no Africans within fifty miles of the camp apart from the employed staff, which includes a team of experienced searchers who actually find most of the fossils. Their chief qualifications are sharp eyes, a knowledge of likely looking stones, and the ability to pass day after day in wandering across the lava beds beneath the sun. Their motives in undertaking this work, apart from the need to earn a living, are obscure. Scientific curiosity is unlikely to be among them since the searchers have little scientific knowledge. Apart from their eyesight, their true importance to the proceedings is political.

Just as "Nutcracker Man" played a prominent role in bolstering the infant culture and national self-esteem of Tanzania, so the association of Kenya with hominid paleontology, through the African team that actually looks for the fossils, is emphasized whenever possible. The leader of the searchers has even been appointed deputy leader of the expedition. He left school after four years because his father could no longer pay the fees. In 1960 he began to work for L. S. B. Leakey, grubbing around for fossils in Olduvai Gorge. At Lake Rudolf, where he moved after old Leakey's death, he has had considerable success and has found many of the most interesting objects. The directors of most expeditions tend to monopolize publicity, but at Koobi Fora there is a recognized courtesy now paid to the Africans involved in that if they pick up something noteworthy, the first announcement credits them with the achievement. Their essential status, however, remains that of directed onlooker. The leader of the African team, despite the suggestion that he will shortly be submitting a doctoral thesis at the National University, cannot always remember the fossil date of his most important find.

For the scientists working at Koobi Fora there is a more rigorous approach. No matter how inexperienced the director's colleagues might be when they arrive straight from America or Europe and are flown up to the lake, they are expected to conduct their work as though they were as well acclimatized as his African staff. Since the

Africans are in the habit of walking across the volcanic outcrops all day without taking any water, this can be uncomfortable for the newly arrived. Indeed, one young man got lost and died of thirst. It was a tribute to the director's self-confidence that this event did not lead him to modify his arrangements.

The director's net of patronage is extensive; no one can mount an archaeological expedition in Kenya without his authority, and he is frequently absent from Lake Rudolf. When he is away, work can proceed in a more relaxed atmosphere. The hazards, apart from sunstroke, include occasional encounters with snakes or lions, thoughts of which keep some of the paleontologists awake at night. But to study fossil man, it is sometimes necessary to face the hazards of the fossil age. After a meeting with a lion, one English student requested permission to carry a gun, which the director refused. The youth appeared to accept this decision, with the assistance of a daily ration of whiskey, but after his departure it was discovered that the whiskey bottle he had taken to work each day contained gasoline. If he ever met another lion, he intended to bombard it with this cocktail.

So, beset by theoretical and practical problems on all sides, the hominid paleontologist battles on. Any conclusion he draws must be based on a tiny world sample of 120 hominid fossils. If he were to take account of all the skeptical objections raised about his work by physicists, chemists, anatomists, and even fellow paleontologists, he might achieve a rare degree of objective purity, but he would risk losing his sponsors, his site, and his career. The world is waiting for a family tree, and he provides one, sometimes several new ones annually. Methods of dating are imprecise, but the dates can always be revised, usually backward, deeper into the mists of prehistory, half a million years at a time.

Hominid paleontology is engaged in finding the evidence of humanness, but humanness itself has never been defined. Is it inextricably related to brain size or to brain shape, or to the capacity to make tools, or to the ability to walk upright? Evidence relating to all these can be traced in the fossils, and the paleontologists, being human, tend to favor the theory that their personal discoveries suggest. But suppose the essential characteristic of humanness is language. Or suppose it is exogenetic heredity, not the ability to make tools (which is shared by baboons and other species), but the ability to transmit that knowledge from generation to generation through teaching. How can the paleontologists distinguish between the fossils of apelike men with language, and those of manlike apes without it? Suppose one accepted the theory of the bicameral mind. This suggests that conscious thought was not developed by man until 1000 B.C.; will it ever be possible to trace the identifying characteristics of the species' ancestors three million years earlier, if this be the case?

Undaunted by any of this, the hominid paleontologist is capable of producing a matchbox full of fossil knucklebones at a press conference and describing them as evidence of a social unit unlike that seen in any other species and, moreover, a sign that our earliest ancestors were decent, cooperative creatures instead of killer apes.

After supper at Koobi Fora the highly qualified young paleontologists who have just arrived from America to be confronted with the "hominid temptation" can sit on the veranda and recover from the exhaustion of the day. In the vague light of the moon they can just about see the edge of Lake Rudolf, from which, if they are fortunate, a silent hippo may rise. Closer to the huts jackals and striped hyenas loom out of the warm night, waiting for a chance to get at the camp's garbage heap. And it is not only the scampering and snuffling around the veranda that make the new arrivals uneasy. For "the trouble with hominids," as one of the director's more experienced colleagues put it, "is that there are more scientists than there are skulls. I stick to nonprimate fossils. One can be much more scientific; after all, they provide millions, not dozens, of reasonably exact points of comparison. But I have to work with hominid researchers because they get all the money."

Hominid paleontology "does indeed stimulate ambition, though not, unfortunately, scientific acumen," wrote one anatomist.[5] "It is odd," he continued, "that whereas man's knowledge of the stars was one of the earliest forms of science, his knowledge of his own origins can hardly be called scientific even today." In that case it is perhaps not so odd that this putative science should have found its most celebrated location in this part of Africa, under the detached guardianship of the Kenyan people. L. S. B. Leakey was a scholar in three disciplines, but he was also a showman who took shortcuts and had a genius for publicity. And is it so inappropriate that from so gifted a life given to the search for the human family tree the most memorable tree propagated should have been his own? The roguish savant succeeded by his bureaucratic son, their relationship reproduced in the eventual heir to fifty years of learned speculation: Kimoya, the leader of the African team, sitting in the shadows by the campfire at Lake Rudolf, watching the director's face, sucking the same shape of pipe, wearing the same colored shirt and pensive expression, sipping the same brand of whiskey, and muddling up the dates.

NOTES

1. Paul Spencer, *The Samburu* (London: Routledge, 1965).
2. Lake Rudolf has been renamed Lake Turkana by government decree. Here the more familiar name has been retained.

3. It is interesting to note that the group of tribes directly affected by the Lake Rudolf National Park are close neighbors of the Ik people of Uganda, whose story is summarized in Chapter 2. It is unlikely, however, that the people of East Rudolf will suffer the same disaster at the hands of conservationists as was suffered by the Ik in the 1960s. Under African direction the relationship of game wardens and poachers seems to be held in more equal balance. Elephant, poacher, and warden are all permitted to eat.

4. The discovery of more prints was announced in March 1979, and the "footprints theory" is currently enjoying a second airing.

5. Professor J. Z. Young, *New York Review of Books,* May 29, 1975.

CHAPTER 4

THE SMALLEST TRIBE

From Afric's steaming Jungles
    To India's arid Plains
The Natives are dependent
    Upon the White Man's Brains. . . .

Instead of letting him exist
    Just how and where he pleases,
We teach him how to live like Us
    And die of Our Diseases.

We move him from his valleys
    To airy mountain-tops
Where he won't undermine his health
    By raising herds and crops.

The most disturbing nightmare
    Which haunts each White Man's son
Is: "If there had been no White Men
    What *would* the Blacks have done?"

                      Pont, *Lines*

The road to Loyengalani lies by a pass which picks its way between huge black boulders. As one ascends toward the head of the pass, there is no warning of the sight in store. All that is visible are the flat, dead lava beds of the Northern Frontier, their monotony relieved by the occasional solitary zebra, apparently stranded amid the flints without a blade of food for miles. Then suddenly one is at the top, and there is a flash in the blackness ahead and then a clear view of a brilliant inland sea, stretching away northward through the center of Africa, Lake Rudolf. There are desert roses among the rocks

and, far below, what seem to be white beaches fringed
with yellow grass, and as one descends toward them, by
a road that falls like a flight of giant steps, the color of
the lake changes from blue to intense green. Down by the
shore the gentle illusion is maintained. The fine sand
bears the prints of wading birds, spidery tridents beside
the pudgy webbed claw marks of the crocodile, and the
dimpled depressions of hippopotami, which resemble the
outline of crudely cut piecrusts. The hippos pass the day
beneath the water in sleep, but some yards offshore sharp
silhouettes lie on the surface waiting for the beach to be
vacated so that they may rest their long snouts on its
heated softness. Cooled by a gentle breeze, one can look
up from this beach to the volcano, Mount Kulal, which
looms in the distant sky, and just distinguish the pattern
of the forest which always seems to break out in Africa
at a certain altitude.

It is curious to gaze up from the growing heat of the
lake basin, under the volcano, and realize that although
the mountain is completely surrounded by desert, in its
tenuous hoop of trees there live elephants and pigs and
pythons and all the other wallowing animals that profit
from a vegetable dampness. And then the heat pricks,
and the glare of the sun reflected off the lake reduces the
view to a painful cascade of pointed lights, and without
warning the breeze is extinguished by a wind that roars
down the pass like a waterfall and out over the water.

The settlement called Loyengalani lies about an hour's
drive along the lake. It is a place, rather than an anonymous expanse of foreshore, because it has a spring, one
of the few sources of sweet water for hundreds of miles,
and there are palm trees beside its streams to provide
shelter and fuel for the nomadic people of East Rudolph
who are its constant but irregular visitors.

There are also the settled people of Loyengalani, the
Elmolo, whose numbers once sank to seventy-five and
who still amount to no more than three hundred and so

form one of the smallest tribes in Africa. Some years before, an attempt to develop the oasis ended in disaster. A mission and a fishing lodge were started, but before the buildings were complete, they attracted the presence of a Somali raiding party which murdered everyone it could find. This is the sort of incident on which mission societies thrive; but game fishermen are less adventurous, and it was not until the ending of the Somali war and the installation of a police garrison that the lodge reopened. From then on Loyengalani should have become just another flea-bitten settlement on the Northern Frontier, but things did not go according to plan.

The two institutions of Loyengalani, the mission and the lodge, stand in favored positions but are completely surrounded by high wire fencing. This is not to keep out animals or bandits. Rather, it is a precaution against the activities of the Elmolo, the very people who are supposed to be the beneficiaries of the scheme. The most prominent feature of the mission is not the school or the church but the gas pump. The old pump stands just inside the wire as a symbol of ecclesiastical authority; but it proved to be too difficult to guard, so, at some risk to their lives, the good fathers have installed a new one right outside the mission building, and every vehicle that passes through Loyengalani comes to the mission in search of gas. By closing the pump, the missionaries can effectively close down quite a sizable part of Kenya. Furthermore, the pump supplies the mission truck, the only regular transport between the settlement and the world. Even the lodge, which like the mission is under Italian direction, relies on this truck for its regular supplies. And if the missionaries decide that there is a more pressing need for Bibles than for beer (as even today they sometimes do), those staying at the lodge go sober. That is a serious matter in this place.

The mission runs the school and a dispensary, and the lodge employs all the people who can find local jobs, and

between these two centers a small village, quite distinct
from the original Elmolo settlement, has grown. There
is a short street containing a dozen shops and houses for
the Somalis, which have been constructed from flattened
oil cans, and there are two clusters of palm-leaf huts
where the Turkana and the Samburu live. So although
the original mission was intended for the Elmolo, most
of the people who now live in Loyengalani belong to
other tribes and have been attracted to the place only by
the mission. And though the period of Elmolo recovery
is dated from the arrival of the mission, nearly half the
members of the tribe have recently left the settlement.
They shun the mission and even refuse medical treatment.
They are, in the words of one of the missionaries, "running away from civilization." In explanation the present
priest in charge added, "There was original sin here before I arrived. Now we cannot trust these people. They
were given too much free, so they will never stand on
their own feet. That is why we have built the fence, but
we still have always to keep our eyes peeled. They steal
from you and call you friend."

The tourists who come to enjoy the simple life which
the Elmolo have rejected as too civilized are flown in
straight from Nairobi. They land on the dusty strip
beside the lake and are greeted by the lodge stewards
wearing beach clothes, little green shorts and white
T-shirts. But then they have to struggle up the hill
through the eager crowd of residents, dressed in authen-
tic paint and feathers, being warned all the while to keep
a hand on everything they possess. At last they reach the
security of the gatehouse, and the gates are locked behind
them; but the crowd, though silent, continues to press up
to the fence, staring in, numbering the tourists' visible
possessions, and devising ways of acquiring them. The
tourists' sense of insecurity increases again when they
eventually realize that the friendly and considerate Africans dressed up in the little shorts and T-shirts are related

to the painted savages outside and apparently on the best of terms with them. By the time that they discover that the beer is warm because the refrigerator is broken and the hotel manager is more interested in the challenge of survival than in running a hotel, it is too late. The plane has disappeared into the yellow haze above, and they are consigned to four days in this fortified compound under the command of a man whom many of them regard as half crazy.

By day they can hire a camel which will carry them up and down the dusty furnace of the airstrip, or they can take boat trips over the torpid lake, hauling in enormous and unresisting perch. When the day's distractions are exhausted, there is the swimming pool which has been built astride the settlement's main spring. The water comes out of the ground at a comfortable temperature, and the visitors float in it on their backs, perhaps looking for a glimpse of their returning plane. Since they are swimming in the spring which is the main water supply for the people of Loyengalani, its use has to be shared; the women of the community are admitted into the compound to do their washing in the pool's outlet drain.

At dusk the fireflies dance briefly above the pool until they are drowned in the beams of the security lights which burn throughout the compound all night. The wind gets up around two in the morning, waking the tourists and turning the fragile little guest huts into wind tunnels, since the heat requires everyone to leave his ventilation slats open. And the tourists toss about and watch the shadows playing on the curtains and perhaps note one shadow that scuttles across the ceiling like something from a horror film, a spider the size of a crab with hairy legs and a gaping mouth and the ability to jump onto the pillow whenever it chooses. And they may also realize, since it is their first night in Africa, that if they were to be given a map of the continent and asked to point out their own position, they would not know where to look.

It was to this lodge that Willy, a prosperous building
contractor from Belgium, came to shoot a crocodile.

Willy's arrival at the lodge, though worthy of attention,
passed without general remark because it coincided with
the discovery of a theft from one of the tourist huts. Two
hundred dollars in traveler's checks had disappeared from
a locked room. The police had been summoned and had
arrived in a three-ton truck. The man to concentrate on
was the room steward, they decided, and they took
him away to the barracks for full investigation. In
all the excitement the entrance of Willy with his personal safari, cook, and professional hunter and skinners
and advance party of gun bearers, and the professional
hunter's father, also a professional hunter, was almost
surreptitious.

Willy had hunted animals all over Africa and Europe.
He had shot lion and elephant and buffalo and so on, but
he had never secured a crocodile. Loyengalani is situated
in Hunting Block 68 and is a particularly good place to
look for crocodiles since the bitter lake water toughens
their hides and makes them useless for handbags, allowing for an abundant supply. Willy only needed someone
to guide him to a promising spot, and with this in mind
his hunter, Mr. Patel, interviewed the Elmolo chief.

The chief of the Elmolo spoke no English and had
been appointed by the administration. He lived with the
majority of his people on the edge of the settlement,
away from the rest of the village and the shade of the
trees, on a pebbly spot which jutted out into the lake.
Looking for the chief, Mr. Patel understandably went to
the grandest hut which was tall and solid and five times
the size of the others and possessed regular doors. But
they were padlocked; no one answered however hard Mr.
Patel knocked, and only when a small boy who spoke
English appeared could the old gentlemen sitting in the
shade of the grand hut explain that it was empty. Al-

though it was built of doum palm in the tribal style, it did not even belong to the Elmolo.

It belonged to an American girl, an anthropologist, who had come to study the tribe, until she was eventually driven away when they had taken all her possessions. The padlocks on her door remained in place, as useless now as when the hut was filled with her property. And the Elmolo maintained the empty hut carefully, and they still spoke of their departed guest with affection and seemed proud of the impressive structure she had bequeathed them, though they could find no use for it. As for the chief, he lived in a hut that was indistinguishable from the rest, a low round structure containing a single undivided chamber.

Negotiations in the chief's hut took some time. The chief sat on the floor so that his guests might sit on the sprung bed frames. There were some donkey panniers to one side, and a litter of old brooms and fishing floats, and a devotional picture of the Blessed Virgin attached to the palm-frond wall, though the chief was not a Christian. Everything he said was interpreted by the same small boy.

Before they came to Loyengalani, the Elmolo lived on an island out in the lake. It is a large island, and they had lived there since long before the time and events of Lake Rudolf were recorded. It was a safe refuge from the tribes to the north who preyed on them and whose habit of ritual emasculation may have been directly related to their falling numbers. But the island was not self-sufficient. A trade existed between the Elmolo and the mainland. They exchanged fish for goats with the nomadic Rendille (although since the crossing of the lake is always hazardous—the sudden storms are violent enough to sink modern fishing boats—and since the Elmolo had only rafts made from soft doum-palm trunks which become waterlogged within an hour or so, and since the island crossing takes all day by raft, how they managed it is a mystery).

The chief said that the Elmolo still lived by fishing; until recently they had dried lake perch and sent them down to Nairobi on the mission truck. But the market had failed, so they now just caught what they needed for themselves. It was the only way to live since only six of his people had jobs, three at the lodge and three on the game-fishing boats. But they were used to this style of life, and he expected it to continue. The chief did not know how many of the children went to school, but he knew that it was too expensive for most of them. Even the small interpreter, who spoke Turkana, Samburu, English, and Swahili, had not been to school for a year because his father could no longer afford it.

Eventually the conversation turned to the subject of crocodiles, which the Elmolo hunted with harpoons. The chief mentioned how extremely difficult they were to find, and Mr. Patel mentioned how anxious Mr. Willy was to shoot one, and the chief said he knew the only man who could find one tomorrow, but he was very busy, and Mr. Patel mentioned a sum of money, and the chief said for twice that he would come along as well, and the deal was done.

That evening, excited by the prospect of a crocodile, Willy threw a party. He had placed his camp outside the fortified compounds at the central crossroads of the village since he was confident that no one would attempt to rob a man with so many guns. There, while he and his wife and daughter and their friend who was a Belgian judge waited for Baby, the aged cook, to make some curry, Willy settled down to tell the story of his life. His father had always wanted him to be a doctor, but there was more money in building—the judge nodded sagely—and he had never regretted his decision to abandon his studies. Since he could lift a gun, he said, his life had been dominated by hunting. Here he stuck out his leg amid the fireflies and wiggled his toes. That was how he had come to lose one of his toes; he stopped wiggling them for a moment to confirm this intelligence. He had shot it off himself in the Ardennes forest, while out hunting. A wild boar had leaped on him in the middle of winter and had attempted to bite off his face. For a time they had rolled around in the snow, clasped firmly together like lovers, until eventually Willy had managed to insert the barrel of his gun into the mouth of the boar and to pull the trigger. The bullet had passed through the boar, exited at the rear, and carried away Willy's toe. And he had struggled out from beneath the relaxed carcass and walked several kilometers to the nearest house. His wife had supposed that after such an experience he would give up hunting. Nah! He wiggled his toes again.

Mr. Patel became rather impatient during this talk— possibly he had heard it before—and he started to recount a more recent adventure with a lion. It seemed that Willy had failed to kill this lion with his first shot, and so the two of them had been obliged to track it through thick bush in order to finish it off. The bush had been so thick that they were almost upon it before they could see it, whereupon the lion had let out a tremendous roar. Mr. Patel had fired, and Willy had bolted. While it is not unusual for professional hunters to tell tales of their clients' circumspection, it is unusual for them to do it in front of them, particularly when the safari is costing $200 a day, but fortunately Willy had started on another hunting story, this time about his daughter, who that very morning had shot her first gazelle.

She was a frail young woman with a stooped figure and an uncertain expression, which she maintained even when her father smacked her bottom loudly in a moment of sudden affection. She had learned to shoot in his wood at home by shooting his chickens as they roosted in the trees. For the gazelle he had given her his crocodile gun. He had been rather worried for her because the last person he had lent it to had received a black eye from the telescopic sight. Naturally he had not mentioned this lest it make her more nervous. That night Willy, mindful of his neighbors, curled up to sleep with his favorite gun. Mr. Patel told him to put it away; but he paid no attention, and finally, when he had dropped off, Baby stole up and removed it to the gun rack.

The next morning was a Sunday; the mission gates were thrown open, and several hundred people, including the entire staff of the lodge and the pagan chief, arrived for mass. The whole congregation embraced the service with an impressive display of belief, even keeping reasonably still while a sermon, given in two languages which many found equally incomprehensible, lasted for thirty minutes. They sat in their tribal groups, marshaled by nuns and animated during the singing by old Father Mike, who had been an African missionary for fifty years and who took especial pride in the Turkana he had trained because they could sing top C. Once in Tanzania he had trained the church's brass band to play a selection from *Aïda*, but here it was an uphill struggle for him since the Samburu and the Elmolo found it impossible to pick out Northern melodies and remained as impervious to his musical instruction as they were to everything else to do with the mission. The mass was celebrated by the priest in charge, a craggy young man in thick spectacles whose naturally harsh voice became positively painful to hear when amplified by loudspeakers. For most of the week he wore a football uniform, the school team being his great passion, and it was noticeable how his athletic dignity was lost in the ceremonial vestment—just as that of the lodge stewards, who had abandoned their short trousers and T-shirts for suits, was enhanced by the same process. The only obvious peculiarity was that no plate was taken around at the time of the collection; if it once disappeared into the congregation, it would never be seen again. Instead, the whole assembly trooped up to the altar to make its offerings.

After mass there was a social gathering on the church

steps. The children held out rosaries for the old priest to bless, and all seemed united in common purpose and affection. And then Sister Constance, who supervised the infant school, came hurrying up in tears. During mass someone had broken into her store and wrecked it. The children's tunics had been thrown on the ground; medicine had been spilled over them; the room and its equipment were ruined. Nothing had been taken, but everything breakable had been smashed. The crime wave had spread to the mission, but Sister Constance had an explanation that verged on the poetic. "It is the older boys who have done this," she said, "the ones who have just left our school and who have nowhere to go."

To reach the Elmolo people who have "run away from civilization," one has to wade out into Lake Rudolf to the little island where they have settled. They will not talk to strangers, but the chief at Loyengalani spoke to Lanapirr, "the fat one," who was their leader and extremely thin, and a visit was arranged. "They are not worth the time," said Sister Constance when the mission heard of this plan. "Those people on the island won't even take Sister Lorenziana's good medicine. They even refuse it for their children, though they know that they are sick. They are wicked people."

The island is about a quarter of a mile offshore, and before wading into the water, the chief pointed out a long scar on his leg. He said that he had received it as a child when he had been seized by a crocodile. "Many teeth, the crocodile," said the chief, as he hitched up his robe and prodded the water in front of him with his furled umbrella. "Too many, many teeth." The water was soapy to the touch and nearly waist-deep. It was opaque, and one had to feel one's way between the sharp stones on the lake bottom. Crossing it seemed to take a long time.

On the shore of the island there was a litter of fish skeletons and a crocodile skull. The children who lived there were fishing with a net, and unusually for African children, they paid little attention to the party of visitors. There was no drinking water on the island, so everyone who lived there drank the alkaline water of the lake. Eventually their stomachs learned to accept it. There were no trees on the island and hardly a blade of grass. Its surface was covered with volcanic stones, and at the foot of a lava slope the islanders had erected a few palm-leaf huts. This was their village.

Everyone on the island seemed to move very slowly and as seldom as possible. Strangers meant the possibility of food, and in return for this they were prepared to discuss their predicament. To show how they lived, two of the young men poled a flat raft made from palm trunks out into the sound, where they said they fished with harpoons. But it was not an impressive demonstration; they caught nothing, and after ten minutes the raft became waterlogged and started to sink. By the time they had floundered back to the beach both young men were exhausted. The islanders said they were the true Elmolo. They said the Elmolo were neither Turkana nor Samburu but a different people. "The Turkana and the Samburu travel around. But we live and die here. And when the Elmolo are a great people again we will still live and die here"; that was how they explained the difference. They said that they preferred the island because it was "so cool" and that they had no use for the mission. All of them denied any knowledge of the original Elmolo language, though they said one old woman still knew it. She was sitting outside her hut and was almost blind, but she was prepared to say two words in Elmolo, which were subsequently translated as "tobacco" and "tea." Then it began to grow dark, and it was time to wade back across the sound.

The young men said that on the previous night they had seen a fire on the mainland and they had crossed over and driven away a party of Somali raiders. It was an unlikely story, and though it was not impossible, they did not insist on it. They just shrugged and fell silent.

They have another story about a party of English explorers who disappeared with all their stores and equipment on Lake Rudolf in 1936. The colonial authorities finally decided that the explorers had drowned when their boat overturned in a squall out on the lake, but the El-molo murmur among themselves that they ate these men. It is one of the consequences of their condition that nobody believes this confession. The only person left who might know the truth of the matter would be the old lady on the island, with her few teeth and her taste for tobacco and tea.

The hunting party set out after lunch. There were emotional scenes of farewell, for the judge and Willy's wife and daughter were due to return to Brussels first, and they would not be seeing each other for three days. The more jokes Willy made about crocodiles that liked the taste of curry, the harder his wife sobbed, until Mr. Patel eventually succeeded in separating her from his client. Willy was placed between the expressionless chief and the senior fisherman, and the hunting party moved off. But within half an hour of the parting all were reunited on the lakeshore. The chief had been so efficient at finding a crocodile that it had been sighted, stalked, shot, and laid out on the road home before Willy's wife passed by.

Three crocodiles had been sunning themselves by the lake. The chief's sharp eyes had picked them out among the rocks from half a mile away, and Willy had shot the biggest from 250 yards through his telescopic sight. It died while it dozed, the only movement being the splash of the other two slipping into the water.

The judge, who was not interested in hunting but who was an amateur photographer, took several rolls of film to record his friend's triumph. He posed the crocodile in Willy's bush hat and then propped open the crocodile's eyes with matchsticks and its mouth with a knife. The chief and his senior fishermen were put to work hoisting Willy into the air; they weren't strong enough to put him on their shoulders. Willy's wife blew him kisses and tried to stop crying. She had many reasons for her tears. Willy had not been eaten; she was relieved. But she had to leave again, and she was sad. Also, her feet had swollen to twice their usual size because of mosquito bites, and she was in pain.

Furthermore, Willy had just decided to stuff the crocodile and bring it home, and she did not know where to put it. The house was full of stuffed animals: deer, boar, zebra, snakes, leopard, and parts of a hippopotamus. It was true that she could not remember a crocodile. Perhaps they had room for just the head. She tried to bring herself to look at it and burst into tears again. It was to be a full mount. The whole skin had to be removed as quickly as possible, every particle of flesh scraped off, sacks of salt rubbed in, and the skin kept damp all the way back to Nairobi. Only the chief remained unmoved by the storm of emotions around him. It was quite a big crocodile; he was calculating how many villagers would be able to feast that night. He indicated the urgency of getting to work on the skin, and so, at last, Mr. Patel's ramshackle safari triumphantly split up. That night Willy held another celebration supper, and he and Mr. Patel and Baby and old Patel slept exceptionally soundly, and somebody, despite the guns, crept up to their truck and removed several cans of sugar.

At the height of this crime wave the police chief announced that it was time for maneuvers, and he ordered a general mobilization, leaving only a skeleton force behind. Before leaving, he authorized the release of the suspected room steward, who was sent back to the lodge. "Don't worry," the police chief said reassuringly to the tourists. "The incident book is full of cases like yours." He drove off to the surrounding battlegrounds, passing on the road groups of armed Turkana tribesmen, who were coming into the oasis for a ceremony.

Up at the mission Sister Constance was inconsolable. The nursery school was her great pride. The children, up to ninety of them, attended during the dry season. After rain they went off to distant pastures to drink goat's milk. Her main work was to sew their clothes and accustom them to sitting quietly in front of a blackboard. Periodically she turned them out into the compound, where they spent the time rushing around in groups, being herded by a slightly older girl who was equipped with a light whip. Now all the uniforms were ruined, and she would have to start her work again. The sight of the mess in her store had reminded her of the *shiftas* who had raided the lodge before. They had come on an evening like this and shot up all the cars outside the lodge. "Then they caught the lodge manager and the priest in charge. We found their bodies in Room Six. Father was lying in his own blood, and the manager had his hands tied behind his back. There was another man who was building the compound, and he managed to escape in his lorry. He got a long way away, but then they caught him, too, and killed him. There was a road gang working at the pass, and they ran all the way back to the next settlement and told us. And then we came here to get them, and I drove all the way back to Nairobi with Father's body. It was just ten years ago."

The funeral dance was held that same evening, the evening of the day the police left and Sister Constance recalled the *shifta* raid. It was to mark the death of a child, the only child of the suspected room steward who was now revealed as a Turkana elder. It was a well-attended ceremony, the first full moon after the event, and it would cost him a lot. The dance started quietly in the gloomy hour before sunset, almost as if by chance. A small group of Turkana elders in red cloaks sat together under a tall palm. They were joined by a few *morani* and adult men. The men stood in a group, and one of them started to sing. The room steward, still in his T-shirt, came out from the lodge and sat down beside the elders.

Slowly it grew into an occasion. All the men started to sing. They stood in a line, and then one or two of them stepped forward and started to leap up and down in time to the singing, rising and falling on alternate beats. A group of girls joined hands in a line and faced them and also started to dance. A crowd gathered: all the other people in Loyengalani—Elmolo, Samburu, Rendille, the Somali shopkeepers. Even the teachers came down from the school. The number of dancers increased, and several of the lodge stewards, still in uniform, joined in. The young girls wore tribal dress, long gray hides that stretched from waist to ankle, with strings of beads between shoulder and chin. Their hair was caught up into tufts and stained red. The more beads they wore around the neck, the better they were loved, each string being the gift of their lover, a *moran* of their own age. When they eventually married, it would be to an older man whom they hardly knew, and they could no longer wear their beads. Several of the Turkana girls from the school stood by, sturdier figures demurely dressed in frocks and scarves, wondering whether to dance. From a distance they were watched by a sister from the mission. They giggled together and called out to her and hesitated, and then the singing rose again, and the decision was taken from them as they turned into the dance, their expressions changing instantly into the passionate indifference of all the girls of their age. They wore no beads, but around their necks, which were thickened with mission porridge, flapped the rosaries they had held out to be blessed that morning. As the men and the girls leaped, facing each other, they fixed each other's eyes, but their expressions showed that all they could see was the song.

Suddenly it stopped, leaving them leaping without purpose. Then another elder, leaning on a stick, started another song, and the singers drew closer to him, absorbed in their efforts, gazing ahead but noticing nothing else. The dance restarted; people were drawn to it from all over the oasis so that there were three circles: the dancers, the rest of the Turkana—older women and young children—and then, on the outside, the onlookers, people of many tribes alike in their exclusion. The dance grew wilder, the girls holding their line and managing to look both more disdainful and more challenging as the *morani* rushed at them and retreated again. Self-consciousness was lost in a deep concentration. The children at the edge tripping and struggling around the circle, the old ladies kissing each other's grandchildren, the lurching circle of dancers, and the still center of the elders—all were supported by the encompassing security of the song, until the wind began to blow again through the palms, and the dance, in mid-note, stopped.

PART 2

WEST AFRICA

AID AND WARFARE

Famines do not occur. They are organized by the grain trade.

Bertolt Brecht

Modern war is so expensive that we feel trade to be a better avenue to plunder. . . .

William James, *The Moral Equivalent of War*

CHAPTER 5

THE OUTPOST

In spite of existing conditions, there is reason to expect that this region around the elbow of the Niger will have the finest future of any portion of the Sahara, and one out of all proportion to its present wretched state. This future lies naturally in the river itself, a mighty water-course flowing through the midst of the desert and bringing to it tremendous annual floods which overflow and spread across the terrain. It is truly a second Nile, lacking only management to cause it to fertilize a second Egypt. There is not another spot in the whole Sahara where such financial possibilities are indicated.

Émile Gautier, professor of geography in Algiers, 1928

Let us not flatter ourselves overmuch on account of our human victories over nature. For each such victory it takes its revenge on us . . . at every step we are reminded that we by no means rule over nature like a conqueror over a foreign people. . . .

Friedrich Engels, *The Part Played by Labour in the Transition from Ape to Man*

The West African coastline is torn apart by wide rivers. They drain the rain forest of the interior and carry away the wreckage of the life beyond the trees. The greenery that falls into the stream can be seen from the river quays of the coastal towns as it bobs past on the current like the unrealized promise of easy wealth and is swept out to sea.

The rivers were a magnet for the first Northern travelers who reached Africa. From the fifteenth century they provided a route to the gold and ivory of the interior; there was upriver, where the trade was, and downriver to the homeward sea. There was, therefore, no need for a bridge. And since the North did not link the banks, they remained unlinked and still do today. Like the railway map of Africa, the rivers, as a means of transport, have remained untouched since the first colonial enthusiasm exhausted itself.

The trading settlement so tenuously established at the river mouth was the scene of the first stage of the relationship between Africa and the North. It preceded the slave trade and flourished at a time when nothing bound the two parties but the terms of their latest bargain. Sometimes the advantage lay with one, sometimes with the other; it was an equal relationship. In the few towns that have survived from that first encounter, without being abandoned or destroyed by subsequent addition, it is still possible to trace something of that mutual respect, all the more noticeable against the background of the official good manners which have succeeded it. Saint-Louis, in Senegal, is one such town.

Saint-Louis was once the principal town in Senegal, but it is now peripheral to the life of the country, a crumbling seaport which is even bypassed by the road north to Mauritania. But it was built originally to house the French settlers in some style. Then the colony grew too large, and its interests too extensive, and all the administrators had to be moved south to the rocky peninsula where they built Dakar, from which they could supervise the peanut trade and run an empire. Now the stone houses in Saint-Louis are inhabited by some *petits blancs*—poor whites—or by the superior mulatto families who can trace their descent back to the earliest settlers; the houses are decaying, but they remain the grandest in town and recall that brief period of glory.

A hotel has been opened in one of these houses, and beside it there is a walled courtyard which, viewed from the road, seems ready for demolition. A tall corrugated gate swings on one hinge, and the dogs wander in and out at will. But from the upper rooms of the hotel one can look into the courtyard and see that it is a very busy place. Behind the unhinged gate four large families live in the four small rooms of the courtyard which were originally designed as the domestic offices of the adjoining colonial house, now the hotel. Only two of these rooms have an electric light, and there is no light in the yard. At night this is dimly lit by the open fire which the families share. It is a very simple arrangement. One little girl, who tires early, carefully sweeps a corner of the yard, not cleaning it but marking out a form in the dust, unrolls a rush mat, and then lies down on it in her clothes and without a cover. She wriggles around for a moment and then sleeps. Shortly the other children join her, stretched out in the dark in their habitual places around the fire, oblivious to the evening life of the courtyard.

It is too dark to see the ground, but nobody steps on the children; like blind people, the members of this community have learned to live without light. And no noise is loud enough to disturb the sleepers. Beyond the walls of the yard two dogs bark at each other alternately and endlessly, one high, one low; a sick child cries and cries. There are car horns and music from a bar which never closes and a noise which is caused by great numbers of people moving through the darkness close together throughout the night, working, haggling, arguing, dancing—considering their numbers, moving rather quietly, but causing nonetheless a tremendous rustling noise, which ceases only at dawn, when even they go to rest as the cocks and goats, all the cocks and goats of the town, bleat and crow together, and the children sleep on around the dead fire.

The people who live in this courtyard, including the older children, work for the French widow who runs the hotel, which is a very pretty building also built around a courtyard but filled with plants and shrubs. It is a center for the remaining society of Saint-Louis, the widows who call on Madame, the families of *métis* with their intricate order of precedence, the few old colonials who prefer to remain in Saint-Louis rather than return to France and who provide the last link between the town and its original inspiration.

"Did you know," said one of the old waiters who lived in the courtyard, "that Madame was *métisse*? You would think to look at her that she was as white as you. And yet her father was as black as I am." And he stopped to enjoy the effect of this remark, a much-practiced pleasure of his. He seemed to offer the story as a curiosity of human achievement, and then, having drawn his listener into accepting it as such, he added, "Her daughter also married a *métis*, and her children, Madame's grandchildren, are as white as she is. She was so glad." Enjoying his audience's discomposure again, the old man withdrew into the kitchen.

But none of the Africans who listened to him seemed offended by the old lady's preference. They all knew her; she had been born there as they had, and would die there as they would, in the unlisted building which distinguished their street, among her unlisted family, whose proudest achievement was its connection with the civilization that had forgotten it. Saint-Louis was no longer a capital, but it was still more than a place on the road. It remains the center of a society, the dwindling society of mulattoes, the children of the original French settlers who had been encouraged to take African wives and thereby to rear an indigenous aristocracy which would be loyal to France. Once the mulattoes had advised metropolitan France on its policy in West Africa, and at the time of the Revolution they had arranged for slavery to be abolished in Saint-Louis, making it the first town in Africa to be freed of the trade that was to poison all that followed.

While the town flourished, it represented a moment of sympathy between Africa and the North, and there was some hope for that relationship, based as it was on trade and not yet blighted by conquest. The traders were permitted to settle in the fortified garrisons they established on the river mouth. But their security lay not in their fortifications but in the tolerance of the surrounding people. The balance of power was held by the Africans, and generally they did not abuse it, lacking a reason to do so. Later the balance of power changed in favor of the North, and events showed that Northerners, on the contrary, generally needed a reason not to abuse their advantage. The Senegal of coastal trading settlements was succeeded by the land of groundnuts and cash crops and a taxed colony, the Africa of development. But Saint-Louis was inspired by a different intention and a less dishonorable one, and the society that has descended from it has not entirely lost sight of the difference, though it sits now in the half-abandoned town, by the harbor which is peeling into the sea and which has become too dilapidated to receive even famine relief, dozing away the years over its imported apéritif, like an idea that the world has forgotten.

The road that hurries past Saint-Louis is the only road connecting Dakar, the capital of Senegal, with Nouakchott, the capital of Mauritania. It passes through the Sahel, the semiarid shore of the Saharan sea, and reaches the international border east of Saint-Louis on the Senegal River. Nothing urgent has used this road since the great drought of 1973, when it was a local supply route for the international grain convoys. And even their urgency was an illusion, since (as has subsequently become clear) throughout the period of the emergency there was enough grain stored within the six afflicted countries to feed their total populations.

As a political entity Mauritania is insignificant. It has about one million inhabitants, who occupy an area of desert which is one-tenth of the size of the United

States. Its borders follow compass bearings, straight lines on a map, and were laid down after heated argument between two ministries of the same government, the government of imperial France. Its annual rainfall varies between four inches and none, but the great majority of its people still manage to live by stock raising. Nouakchott was originally the site of a Foreign Legion fort, and it still looks more like a camp than a town. The sea is five miles away, but there is no port. The sand blows across the streets and piles up between the shacks of the metropolis; sweeping it into heaps is about the only source of steady employment that the city can offer.

At the time of the drought the distribution of relief supplies to the more remote areas of the Sahel became a matter of intense competition among the various Northern air forces that were involved. At one point the German air force was instructed to fly from Dakar to Conakry, where there was a railhead giving access to the interior. But the Germans did not wish to fly to Conakry, which is the capital of Guinea. Guinea was not a country where Germany, or any Western power, exercised much influence. The Germans said that either they flew to Mali, like everyone else, or they would withdraw their planes. Bamako in Mali was already choked with relief grain, but Germany remained adamant, the other countries gave way, and the Luftwaffe was suitably displayed for a few weeks to the admiring, supposedly starving population of Mali.

As a matter of fact, for all the difference it made to the people of the Sahel, it might not have mattered if the relief planes had flown out over the Atlantic and dumped the grain into the sea. Much of it was never distributed beyond the main reception centers until more than one year after the drought had ended, by which time local food supplies had been restored.

But if the supply of free grain was irrelevant to the predicament of the Sahelian people, the camps supposedly set up to distribute it were not. The terrible aftereffects of the relief operation can be seen in Mauritania today. Once one is across the river, the journey is punctuated by the sudden rushing of men out of the desert and toward the car. Their tents are usually hidden from view, and the first sight the driver has is of a robed figure flying over the sand toward the car, arms waving, voice raised. These desperate sorties are not in search of food, which is distributed from government trucks at regular intervals, but of photographers. The refugees have discovered the only means whereby their predicament can be turned into a source of income. Until the drought of 1973, 900,000 Mauritanians were engaged in nomadic pastoralism; it provided for their own requirements and allowed Mauritania an export revenue. Then the herds were destroyed, and many of the pastoralists became destitute. On the promise of free assistance thousands of people abandoned their traditional resources and went to Nouakchott or camped along its approaches. And many of those who were supplied with free food in 1973 are still there. There is nothing for them to do, their economy has been destroyed, and there are no schemes to rebuild it. They are refugees in their own country, and their government, which lacks the resources to offer them any hope of improvement, is finding the burden of this influx of modern citizens so heavy that it is increasingly unable to assert its authority outside the capital. The secessionist war which broke out in the north of the country has drained national resources still further. The plans for peaceful development, for roads, ports, railways, towns, industries, and a soccer stadium, remain plans. All that has materialized in Nouakchott has been a vegetable allotment to supply the new dwellings of the international bureaucracy that follows in the

train of disaster. These dwellings at least have the advantage, from the refugees' point of view, of being
worth burglarizing.

Even the equipment donated during the drought has
proved useless. Encouraged by the existence of the road,
the relief organizations decided that convoys of trucks
should be supplied to distribute the free grain. But the
road had never been intended to serve the people of
Mauritania. It was a way of linking the French colonies
of Algeria and Senegal across the Sahara. So in order to
reach the people of Mauritania, the trucks had to leave
the road and go across the sand, a process that destroyed
most of them within a year. And during that year the
efforts necessary to keep them in working order, to train
men to drive them, to supply them with fuel, became part
of the process of national disintegration. The trucks were
gifts to Mauritania which made the country poorer.

Nor did the other conventional remedies work. At the
time of the drought a perceptive camp administrator who
foresaw the likelihood of growing dependency believed
that much of the problem could have been avoided if the
large herds of nomadic cattle had been regularly culled.
The herds had increased so quickly because they had been
inoculated against rinderpest. The administrator therefore advocated more abattoirs. His inspiration came from
Kaédi, on the Senegal River, where an imposing modern
abattoir had been erected with the intention of refrigerat-
ing the meat where it was slaughtered and exporting it
to Europe. But the scheme went wrong from the start.
During the years of drought, when the pastoralists were
eager to sell, they drove their herds to Kaédi in great
numbers, and the grazing was destroyed for miles around.
Subsequently they have largely abandoned the abattoir,
preferring the traditional markets of the West African
coast, to which they travel with their herds annually.
The problems of drought and overgrazing and avoiding
starvation have once again evaded the imported solution.

For Mauritanians the refrigerated abattoir symbolizes all the improvements that have served only to worsen their predicament.

During the drought the land on each side of the Senegal River provided the best illustration of what had occurred. Nothing grew then but thornbushes; the land was dust; the streams were dry; there was no pasture, no herds, no crops, and few settlements. And the river water ran past and wasted itself into the sea. It was the sight of rivers such as the Senegal and the Niger which aroused Émile Gautier in 1928, the contrast of water and sand having the usual fatal effect of overexciting the Northern mind. So much water in a dry land cried out to be used, and a great river flowing through a desert was plainly an opportunity, through irrigation and engineering, to sow a grassy plain, patched with fields of corn. All that was preventing the realization of this vision was the backwardness of the inhabitants. All that was necessary to improve the existing arrangements was superior knowledge: management, investment, and, eventually, profit.

The practical results of this notion, the idea that the world has not forgotten, are displayed to advantage on the journey between the Senegal River and Dakar. This is the land of commodities, the cropped land which stretches the length of the African shore from here to the Cape, the wasteland of sugar and cocoa and coffee and tea and peanuts and cotton and copper and tin and rubber and zinc and palm oil, the land of plantations and mines which has replaced the fields where food was grown for local consumption. "Will our labouring people, then, still insist upon lapping up tea-water, expensive villainous tea-water, sweetened with the not less expensive result of the sweating bodies, the aching limbs, and the bleeding backs of the Africans?" asked William Cobbett in 1825, and the answer has never been in doubt. Cobbett strug-

gled on behalf of the prosperity of the English "in-
dustrious classes" and proposed a simple and sustaining
diet for them, satisfying both "the love of a bellyful and
the love of ease." At the same time he mocked "Parson"
Malthus for his predictions of worldwide famine, believing him to be a pessimist and an oppressor of humble
people.

Cobbett had the better of the argument, but only
for reasons that ultimately proved Malthus right. For
famine among the growing population of England was
avoided by the adoption of a policy that seemed at first
so fantastic that Malthus treated it as a joke: the
importation of the nation's food. "There is no occasion
to wait till our own crops come: there is plenty to be had
from America; and plenty from Canada too . . . ,"
urged Cobbett.

"In the wildness of speculation," Malthus replied, "it
has been suggested (of course more in jest than in
earnest) that Europe should grow its corn in America
and devote itself solely to manufactures and commerce
as the best sort of division of the labour of the globe."
But Malthus's jest and Cobbett's inspiration became
reality, and after America had supplied Europe's wheat,
West Africa began to supply its luxuries.

The land that was chosen for this task was, historically,
a land of famine. With the exception of a period of
stable government in the fifteenth century[1] the Sahel and
its adjoining savanna were regularly subjected to dis-
astrous crop failures. Traditionally the Sahelian people—
lacking written records—have distinguished these events
by nicknames. There was the famine of "leave the wife;
push her aside," for instance, and another called "carry
off and throw away," because there was no time to bury
the dead, and another called "grinding up the water
gourd," to eat it. In 1795 Mungo Park, on his journey
to the Niger, nearly died of hunger when he passed
through an area of famine and was saved only by the

kindness and generosity of the wretched and supposedly savage men and women who allowed this helpless stranger to travel across their land. Even then attempts to develop the Sahel had drastic side effects. Park noted that one town, Kaarta, was "situated in the middle of an open plain, the country for two miles round being cleared of wood, by the great consumption of that article for building and fuel."[2]

It was to this land, where people had to struggle so hard to provide their own food, that the North brought its expectations of "financial possibilities" and its commodity seeds. The backward people were to be instructed in the knowledge of growing even less food. They were to surrender their most fertile ground for the cultivation of the inessentials of Europe and America, the commodities that could be shed in hard times when their price rose and purchased cheaply in good times or when fashion favored them. The wealth the Africans gained from this bargain was to be spent in purchasing Northern grain, and any grain they could still grow themselves, or any other money they acquired, was to assist them in paying taxes to the philanthropists who had devised this economic miracle.

Dakar is approached across a bald plain from which 150 years of urban growth have removed much of the vegetation. During the drought it was to Dakar that most of the international bureaucracy were "outposted," to use the United Nations term with its hint of hardship and its promise of increased remuneration.[3] For the city, which was once the pride of France's African empire and which still has tourists and official receptions and motorcades and guards of honor, is in decline. In the 1930s it suffered from endemic plague, and it is still considered an unhealthy place. The rats peek out of the holes in the pavement surrounding the broken traffic lights and collect in hordes around the overflowing refuse bins. One rat expired outside the British embassy, and someone wrapped it in a children's comic and placed it on the embassy window ledge. He was not making a political gesture, just tidying up. In order to assist with the problem, the United Nations dispatched an international team of ratcatchers, one of whom had to stay behind after the emergency, having drawn the short straw and been "outposted."

"Dakar, Senegal. Beautiful new house in residential district, lovely views, four bedrooms, sunken living-room, dining-room, two baths, servants quarters, carport, one-acre landscaped garden. Rental returns $500 a month, priced $55,000. Apply J. Smith, World Health Organization, Geneva."

Fortunately there was a place for the ratcatcher, where he could catch some rest from his rats. And there was a technical community which he could join. There was Harry from UNICEF, who said he was nine pounds overweight "approximately," who had his own sauna. There was Hans, an engineer who had become attached to UNESCO, who was really "into" African art. His work, building silos for grain storage, took him into some of the most remote regions of the Sahel, and he had amassed an exceptionally valuable collection of masks. He was a name, now, in New York primitive circles. And then there was Georges, who gave a dinner party for the ratcatcher at which rats were discussed at length. The ratcatcher's main task was not to deal with the rats of Dakar, but to advise on what to do about the plague of bush rats which were ravaging the irrigated, intensively cropped lands beside the Senegal River, the area which had just recovered from the drought.

There were many theories as to why there should have been this outbreak of rats so soon after the previous disaster. The ratcatcher said that nobody had ever explained an outbreak of rats. Georges thought it was because the drought had killed all the snakes which

usually ate the rats. Georges's wife who went to evening
classes in ecology suggested that it was because there had
been no locust plagues for twenty years in Senegal. The
locust had been controlled by insecticides, and the rats
were now occupying the niche of the locust. If there were
abundant crops in a fragile environment, a pest would
arrive to consume them and prevent the soil from being
exhausted. The theory was dismissed as naïve.

But Georges's wife persisted. "What about the lions?"
she asked. Since the drought the numbers of lions in the
south of Senegal had increased enormously. The week
before they had taken fifty cows from one village alone.

"That is normal," said Georges. "This is Africa.
There are always hitches."

At this point his wife abandoned her attempt to introduce some new ideas into the conversation. "Did you
know," she said to the ratcatcher, "that in some of the
villages my husband has been to, they eat these rats?"

But this was not a success either. "And in my village,
madame," said her only African guest, "which is only
ten miles from here, we eat such rats." And he smiled,
like the waiter in Saint-Louis.

The evening was over. There had been some awkward
moments. Georges's wife had gone to some trouble to
serve the national dish of rice and pepper, but Georges
had pointed out that it was no longer possible to make
it without imported rice. As his guests started to leave,
the insects came buzzing in through the open glass door,
and Georges began to squash them. "What are you
doing?" asked his African friend. "Don't bother with
those."

"I don't like them," said Georges.

"This is Africa," his friend replied.

"Not in my house," said Georges.

The ratcatcher's office was set up in the Place de l'Indé-
pendence, in a modern air-conditioned building with

elevators and double glazing. In the corridors there were iced-water dispensers and power points for vacuum cleaners, and there was an uninterrupted view over a parking lot which had been provided for the convenience of the members of the technical missions. The building was the place where the future of West Africa was being planned. In order to avoid another disaster, it was proposed "to roll back the Sahara Desert" by 1982. Plans were already under way which would increase irrigation and food production, increase the number of boreholes for watering cattle, protect crops, and increase agricultural productivity fourfold. The per capita income was to be doubled by 1995, life expectancy at birth was to be raised from thirty-four to forty-four years, the gross national product of all the Sahelian countries was to be increased by 5 percent each year, 2.1 million acres of new land would be brought under cultivation, literacy would be raised from 5 percent to 50 percent, and not only would the area become self-sufficient in food, but individual food consumption would itself be doubled. The quality of life in rural and urban environments was to be quantified—the distance that separated the average Sahelian from a doctor or from the post office, the number of households with electricity, a radio, and a lavatory was to be calculated. And when the needs had been measured, targets would be set, and $1 billion would be spent every year for ten years to bring all this about.

If the men in charge of this grand design had possessed the time to look out the window, they might have seen, far below in the parking lot, a person who spent the day behaving in an unusual manner. The lot was shaded with mature trees and ringed by lockup garages, and it had neat yellow grids painted on its new tarmac surface to assist drivers to park in orderly lines. At the shady end there was a filling station laid out just as in France or America with a central aisle of pumps, a water line, a grease pit, a glassed-in office, and a low white-washed wall with shrubs. The men who worked there wore clean blue overalls with a company badge on their chests, and the same badge was displayed in a lighted glass emblem above the canopy of the station—Texaco; the same name, the same colors, identical in every way to thousands and thousands of gas stations all over the world.

The peculiar thing about this station was an African male in the physical prime of life. He was dressed in ragged dungaree trousers and a tattered cloak made out of a piece of salvaged denim. He was a lunatic. His most obvious symptom was Saint Vitus's dance. He could not keep still. If he sat on the wall between the shrubs at the front of the garage, one leg jiggled wildly, and his head and neck twitched: one, two, three; pause; twitch, twitch. If it was raining, he could not stay beneath the shelter of the canopy but had to rush out into the rain like a man with an urgent purpose and hurry up to the corner of the street and then hurry back again. At night he went away but not very far, because he lived in one of the lockup garages; the parking lot was his home. Each of the garages with the international No Parking sign stamped on the corrugated roll-up doors was an ideal dwelling for the poorer citizens of Dakar. Few of them were occupied by cars; the technical experts had long since moved out of the city center to the lovely views and sunken living rooms of the suburbs. They left behind these capacious interiors, which were larger and better built than the houses inhabited by thousands of Senegalese. The lunatic had No. 97.

Two hundred yards away on the far side of the parking lot lived a young man with a locked knee. The two beggars rarely spoke to each other. The cripple apparently looked down on the lunatic. He was always well dressed in a freshly washed robe, and he had a trade, selling trinkets to tourists in the streets. Sometimes, if the lunatic was not shaking too much, the cripple told him to fetch water, but mostly he ignored him.

One of the gas pump attendants had given the lunatic a bottle of methylated spirits, and he kept this hidden in another garage well away from his own. He had a use for each part of the lot; he liked to spread himself around because it gave him an occupation. If he got wet in the rain, he walked to the middle of the lot when the sun came out and laid out his cloak on the yellow grid to dry. If he wanted a sip of meths, he had to walk several hundred yards. The lunatic was house-trained. He shat on a rubble heap at the back of the lot, right under the offices of the United States Agency for International Development, and he pissed like a dog on any tree, wall, or car he recognized as familiar.

He was also ingenious. He had found a domestic use for virtually every mechanical service the filling station provided. The high-pressure water hose supplied his drinking and washing water. The tire-pressure gauge was a much-used toy. The shrubs gave him shade when he wanted to sleep. The trash cans were his larder; he sorted through them every day. The filling station gave him shelter, company, and refreshment. What had been so carefully designed to entice the fickle eye of the international motorist had, at long last, reached a human who could put it to serious use.

The parking lot was also the lunatic's place of work, for like all the beggars in the city, he was a hard worker. All day he stalked around the lot, threatening, disputing with, rebuking, or laughing at the mostly invisible occupants of his world. When he met a visible face, he usually failed to notice, unless it was a white one, in which case he set to work. Like a negative of the guard dogs trained by Europeans to attack only Africans, only a white pedestrian could start him off. First he cackled in delight; then he pointed, threw up his arms, and cavorted toward them, shuffling sideways like a crab, cracking his knuckles, and weaving across the pavement. As a begging tactic it was a failure; he frightened and revolted most of his hoped-for patrons. The young Frenchwomen heading for the *patisserie* in their white high heels and summer prints became slightly hysterical when he stumbled between them and the *brioches* beyond the glass doors. It was a bad thing for this lunatic when he was rebuffed. His expression changed to disappointment and then to rage. He growled like a dog. Tears started to run, and he pulled at his face. He showed no restraint. It was as if he were incompletely controlled by one small area of the brain. He sobbed and walked away, looking at no one; he mumbled and twisted his head to one side in violent dissent. The disappointment stunned him. What had happened to him was very bad. It was unbelievable. Each time it happened it was as serious a calamity as if it had never happened before. He hid himself among the shrubs and moaned softly in his grief.

The lunatic recovered from these catastrophes by allowing his mind to devote itself to his other interest. As he sat on the wall half-hidden in the leaves, his legs dangled down on either side of a stout dark root, its end plumed and black. Underneath his tattered cloak his trousers had no crotch. Choosing his moments with some care, he would hitch up his cloak and reveal this fact to approaching passersby, usually Frenchwomen. They saw nothing. They seldom glanced in his direction. If they did, he was always quicker. He dropped his cloak and smiled and fluttered his fingers at them. Sometimes, relieved to see that he was not too close, they waved back, making him laugh. Someone, perhaps someone from the mosque which was supposed to look after him, would occasionally supply him with a more complete pair of dungaree trousers. But before long he was discouraged again and had to retreat to the wall and work away at a hole in the seam.

In the evening the technical experts left their offices

and went to their cars. Then they drove home from the well-maintained lot, over the garage's trip-wire bell, past the high-speed electric pumps, and out onto the potholed roadway of the public city. They drove through the gloom of the prewar streetlighting, past the lines of lepers sleeping on flattened whiskey cartons, past the peanut vendors and the cigarette vendors and the news-stands selling *Newsweek* and *Le Monde* in the light of flaring lamps, past the groups of pickpockets and high steel bars of the banks. They left the lunatic blinking in the glare of the dry cleaners sign, his tumultuous day, with its abysses and peaks, now enriched by their coins. For the technicians who stopped for gas were prepared to show that they knew Africa and were not discoun-tenanced by this wretched commonplace. They gave him money, and they knew enough to laugh when the lunatic was refused by someone less experienced and was driven to weep so hard that he could not catch his breath and could only mutter, "No need for trouble, no need for violence"—a snatch remembered from some institution in his past. They laughed at him—there was nothing else to do—but they did not enjoy this necessity, and so even they avoided him when they could, agreeing to forget the frightful things, buying their gas and laying their plans for changing the continent, their eyes as selectively blind as the lunatic's own.

NOTES

1. Jeremy Swift, "Sahelian Pastoralists," *Annual Review of Anthropology*, vol. 6 (1977).

2. Today Kano in Nigeria has an annual consumption of firewood of seventy-five thousand tons, which is taken from a circle whose radius extends twelve miles from the town. The citizens of Ouagadougou in Upper Volta have almost exhausted stocks of firewood within forty miles of the city, and on average

they spend 25 percent of their income on buying firewood
from farther away.

3. One visiting team of forestry experts who spent three weeks
in 1974 considering the question of reforestation cost the
United Nations $110,000. The leader of the team was paid
$4,000 a week and all his expenses. Naturally the fee was free
of tax. The team's recommendations did not result in any
visible action.

CHAPTER 6

THE PET CHILD
OF CALAMITY

We have to discipline these people, and to control their grazing and their movements. Their liberty is too expensive for us. This disaster is our opportunity.

Secretary of the International
Drought Relief Committee, 1973

If the President orders us to go home, we will go; if he orders us to stay, we will stay; it is his right. Since we gave up our forefathers' traditions and came here, we now depend on him and will obey him. . . .

Interview with a Tuareg refugee
after the drought, 1973

Whoo-oop! . . . the kingdom of sorrow's a-coming! . . . When I range the earth hungry, famine follows in my tracks! . . . I bite a piece out of the moon and hurry the seasons. . . . The massacre of isolated communities is the pastime of my idle moments, the destruction of nationalities the serious business of my life! . . . Bow your neck and spread, for the pet child of calamity's a-coming!

Mark Twain, *Huckleberry Finn*

Bamako is the terminal city of the railway line from Dakar. For the French it was the next step. Just as Dakar replaced Saint-Louis, Bamako was better suited for the administration of the empire of West Africa as it grew into the interior. The city is laid out in an even more leisurely and imperial manner on the banks of the Niger River. There are avenues of tall trees, white colonnaded buildings with marble floors, villas and gardens for the clerical class, and still enough French restaurants to make life diverting—although an increasing number of them are locked up, with a sticker across the door: "Closed, for nonpayment of taxes."

But while the buildings and vistas of France still stand, they are not still in use. Instead, beside the peeling structures the people of Mali, who have inherited Bamako, have created a separate city of the open air. On the spacious plots between the boulevards, where the French cultivated herbaceous beds, there are bicycle repair benches and photographers' and barbers' establishments. The bicycle mechanics arrive each morning with a bag of tools, a sack of spares, and a bench. Then a line of bicyclists and motorcyclists forms, and a day's business is arranged. The last to arrive will wait, as is normal, all day. The photographers have far bulkier equipment, cumbrous teak-cased machines on iron pedestals with long brass lenses like antique telescopes; their numbers are swollen by the astonishing number of forms and identity cards which are necessary in Mali. The barbers have their scissors, collapsing stools, and broken pieces of mirror which they suspend from trees. This is the commerce of the parallel city which has been organized by those who cannot afford to pay the taxes which, together with the administrative regulations, are the most dependable fruit of independence.

The dwellings of this parallel city are constructed from the traditional materials of urban Africa, old tin cans, rusted corrugated sheets, cardboard boxes, rubber tires, and Coke bottles. Their inhabitants rarely consume the original contents of these packages; their chief ambition is to live in them. But even when sufficient quantities have been acquired, there remains the problem of where to build. Since they are not permitted to use the abandoned herbaceous borders within the town, the people build on the edge of town, in the fields of the farmers.

Since this is also illegal, they build at night.[1] In the

morning the authorities frequently come with a bulldozer and destroy their work; but they start again on the following night, and if they are sufficiently persistent, the army's bulldozers may eventually be called away. Building in the fields at night is the only way in which the citizens of Bamako can bypass the network of customary and inherited regulations dealing with planning, taxation, and land tenure. To reach an acceptable accommodation with the law, they cannot sleep when it is dark if they ever wish to sleep beneath a roof. And if the urban code were rigidly enforced, half the population might have to sleep in the open, like the animals or a few eccentric Europeans or the men who existed before shelters were invented.

That the law is not rigidly enforced is largely thanks to the police whose internal hierarchy is founded on the opportunities that each department has to accept bribes. The border police are the *crème de la crème* because they have unrivaled facilities for increasing their official income through mild but regular extortion. Lowest of all are the gorgeously attired *gendarmerie montée*. For this depressed force there is very little contact with the general public, and their self-respect has ebbed to such an extent that they rarely bother to exercise their beautiful horses and no longer teach recruits how to ride. They rose slightly in public esteem when they obtained a large shipment of famine relief millet from America with which to feed their mounts. Despite this, the humblest unmounted policeman can look down on them with contempt from the grandeur of the splendid building near the center of town which acts as police headquarters. Inside this structure the original wooden counter still runs the length of the hall, its colonial ink stains still visible, and although supplies of paper and ink have been exhausted, the counter is much in use. If you enter the *poste de police* at most any time of day, you will find a correctly uniformed constable stretched out asleep on its varnished expanse.

The idle police post, the locked premises of the tax debtors, and the army's bulldozers represent a promise to the people of Bamako about the conditions of life they expected to enjoy after independence, another promise that has not been kept. But there are people in the city who are preoccupied with this problem. They are the foreign technical advisers, many of whom live in a newly built suburb which looks out over the Niger River. It is the last thing the builders of the night see at sunset and the first they can make out in the morning, and they have nicknamed it, after the event that financed its construction, the District of the Drought.

The project on which Mali's foreign advisers are engaged is the National Plan, a comprehensive document whose modest intention is "to enable the whole population to reach a standard of living which will provide for all its cultural and material needs." The first obstacle to this goal from the planning point of view is presented by the existing people of Mali, in particular by the country's minority of nomads, whose distress at the time of the drought had originally attracted the great windfall of foreign aid. The Malian official who spoke of that disaster as "an opportunity to discipline the nomads" had been waiting for his opportunity for many years. Before French rule the settled people of the Sahel had frequently been plundered or enslaved by the nomads, and almost the first event of Malian independence was a massacre of dissident but defenseless Tuareg in the north of the country. Even during the drought some government officials mistreated the victims of the disaster.

But there was a stronger reason for this discrimination than historical enmity. The nomads never wanted to belong to any of the six independent Sahelian countries, with whose governments they had as little in common as they had with the colonial authorities. But it was no defense for them to say that they neither contributed to nor demanded anything from the state or that they sought neither taxation nor representation. By demonstrating that they were capable of surviving independently of the state, and without committing themselves to its monetary economy, they challenged the necessity for both. So they were forced to enter into the market economy, to produce a surplus, and to sell it under supervision.

In the National Plan some of the most ingenious reasons were produced to justify this coercion. The plan suggested that there should be a strategy "to reduce the vulnerability of the economy to a hostile climate." The economy, it asserted, would be at the mercy of the climate for as long as the purchasing power of that 90 percent of the population which could be classified as rural continued to fluctuate in accordance with annual climatic variations. The self-consumption of subsistence was inflexible, and so the whole effect of climatic variation was being thrown onto the commercial sector of the economy. Instead, there should be a production and accumulation of the surplus food produced in good years which would help balance the bad ones, and this would eventually liberate the economy from climatic restraints. What this amounted to was a suggestion that food should be stored, not a new idea in the Sahel, indeed one that had occurred to the people long before the arrival of the French. But they had never supposed that the practice of food storage would enable them largely to abandon agriculture, the aim of the National Plan, even though there was already a chronic food shortage in Mali when as little as 10 percent of the population was not producing its own food.

Where ingenuity did not work, abuse would serve. "The nomads," said the same official, "are marginal to our national life. They are illiterate, lawless, and destructive. They use very ill-advised grazing techniques, and they are destroying our pastures and wells. The first thing to do is to shoot all their goats. The goat is a mountain creature; when the nomads brought the goats down from the Atlas Mountains, look what happened—the Sahara Desert! The goat is a bandit; it rips plants up. We have a shortage of wood in the Sahel, and this too is made worse by the goat. As far as the nomads are concerned, it is a transitional animal on the way to the cow. We will replace the goats with cows. The whole Sahel will be divided into managed or unmanaged areas, we will introduce beef-fattening stations, and the trans-Saharan highway will be built to facilitate our access to the markets of the world because after we have rearranged our agriculture, we are going to develop both light and heavy industry, based on the increased consumption of an internal surplus and an increase in internal demand. If you don't understand how this can be achieved, you must read the National Plan. It's all there."

And he indicated the volume, which was indeed handsomely printed and very fat, although Malian industrialization had not yet reached the stage where it could be produced in Mali. Instead, it was printed in France and written by a Frenchman and paid for under the French aid program. Its most obvious use was to adorn the bookshelves of officials such as this one who were sufficiently important to live with the foreign advisers in the District of the Drought.

But the official had reason for his self-confidence. He stood in a great tradition, the tradition of cooperation with the North, which has dominated Africa for a hundred years, since the rulers of Africa took the advice of the Northern missionaries and traders and ceased to oppose the colonial division of their continent. The only modern touch that the Malian official added was the contempt he had learned to feel for his less educated countrymen, a contempt that was most obviously revealed in his oversimplified account of the workings of a pastoral economy.

* * *

For a Malian to be born in the drought and to die in the District of the Drought one common means of transition is the school. Education is expensive in Mali. A native teacher receives £85 ($170) a month, but the native teachers are reinforced by Frenchmen, and merely to house an expatriate teacher costs Mali at least £170 ($340) a month, money that could be used to employ two native teachers. For the expatriates there are certain irregularities to be accepted. First, even in the top secondary-school grades and the universities much of the teaching has to be done without books. There are very few books anywhere in the country, and although everyone who enters the university can read, many of them will have had very few opportunities to read a book from cover to cover.

The Malian teachers are as heavily handicapped by this inadequate system as are their pupils. A demand for a pay raise for teachers was countered by the government with a question: why should teachers be paid more than uniformed policemen? The teachers did not suggest that teaching required higher qualifications than street policing. Instead, they said that policemen were actually paid much more than the teachers since they had much easier access to bribes. It was a tactical error. The government replied with their old entreaty. The teachers should leave Bamako and go out into the remote parts of the country, where they were so badly needed. There they would be important figures with the right to participate in all sorts of rackets.

There is no likelihood of public criticism of this system even if the Malians should wish it. In the higher classes there is an unspoken embargo on political discussion. Contentious matters are never raised; if they were, the class would get out of hand, and the incident would be reported to the police by those students whose fees the police paid. And there is a further discouragement to dissent.

Far more students qualify for the university than there is room for. So after the first year 80 percent of the university students are failed. They are turned out into the town without a job and without the qualifications they need to find one, filled with all the ambition they have been encouraged to foster since they first went to school. Their literacy has ensured that they will be unemployed. If the students strike and demand guaranteed jobs, the university is closed, or no new admissions are taken, or the leaders of the strike are offered jobs provided that the strike ends. The strike always collapses.

The ministers who run the country are naturally as deeply committed to the system as is anyone below them. In a sense their success is evidence of their exceptional skill at profiting from it. When a Cabinet minister took a mistress who wished to attend a Northern foreign language institute where there is a long waiting list, he recommended her for priority. The director of the institute interviewed her and saw that her reason for joining was that she was bored and wished to make new friends. When he refused to advance her up the list, the minister threatened him with deportation. The director complained to his own embassy, which rebuked him. It considered the minister very influential and had been trying to cultivate him for months. The minister's mistress was admitted. At the same institute there is an annual examination on the results of which the institute offers scholarships to the best pupils for a year's study abroad. Naturally the list of successful candidates has to be approved by the ministry, and it is approved every year, except that when the list is returned from the ministry, all the names on it have been changed. Influence overcomes merit again and again.

For the ministers in Bamako some of the most satisfactory opportunities lie in the housing arrangements made for the expatriate advisers, or *coopérants,* as they are called. The ministers decide how many advisers will be admitted. They decide where they shall live. They own the houses that are rented by the advisers, and they fix the level of rents. French *coopérants* who pay the monthly salaries of two Malian schoolteachers in monthly rent alone are good tenants, but American advisers are even better. An American adviser pays in monthly rent the salary of four Malian teachers for his rather larger house, and he also requires a refrigerator, a freezer, air conditioning, and sometimes a filtered swimming pool. For the Malians who provide these facilities it is possible to build a palatial house, rent it out to expatriates, and recoup the cost in five years' rent. The money that changes hands is, of course, budgeted by the foreign governments as part of their aid program; that is why the people of Bamako, gazing up at dawn from their just-completed shanties, waiting for the bulldozers to arrive, have christened the new suburb the District of the Drought.

A large part of the program to implement the Malian National Plan is paid for by foreign countries, in particular by France and America. American assistance is administered by the Agency for International Development —or USAID. The symbol of USAID is a stars and stripes shield surrounding the clasped hands of international friendship; one sees it in all the West African capitals, painted on the cars that are parked outside the cool, new embassies that the American government is erecting in this part of the world. As one becomes more familiar with the purpose of USAID, one can never see the clasped hands without wondering about the rest of the picture: what is the other transatlantic hand up to, clubbing the unfortunate recipient of all this attention or just tickling him into submission?

In Bamako USAID employed a very correct and serious young man named Alvin Roberts. He was especially serious on the subject of the American Indians. On his wall he had pinned a copy of the speech made by Chief Seattle of the Dwamish League in 1854:

"The white man treats his mother, the earth, and his brother, the sky, as things to be bought, plundered, sold like sheep or bright beads. His appetite will devour the earth and leave behind only a desert. . . . We know that the white man does not understand our ways. . . . Man did not weave the web of life: he is merely a strand in it. Whatever he does to the web, he does to himself. . . . Continue to contaminate your bed and you will one night suffocate in your own waste."

Alvin Roberts identified the pastoralists of Mali with the American Indians, although he blushed when saying so as though he had mentioned something of personal importance. He was not a man to feel contempt for the nomads.

Since the head of his mission was absent, Alvin agreed to be interviewed about the activities of USAID in Mali. He was as straightforward about being interviewed as he was about the rest of his life. He had read the Freedom of Information Act. As far as he was concerned, an interview was an exchange of information. He got out the master file from his desk and proceeded to read through it, project by project, with dates, financial details, criticisms of other agencies, and all problems that had occurred. For instance: "We drilled twenty wells in this region. We have now blocked them all up again. The reason is that the villagers don't have enough money to pay for the necessary electric pumps. New wells of a different design will have to be drilled instead. This will take a lot of time. So far the project has cost us $525,000, $20,000 of which paid for the part-time services of one UN expert for one year. He was four months late in starting. The UN sold us six trucks three years ago. They arrived this year. Only one of them is serviceable. We frequently have a problem with the UN coming through with its obligations." He continued for two hours, never smiling once, to spell out the daily realities of the agency's attempts to improve the lot of the Malian peasant. The program, he said, had now reached its second stage, which was called "Accelerated Impact." Listening to him was like presiding in a confessional.

Pit silos had been provided at a cost of $250,000. The French colonial authorities had devised them in the 1930s for feeding draft animals. But they had been intended for a different part of the empire, and USAID had dug them in the sandy ground near the Niger River. During the river's annual flood the silos also flooded. In any case there were few draft animals in the region. Wells that had been newly bored were unusable because they were filling with nitrate. Nobody knew why. The grain storage program had also been delayed because the only lecturer on the subject spoke no French and had to lecture in English, a language spoken by almost no Malian agriculturalists. The road from Mopti to Gao had been improved because the old one was unusable during the four-month rainy season; $300,000 had been spent. The road was still unusable during the rains.

When it was eventually ready, three trucks and twelve Land Rovers would use it to supervise the beef management schemes, to impose veterinary regulations, to distribute animal feed supplements, and to popularize these new methods with adult education courses. The annual fuel costs of this might be as high as one-fifth of the capital cost of the road. A warehouse had been constructed in Mopti at a cost of $140,000. It was designed to overcome the problem of contaminated grain. He continued with the list and then interrupted himself. "I have to say something more on that warehouse. It fell down on completion. One man was injured, and a court case is pending." And so on, until the catalogue was complete, the file closed, and a penance imposed. The penance was anonymity; that meant that Alvin Roberts would com-

plete his tour of duty in Bamako instead of being identified and dismissed. Two more years in Bamako, the
weekly round of meetings, the Marine Corps spaghetti
parties, bridge in the evenings, the endless debate about
how long the water should be boiled, the intermittent
gastric agony which occurred anyway. It was a severe
penance for trying to change the world. But Alvin knew
the likely effects of his program on the nomads.

In 1931 there was a terrible plague of locusts which
caused a famine in the Sahel. The French authorities
were aware of the seriousness of the situation, but they
kept their heads. Throughout the crisis, taxes were collected, and where money was short the villagers were
forced to sell their emergency stocks of grain. No effort
was spared to improve on the ravages of nature. Although food was growing scarcer all over the empire, one
governor, M. Blacher of Niger, declined to distribute his
emergency stocks, which were intended for just such an
occasion, and confined his precautions to a reduction in
the rations allowed for prisoners and horses. When
Blacher was asked by the governor-general of French
West Africa to report on the harvest, he replied, at a
time when people were dying of famine all over Niger,
that he was resisting all extravagant proposals for reprovisioning areas away from the capital and that crops
were plentiful across the whole colony. He seemed, understandably, to regard famine as something for which
he would be held personally accountable. "Do not suppose," he told a worried subordinate, "that I am going
to shout from the rooftops that there is famine in Niger."
As a result of his measures, twenty-six thousand people
were estimated to have died of famine in western Niger
alone, and a further twenty-nine thousand to have left the
area of Governor Blacher's supervision, a combined total
of one-tenth of the population under his care.[2]
When the famine was over and Governor Blacher was

asked to explain why his methods had failed, he blamed it on "the idleness, nonchalance, indifference, inaction, apathy, and fatalism" of the natives. Three years later an English traveler[3] reported that French West Africa was becoming depopulated by famine and by the flight of the surviving population into neighboring British colonies to avoid taxes. In Upper Volta the administration would burn whole villages and flog the menfolk if taxes fell short. In the Ivory Coast children were taken away for years at a time as hostages for unpaid taxes. Sometimes all the corn and livestock were seized, and the villagers were left to starve; in Upper Volta they had to catch ants to survive. And when the people were ordered onto public works and protested that they could never pay their taxes if they had to leave the fields, they were brutally mishandled.

M. Blacher was a bad governor (though not exceptionally so), and this was recognized, at least implicitly, by the French authorities, who drew up a memorandum after the events of 1931 on measures to be taken in future. It was written by the minister of the colonies, Albert Sarraut, a man whose policies were regarded as enlightened and visionary, even rash. France, in his view, was under an obligation to carry its colonial subjects forward; economic development was to take place, but it was to be for the good of the colonies as well as their rulers, and it was to be based on modern schools, hospitals, and farms. For the Sahel, M. Sarraut insisted on new roads, new wells, irrigation channels, fertilization of the soil, the introduction of new crops following experiments with local varieties, measures to control the locust, agricultural education, grain storage, and the reprovisioning of the impoverished areas. It was a model scheme.

"For ourselves," wrote Sarraut, in order to defend himself from those critics who might accuse him of improvident generosity, "we will have the proud awareness of accomplishing our mission, [and] of civilizing peoples whose protection we guarantee: for improving the condition of mankind is the true objective of our skill, and, in the name of human solidarity, the highest end of colonisation."

Today one can see the similarity between the measures taken after the emergency of 1931 and the present aid schemes. There is even an echo of Governor Blacher, the stage villain of colonialism, in the comments of a Malian district commissioner responsible for the nomadic refugees, who described those in his charge as "tax evaders" who were characterized by "idleness and sloth."

The colonialism of the early 1930s is now an admitted, obvious example of exploitation. Public works were carried out by forced labor, and payment was either nonexistent or given in the form of tax commutation. Economic development in the days before Sarraut was undisguised theft. Since then the colonies have been disbanded and succeeded by independent African governments, and forced labor has been replaced by development programs, freely entered into on the supposition of mutual advantage. But it would be a mistake to suppose that anything fundamental has changed.

"Before we came," said Alvin Roberts, "the nomads had to choose between pasture and wells because there was no grass around the wells. Now we tell them, 'You find the pasture, and we will develop it for you and install wells.'" But he knew that the reason there was no grass around the wells was that the enormous herds that used them overgrazed the surrounding land, and he must have realized that the only effect of drilling new wells in areas of unspoiled pasture would be to turn that pasture into another bare strip. He wanted to respect the independence of the nomads, but the techniques he had been trained to deploy could only destroy it. He knew that the locust had apparently been controlled by the use of pesticides and that there had not been a serious plague of locusts for twenty years. But he did not wish to know that this had been achieved by the massive spraying of DDT and BHC, both chemicals that were banned in America as being too dangerous to use at all, and that in the Sahel they were sometimes sprayed eight times as frequently as they had ever been used in America.

Alvin Roberts said that the technology he was install-ing was intended to produce more food, but he preferred not to mention that in every one of the previous seven years food production throughout the Sahel had fallen farther and farther behind the growth of population. He admired the stated intention of the Malian National Plan "to liberate the economy from the annual effects of the climate," but he did not consider that since this in-volved persuading Malians to work for money rather than grow their own food, it might be directly connected with the falling food production. He was committed to the proposition that the only way to solve the world hunger crisis was to persuade peasants to stop farming and buy American grain, but he tried to avoid thinking about that. Alvin wanted to be useful but was succeeding in being used.

There had been a time in the past when the Sahel was the cereal-growing area for much of West Africa, and up to fifteen years before the drought of 1973 Mali had produced and exported an annual surplus of grain. But the methods used to achieve this had included practices that were incompatible with those favored by USAID. Alvin Roberts found them as baffling as he had found the apparent indifference of the herders during the drought. It was as though no one had told them that they faced disaster. Later he realized that their calm was not based on indifference but was an attitude that helped them accept their fate and so bear it better. He called this attitude fatalism. Then he heard of the prayer of the Somali nomads: "You who give sustenance to your creatures, O God, put water for us in the nipples of rain. You who poured water into the oceans, O God, make this land of ours fertile once more. Accepter of penance, you who are wealthy, O God, gather water in the rivers whose beds have run dry."

Alvin thought this was a beautiful prayer, but he disapproved of it. It was worse than fatalism; it was masochism; the people suffering from drought seemed to regard their suffering as a penance for their sins. Then he heard that the Tuareg nomads of Mali also believed that drought was a punishment for sin and could be broken by the prayers of the people and the intercession of holy men who were particularly skilled at rainmaking. This was clearly superstition of the most primitive kind and an impediment to any form of self-assistance; it had to be stopped.

Alvin's conclusion about the inadequacy of the natives' response to their predicament was very similar to the criticisms of Governor Blacher, a man whom he despised. Their attitude revealed how much the North has forgotten in its attempts to understand Africa since the early days of contact. For if drought is caused by sin, the remedy for it lies in man's behavior.[4] And it may be possible to avoid the consequences of drought if behavior is virtuously regulated. Mungo Park noticed an example of this strategy when his soldiers ate some mimosa seed at a friendly village. The headman protested strongly and tried to drive the party away for this offense. Until:

> Finding that we only laughed at him, he became more quiet; and when I told him that we were unacquainted with so strange a restriction but should be careful not to eat any of them in future, he said that the thing itself was not of great importance if it had not been done in sight of the women. For, says he, this place has been frequently visited with famine from want of rain, and in these distressing times the fruit of the [mimosa] is all we have to trust to, and it may then be opened without harm; but in order to prevent the women and children from wasting this supply, a *toong* is put upon the [mimosa] until famine

makes its appearance. The word *toong* is used to express
anything sealed up by magic.[5]

Since Park's accurate observations and patient attempts
to understand, the North has come a long way. Alvin
Roberts scorned the irrational beliefs of the people he
wished to help, but he accepted the tenets of modern
agricultural technology with the same uncritical fervor
that greeted the revealed truths of medieval theology,
though even a small degree of Park's perceptiveness
might have assisted him to a different conclusion.

The evil effects of the development policies which
were suggested in the thirties by Professor Gautier and
M. Sarraut were visible within ten years. In 1938 the
consequences of increased human pressure on the fragile
Sahelian environment—in the form of urbanization,
intensive cultivation, industrialization, and higher human
and animal population—were reported in the *Geograph-
ical Review*[6] to be deforestation, overgrazing, and in-
sufficient fallowing of cropland, and the result was the
process now known as desertification. But more was understood about this process even in 1938 than today.
There was no question of the Sahara's "expanding" or
"advancing"; instead, the author emphasized, "the desert
was not invading from without, the land was deteriorat-
ing from within."

Alvin Roberts, on the other hand, forty years later,
was committed to "rolling back the desert," and he proposed to achieve this feat by employing exactly the
methods that would most encourage the opposite effect.
For years and years his predecessors had increased the
pressure on the Sahelian pastures. The herds of cattle in
the six Sahelian states grew larger and larger as one
miracle of veterinary science and irrigation engineering
succeeded another. The countries grew to depend on
these massive herds; in one case, that of Chad, 80 percent
of its total annual exports came from meat, and eventually 750,000 head of cattle were being driven every year

from the Sahel to the coastal states. But all the time
the herds were eating out the pastures, particularly
around the wells, so when a prolonged drought occurred,
as it does regularly in the Sahel, there were no dry-
season grazing areas left to assist the herders. A huge
number of beasts died. All those cattle, and all dead.
This was calamity indeed; it was an economic and social
disaster, and to cope with it, Alvin proposed more of
the same.

Ranches owned by multinational hamburger companies,
to employ the herders who had formerly owned their own
cattle; more veterinary schemes, waterworks, settlements,
high dams, heavy industry, national parks, trunk roads,
fruit farms, high-bearing hybrid grains, inorganic fer-
tilizers, insecticidal spraying programs, new forests and
towns, full employment, higher education, universal literacy, long life, fatter people, protein minimums, chess
tournaments, ideal weights, leisure hours, day nurseries,
dogs' homes, a regulated climate—everything is in the
plans except mumbo jumbo,[7] the irrational ingredient,
the acknowledgment that people cause famine by their
wrong actions. That was the one proposition that Alvin
Roberts could never accept. The people he dealt with had
to be "helpless" or "desperate." Their way of life had
to be "a form of intolerable suffering."[8] The "fatalism"
of Governor Blacher's natives was replaced by the
fatalism of the Northern technical advisers, who insisted
that drought and famine should be synonymous.

The equilibrium of man, animals, and land had been
upset; the structure of the soil, degraded; the supply of
water, disturbed.[9] Cash crops had been substituted for
food, a burdensome taxation had been imposed, and then
the victims of this lethal patronage had been blamed for
suffering from it. The nomads of the Sahel are "a heavy
social, economic, and political burden on their countries,"
said a United Nations spokesman in 1973, and Alvin
Roberts for all his romantic impulses had to agree. The

nomads would not labor; they would not pay taxes; they would not vote; they violated the Napoleonic Code in favor of their own laws; they failed to treat fencing and machinery with the respect both deserved; they ate too much cheese and not enough chocolate; they bought no life insurance and borrowed their needs from each other rather than incur a debt to the bank. They were dependent on no one and, therefore, a burden on everyone. They threatened Roberts and all his schemes. Supermarkets were coming, to a country that could scarcely grow an ear of corn; towns would be built in places where there was not enough fuel to roast an ox. Alvin Roberts was making a desert out of savanna and calling it development. He deserved his penance.

In the offices of Air Mali, in the center of Bamako, there are only two visible documents. One is a framed copy of *la Constitution,* the two tightly packed columns of print, with their endless articles and subarticles (each correctly numbered according to the system of ancient Rome, each correctly stated in a tortuous, legalistic French), being rather difficult to read with enjoyment. The other document is scattered all over the floor. It is a world timetable for Japanese Airlines, a company that does not land a plane anywhere within five thousand miles of Bamako.

Air Mali has Russian and American jets. They are the most complicated machines the country has yet enjoyed. In his novel *God's Bits of Wood,* the Senegalese author Sembene Ousmane described what it was like in Bamako in 1947 when the railway workers came out on strike and the trains stopped running.

> An intangible sense of loss weighed on everyone: the loss of the machine. . . . They remembered when not a night had run its course without the sight of the flickering coloured lanterns of the teams at work in the marshalling yards, or the sounds of steel against steel. . . . All that had been their life. They thought of it constantly now . . . they were conscious that the machine was the source of

their common welfare. . . . And it seemed to them that
the wind was whispering a phrase they had often heard from
Bakayoko: "The kind of man we were is dead, and our
only hope for a new life lies in the machine, which knows
neither a language nor a race." They said nothing, though,
and only their eyes betrayed an inner torment brought on
by the mounting terror of famine and an inconsolable loneliness for the machine. Sometimes as they watched, a storm
came up, and in the distance they could see the tops of great
trees bending before the wind . . . the doors of the railway cars flew open, grinding and clashing on their unoiled
hinges, revealing a yawning emptiness. And the trespass by
the forces of nature into the land of the machine tore at
the men's hearts and left them humbled . . . their fellowship with the machine was deep and strong.

For Ousmane's strikers the machine is alive and has
a soul like other inanimate objects in their world. But
for the teacher who has lived in Mali for twenty-five
years the Africans "know nothing" of machines. "They
have no understanding of technology at all. If the cook
has family problems, he will break every gadget in the
kitchen. It is because he can do none of his tasks spon-
taneously or by reflex. He always has to make an effort
of will and concentration. It is the same with the drivers
and pedestrians in the street. Their behavior when they
are thinking of something apart from their physical
movement is completely abstracted. It is not a question
of intelligence. Mali has intelligent and subtle men who
know very well how to play foreign agencies off against
each other to the national advantage.

"But with machinery it is another matter. Even jet
pilots sometimes forget the rules of cause and effect. If
I wish to buy a single spare part for my car, such as an
inside door handle, I cannot order it. Instead I have to
set aside most of the day to this task. First I go to my
regular garage and pick up a mechanic. Together we
drive round all the stalls enquiring for the necessary
handle. Then, after several hours of being passed between more and more distant members of his family,

we find the man who has cornered the market and obtained every handle in town. A price is agreed, the part is produced. It is not a door handle, it is a window-winder. And it is not for my car, it is for a Renault. Several hours later we find the only man in Bamako who has discovered how to fit one to the other. And so after a day, and for three times the official price, I have the wrong second-hand part in my car, and every time I want to open the window the door flies open. After a while most people stop buying parts for their machinery. They succumb to Africa."

At Air Mali there is the same improvidence. One of the company's Russian jets crashed; but the company's flight schedule has not been altered, and in the booking office itself there are no timetables, apart from the Japanese one. There is a very long counter and an impressive number of people behind it; but they cannot deal with any inquiry without application to either a calculator or a stapler, and since there are few of both and much time has to be spent repairing them, a very long line of customers builds up. The one daily certainty with Air Mali is that at some point this line will be informed that a flight has been canceled. Some of those waiting so patiently have been waiting for a week to return to their homes in Gao, a town at the other end of the country. It is the rainy season, the road is cut, the river ferry is not running, and Air Mali is their only chance. Eventually, on Friday, a "special flight" to Gao, which will clear the backlog, is announced. It will be on Saturday, and everyone is booked onto it. On Friday evening the "special" is confirmed, and on Saturday morning it is reconfirmed. At midday the passengers are checked in and told to board the bus as soon as it arrives. At 3:00 P.M. the bus has not appeared, and it is one hour after the flight should have taken off. Then it is canceled. There is no announcement, just a muttered aside to the next man who makes an inquiry about the delay. It

seems that there never was a "special." It was all a
mistake; there are not enough aircraft for such extrav-
agances; it was all fantasy, a ploy by a junior member
of the staff to encourage the patient line.

But this is too much for one of the men from Gao. He
remonstrates with the imaginative booking clerk, politely
but loudly, and waves his ticket in the air. At once the
head of the bureau emerges from his room. The manager
is much angrier than his passenger. "You," he shouts as
soon as he begins his advance on the counter, and the
crowd of would-be travelers falls silent. "You," he says
again, and then he snatches the upraised ticket from the
protesting client. "This. . . . Look. This! Why have
you done this to your ticket? You have folded your ticket.
This habit is the cause of great inconvenience to the airline." And he puts the ticket into his pocket. The passenger is appalled. He is about to lose his ticket, and he
cannot remember the answer to this question. Why? Why
is his ticket in this unauthorized condition? Then he
remembers. It was the wife, back in Gao; his wife folded
it. It is a return ticket. He is merely traveling on it, but
it was his wife who folded it. Certainly. This information mollifies the manager at once. All is explained. His
relief spreads to the crowd, and the reservations office
empties for the weekend in orderly fashion. Two more
days have been wasted beyond a doubt, but there will
be a flight when there is a plane. *La Constitution* is left
suspended on the wall of the empty office, a silent en-
couragement, in moments of doubt, of the feasibility
of the whole adventure—office, airline, capital, country
("One people, One goal, One faith"), even the correct
disposition of an air ticket.

Outside, the streets too begin to empty for the weekend. A last convoy of heavy trucks, carrying building
materials to the District of the Drought, races over the
potholes of the boulevards, splashing sheets of water
over anyone it passes. The final truck carries sugar, not

bricks, and it is so overloaded that several soldiers have been placed on top of the load to keep it in place. The truck hits a pothole at speed, the jolt throws a box of sugar lumps into the road, and the truck passes on, the soldiers on top being too preoccupied with staying in place to signal a warning. The moment the sugar hits the road the box bursts, and a man in a suit and tie who is still dripping from the splashing of the truck runs out into the traffic and, crouching down on the road, begins to pick up the lumps of sugar and place them in his upturned hat.

Over the town there sounds the constant hoarse double note of the railway engines at the station, until this too falls quiet and the only noise is the grinding of a pony cart moving toward the bakery, the Boulangerie du Trésor. The cart is laden with sacks of flour, fine white flour rises over it in a haze, and the sacks are stamped "A gift of food from the Federal German Republic." The flour is used for making the bakery's excellent French croissants, which are popular among the technical advisers who inhabit the District of the Drought. They, dreaming in their air-conditioned palaces of what they have decreed—in a country that is still grappling with the technology of 1920, where society is so ill adapted to the institutions it has inherited that it has been forced to reduce each to a travesty of its original, where the people cannot at the moment even erect shanties, and where the domestic production of food is at the point of collapse—envisage, as they munch their breakfast croissants, numerous stately pleasure domes, little noticing that they have themselves become the self-consumers of the very food they give.

NOTES

1. See A. Deyoko, *African Environment,* vol. 2, no. 1.
2. See A. Salifou, *African Environment,* vol. 1, no. 2.

3. Geoffrey Gorer, *Africa Dances* (London: Faber, 1935).
4. "An evil society is rewarded by drought. Drought calls for social and personal reform not technical progress . . . if science and technology are to be servants and not masters of the human situation, then issues of value and purpose must come first." This perception is the work of Paul Richards, from whose essay in *African Environment,* vol. 1, no. 2, this quote is taken.
5. Mungo Park, *Travels in Africa* (London, 1799).
6. Quoted by I. Campbell, in "Human Mismanagement as a Major Factor in the Sahelian Tragedy," *The Ecologist,* 1974.
7. The story of the English understanding of the term *mumbo jumbo* is a symbol of the relationship between the North and Africa. Since the nineteenth century it has meant "an object of blind unreasoning worship," derived, according to *Brewer's Dictionary,* "from some lost native word." But the first appearance of the words in English was in Mungo Park's account of his travels in Gambia in 1795, when he gave a very exact account of its meaning among the Mandingo people and of the social uses to which the mumbo jumbo idol was put (it was employed by Mandingo husbands to discipline nagging or quarrelsome wives). The only element of "unreason" lies in the English perversion of its meaning.
8. Director General of the United Nations Food and Agriculture Organization, May 1973.
9. Looking at the land on each side of the Senegal River during the 1973 drought, one technical expert from the United Nations foresaw consequences as dramatic as Professor Gautier's and declared that there was a danger of the river's drying up completely. But this did not happen either. The end of the drought came as unexpectedly as its arrival, and within a year, after only one rainy season, the pasture was restored, the crops were succeeding, and the same man who had foreseen a dry riverbed was declaring confidently that the speed of recovery was entirely due to the international rescue operation.

CHAPTER 7

THE COUNTRY WITH
NO PSYCHIATRISTS

The farmer's life is not only strenuous, boring, and poorly
paid; but brutal. Through most of the world successful
efforts to reach him and raise his productivity have been
accompanied by some sort of coercion.

Spokesman for the Green Revolution,
New York Review of Books, vol. 23, no. 2 (1976)

The United Nations Food and Agriculture Organization
is featuring Shirley Temple Black, the U.S. ambassador to
Ghana, as Ceres, the Roman goddess of fertility, on a medal
specially struck for the occasion.

Official announcement from FAO
headquarters in Rome, 1975

The River Gambia sparkles even on a dull day. It
is one of the great rivers of Africa and so broad at the
mouth that a newcomer who reaches its bank is not
certain at first whether the sea is to his left or his right.
But the country named after it is one of the smallest
in the world. Such a vast river has brought forth such
a small nation—as though the effort needed to unite
the people on those distant banks prevented any subsequent expansion.

The ferry that proposed to cross this mighty river
was a most filthy object. It was caked with grease and
smuts, and the volume of black smoke it belched out
revealed the degree of skill that was applied to the ad-
justment of its engine. Long before the time of departure
the vessel was completely packed with passengers, bag-

gage, and vehicles. There was nowhere to sit and almost nowhere to stand. Only the officers had a little space. A wooden balcony had been erected over the engine room, and at the front of this an awning was stretched across. Here was the bridge and the wheelhouse, and here was Captain John Cole, in command. The bridge was separated from the rest of the balcony by a little wicket gate with a string catch, the sort of contrivance normally seen at the entrance to a vegetable plot.

Captain John Cole was distinguished from his fellow officers by his hat, a black felt trilby punched out into a dome and secured to his head by a silk ribbon beneath the chin. He showed no interest in the proceedings around him. No nautical preparation could hold his attention; instead, he sat at the back of the bridge, sucking on a pipe and deciding who should be allowed to pass through the wicket. The competition for this honor was all the greater for the discomforts of standing anywhere else in the boat, but few who applied were chosen. Just before departure a man limped down the quay, leaning on another. The limping man was dressed in blue overalls which were covered in blood that had seeped from a heavily bandaged wound in his head. His face was gray, and he could hardly stand. The captain beckoned him to join the party on the bridge, and he stumbled up the steps and into a corner, where he fell in a heap and bled quietly for the duration. The ferry tooted its steam horn, the drawbridge bows were slowly pulled up, and under the direction of a man in an orange vest, the first officer, the voyage began.

A few years ago one of the Gambian ferries met a large wave in midstream and overturned. There were no survivors; by the time anyone on either bank noticed that the ferry was overdue all trace of it had disappeared. On this occasion the ferry chugged away from the quay while its bow gate was still low enough for water to flow over it past the car deck and back to the engine-room door. Captain John Cole remained calm and continued to suck on his pipe and gaze ahead while the bows were adjusted and the surplus water slowly drained away.

After a short while the chief engineer, in fact, the only engineer, abandoned his post and came to the bridge to dry out. As he passed through the wicket, there was a rush of passengers behind him, led by a voluble and rather Parisian Wolof who insisted on addressing his fellow Wolof in French, the second language of Senegal. It took minutes of detailed and elegant argument, he in French, the officers in English, before he agreed to withdraw, and while this took place, the gate remained ajar, firmly wedged into the helmsman's back so that he could hardly manage the wheel. The first officer all the while pointed out rocks and reassured all who would listen that though the river appeared to be so broad and deep, its navigation required calculations of the greatest delicacy. When the helmsman was eventually free again, the ship answered to the helm very slowly. A glance at the wheel cable showed that it was looped together with brittle wires in several places. But Captain Cole's calm was not disturbed, and until the very last moments of the voyage it seemed that he would not once need to remove his pipe from his mouth. Then, as the ferry approached its destination, disaster loomed.

As the quay drew closer, the first officer rang the engine-room telegraph for half speed, forgetting that it would not be answered because the chief engineer was still beside him on the bridge. Consequently the boat reached the quay at full speed. No sooner was the bow rope in the hands of the dockers than it was wrenched back again as the bows raced on toward the beach. The chief engineer in his haste to stop the engines, and not feeling up to further discussion with the Parisian, who still blocked the gate, jumped off the edge of the balcony and began to fight his way back among the passengers and cars and goats.

Then Captain John Cole came to life. He jumped to his feet, pushed the helmsman aside, seized the wheel, and ordered "full astern" on the telegraph. There was no response since the engineer was still some way from the engine room, and the captain, assuming that the telegraph was jammed, began banging the brass handle back and forth from "full ahead" to "full astern" like a motorist trying to change gear.

The first officer, meanwhile, was shouting at the dockers, who had somehow made the stern rope fast, to let it go or it would break. Just before the engineer reached his controls, the stern rope went taut and snapped, to lie in the wake of the ferry (directly in line with the propellers) as the vessel at last proceeded to reverse full astern away from the beach and back toward the quay, once more showing an excellent turn of speed. As it whipped past the quay again, a number of passengers, deciding that this might be their last chance, started to leap off. Children, old men, goats on leads, enormous parcels, enormous women crossed the divide between the pitching boat and the concrete dock. By some chance none fell between the two. The chief officer continued to shout instructions at the dockers, the dockers at the engineer, and Captain John Cole at the chief officer while he banged the telegraph handle. Backward and forward went the telegraph, back and forth went the boat, now threatening to hit the beach, now to make for the deep water and the other shore.

At last the engineer decided to ignore instructions and to dock the boat himself with the aid of the dockers whom he could see through his open door. As he did so, the rush of passengers for the rails increased, and those who could not risk their lives by jumping ran, instead, insofar as they could, from side to side of the deck, adding considerably to the existing instability of the vessel. There was only one calm place in view. On the car deck just below the bridge there was a new police truck. The constables inside it, in their crisp uniforms, ignored the surrounding panic. They sat upright and gazed straight ahead through the spotless glass, while the bows clanged onto the ramp behind them and the passengers scrambled across their cab. All correct they sat, not a scratch on their paintwork, not a thread out of line, like new toys on a shop shelf. Attached to their windshield was a little sticker—"This is a wide zone toughened windscreen"—which recalled the world of accident prevention and road safety and correct procedures in the event of approaching the quay too fast and which seemed as remote from the society they were supposed to control as rescue must have seemed to the occupants of that earlier ferry which had overturned in midstream while nobody noticed. The last person to leave the boat was the gray-faced man with the bandaged head. He stumbled off as he had stumbled on, still bleeding steadily, and made his painful way toward the town, and the police drove past him unhurriedly, models of detachment and moderation.

The streets of Banjul are paved with seashells. The road gangs leave them piled up in heaps by the side of the road, their original use as coinage long since superseded by the glinting products of the Northern mints. The town is even less changed than Saint-Louis, though it is still a capital city. The broad streets are laid out on an eighteenth-century grid and bear their original English names, chiefly drawn from the Napoleonic era. The well-proportioned houses have handsome stone facings and wrought-iron balustrades, and they are built around courtyards and stables which are linked by high stone arches and surrounded by high stone walls. Only the drainage system which runs down each side of the road and is built on the scale of a miniature urban canal is beginning to show signs of general collapse. The rest of the town still gives off something of the prosperous content which it must have inherited from the heyday of the colony. Even the cricket ground is laid out on the original generous lines beside the governor's house, now the presidential palace. The country has no army, has an annual balance-of-payments surplus, and, above all, is traditionally self-sufficient in food. It makes its money by exporting peanuts, but unlike Senegal, the much larger country which surrounds it on all sides, it is able to raise and sell this cash crop without having to spend the money on essentials such as imported wheat or rice. Or that was at least the position until 1977.

Gambia is a country with eight barristers and no psychiatrists. When the British ambassador had to choose which project to support with a grant, he invited suggestions and was asked to make a contribution to the mental hospital, which had few modern facilities. He donated some cricket equipment.[1] The British influence continues, in particular the links between politics and the law. Each of the country's eight barristers has at one time wanted to enter politics, and in so small a country there is only one political post that a lawyer trained in London considers to be worth his attention, the presidency. But all eight lawyers have been frustrated in this ambition, because, ever since independence, the office of president has been filled by a veterinary surgeon whose great achievement has been to authorize an entirely new Gambian industry—package tourism.

It is the fate of any traveler through a new country to be considered for much of the time an idiot. He knows nothing, understands little more, and whenever he passes his new knowledge through his old understanding, he is likely to get it wrong. And of all travelers the most idiotic is the package tourist.

In Africa the package tourist is perhaps more idiotic

than usual. He is the man who will be charged $10 for a shoeshine and, if he hesitates to pay, will be told that his shoes have had "special medicine" and threatened with the police. He is the greater fool who not only will decide to change his money on the black market but will do it in the streets and thereby get the worst rate of exchange, finally managing to do it with a man who will sell him wads of useless paper. The package tourist is always worried about money. "How much?" says his hotel phrase book. Then "Very expensive," then "Give me discount." The package tourist may feel very poor because he has tried to buy too much for too little, and it takes him the full length of his trip to discover how wide the gap was. But although he feels poor to himself, he looks rich to the citizens of his chosen playpen. "Welcome to the Hotel," says the little notice by the bed. "To ensure a more pleasant stay, we suggest that you keep the door locked when you are in the room and do not discuss your hotel or room number in front of strangers. Welcome!"

Almost everything about package tourism in poor countries is potentially idiotic. In Kenya the motorcar manufacturers hold a road rally every year. It is very unpopular with the people of Kenya, who object to dozens of cars racing past their houses, so they stone the rally drivers. When, as not infrequently happens, an anonymous African is killed while crossing the road by one of the rally cars, he is described as "an elderly spectator." The tourists watch the race.

When a pack of hyenas terrorize a remote location in northern Kenya, attacking huts at night and dragging people out, the authorities are at a loss. Then a bright idea is suggested. Why should the government not transfer these hyenas to a nearby game reserve so that the tourists can see them? It is done, and the hyenas are even given pet names—Prince, Jumbo, Podge.

A German jumbo jet crashes at an African airport, killing many of its passengers, including dozens of tourists. The people of the nearby slums gather at the scene of the disaster and, with the greatest courage, rush into the flames to drag the bodies clear. Then they strip them of everything they can find. They have found their dream tourists. A local photographer takes several rolls of film, recording every detail of the event. His pictures are displayed for months afterward in the center of town, just beside several tourist hotels. It is a big attraction for shoppers. The photographer's work is highly commended. As a reward he wins a free package holiday in the Seychelles, to mark the inauguration of a new tourist air service. The chief minister of the Seychelles marvels at the pictures and immediately pins them up outside his party headquarters. "It was a slice of heaven," says the photographer when asked to summarize his experience.

But tourists ask to be idiots. They want to be happy because they have invested much money in two weeks' happiness, and in these unnatural circumstances happiness is more easily achieved in the absence of all normal mental activity. Tourists do not want to consider the reality of their surroundings; they have come for the illusion. They seek to be deluded, the condition of idiocy. They are treated accordingly. "Do not," say the notices in game parks, "wind down the windows of your car," even if you can see forever. "Do not cross this path." But she did, her first day out on the African plains, and there, a few hundred yards from her room, was a blue lake. She wanted to look at the lake; it was, after all, an inducement placed directly in front of her room. So she took her camera and put on her safari hat because she was a careful person and had been told about the sun, even at six in the evening, and she crossed the path and walked down toward the lake. How embarrassing to be the only person in the party who has not seen the lion. And she still hasn't seen it; this is her first day in Africa, and she would not recognize a lion at fifty yards lying by a bush. Look, there are all your friends, on the terrace outside the bar; they are all waving at you and calling, "Trudi! come back!" But no, there is half an hour before dinner, and she needs to photograph the lake before it gets too dark; they are moving on early next day, and these African sunsets can, it seems, be very sudden. Very sudden.

Locked into their rooms overnight, like stamps in a safe, the tourists refresh themselves with sleep. In the morning they rise and go to their balconies, which all look out in the same direction; they have to because that is the direction of the sea. Look, just below the balcony, what is that on the grass? A snake! No, it is dead. It is just a dead snake. How strange that it should die there, just below the balcony.

Actually it did not die there. It was killed by the gardener on the other side of the lawn in the thick shrubs. He carried it over here because he thought it would interest the tourists, who seemed to enjoy looking at such things, and because it might reassure them to know that he had killed a snake in the garden—just near the path where they walked barefoot to the pool.

The warden of a Gambian snake park, an amiable eccentric, took a party of tourists for a walk among the snakes. After a while they reached an enclosure containing a pack of hyenas. The warden approached the wire and tickled one of the beasts under the jowl. It drooled onto his hand. The warden was able to do this because he had known "Sausage" since it was small and had even taken it for walks on a chain. Eventually it grew so strong that he had to take a gun on his walks as well because if he had tried to pull it off the neighbors' dogs with the chain, he would have skinned his hands. One of the visitors, seeing the warden tickling the hyena and knowing only that hyenas have a bite that can remove an entire human face in one, became overwrought. The warden turned around to see what had happened. His visitor, a tourist, was lying on the jungle path, twitching and moaning for a lost Africa.

When the tourist looks out his picture window across the main street of Banjul, he will see the wide river and the far shore and, interrupting this view, the shanty homes of his new neighbors. The people directly opposite occupy a corner site. They have driven tall stakes into the earth around the edge of their plot, and they have erected a tall stockade of corrugated strips and packing cases and old doors. There is one object in their compound which is incongruous in its beauty. This is a high tree with wide branches and feathery leaves. It is gashed on each side because its owners are using the living tree for firewood.

There are two houses in this compound, and the smaller one, which is occupied by eight people, is about the same size as the tourist's room. Both houses have open drains. Outside the compound, sticking up from the broken pavement, is a water standpipe. It is about three feet high and provides water for the whole district. It has a heavy brass tap, a stone step beneath it, the clogged gutter beside. People wash at it. The boys who are small enough take showers beneath it, with their trousers on. The women fill enormous bowls or buckets of water from it. Sometimes they wash clothes there. While they wait to use the tap, they plunk their upturned buckets down onto the dirt and sit on them. Stray dogs piss on the standpipe. Nobody ever cleans this tap.

As he looks out on those hovels, the tourist may realize that the room he is sitting in, which is exactly like so many tourist hotel rooms throughout the world and which shelters him and perhaps one other person, would suit one of those crowded households very well. After all, he is looking out on one of the more desirable residences in the city: a corner site with its own fuel supply. Think what those people could do with this well-appointed chicken coop which he is occupying. He has a shower and a basin and a toilet, as well as running water and drains. And these are all set into one corner with a solid hinged door for privacy and a ventilation shaft for rubbish. Then there is the bedroom with its desks, beds, and cupboards. The cupboards would make bunk beds for four, and the balcony could be boarded in to make a kitchen. He, a visitor, is occupying a model housing unit in a country where thousands of citizens are living in cardboard boxes. It is possible that this will occur to the tourist, but equally possible that it will not.

One tourist, a Norwegian girl in a wheelchair, fell in love with a beggar who was on a soapbox. They experienced such a strong mutual attraction that they were married before her time came to return to Norway. After the wedding there was a ceremony attended by all the beggars in town. They came to the girl's hotel to speed the bridal couple on their way; all the lepers and tuberculosed and amputees and blind and half-wits of the region assembled on the steps of this hotel and attempted to enter the foyer and make for the elevator and get to the party. For the management it was a nightmare. No leper on a soapbox had ever before been admitted through the glass doors. It was enough to frighten away every other guest in the building. Eventually the manager locked the revelers out and asked the bride to leave. He had thought she was a bona fide tourist, and she had turned into an immigrant.

The Gambian tourist industry has grown from 300 tourists in 1965, the year of independence, to 23,000 tourists in 1975, and the target is 100,000 tourists a year.[2] Most of the tourists are from Scandinavia, and their arrival has brought many problems to this small country—as all the politicians who are not in the government will agree. "The tourists are consuming more and more of our resources," said one of the politicians. "They need houses to be built for them; they use up fuel and transport. There have been so many attacks on them that we shall soon need to employ more policemen. We may even have to recruit an army. They also corrupt our children, both boys and girls, and this leads to violence in the family. For instance, two Gambian girls, both from Moslem families, were persuaded by Swedish tourists to take part in a blue movie. When this became known in the Gambia, one girl was murdered by her relatives, and the other committed suicide. And the tourists are also beginning to affect the food supply. They eat a lot you know, these Swedes. And this country does not easily provide the sort of food they eat."

The traditional economy of Gambia, which remained relatively undisturbed by both colonialism and independence, is subsistence agriculture. It is a system that has largely failed to provide a comfortable or secure life, but it has enabled people to live. It has also proved capable of unexpected subtleties, unexpected to the early advisers, who were surprised at signs of native intelligence, and still more unexpected to the highly trained Northern experts who followed them, to the point that the modern experts on how to improve the human condition in West Africa seem to have forgotten the native skills completely.

Some of the former customs of Gambia show that people were well aware, for instance, of the problem of population growth and had devised methods to check it. "The Negro women," wrote Mungo Park (two years before Malthus published his *Essay on the Principle of Population*), "suckle their children until they are able to walk of themselves. Three years nursing is not uncommon; and during this period the husband devotes his whole attention to his other wives. To this practice it is owing, I presume, that the family of each wife is seldom very numerous. Few women have more than five or six children."[3]

The same skill at regulating the birthrate was to be found right across Africa,[4] and the consequences of Northern interference with these customs were not confined to an increase in births. Geoffrey Gorer wrote in 1935:

The successful efforts of missionaries have largely added
to the infant mortality. It was the custom of negro mothers
to suckle their children for three years, for animal's milk is
scarce and the ordinary diet is not sufficiently nutritive for
young children. During that period the husband would not
have intercourse with her, for otherwise she would become
pregnant again and stop lactating. Under monogamy this
practice obviously falls in desuetude. The heavy work which
pregnant and nursing mothers are in some parts made to do
is a contributory cause.[5]

The North, in effect, by its advice, first raised the birthrate and then ensured that most of the surplus children
died. Next, it offered birth control programs to deal with
the first problem and expensive drugs to deal with the
second.

One group of American Baptists which continued this
practice in 1975 enjoyed the assistance of USAID. Every
week the people selected by the Baptists for enlightenment attended a service at the end of which the minister
preached a sermon. For those who stayed till the end of
the sermon there was a blue ticket which they could take
to the mission dispensary—run by the minister's wife.
She was naturally opposed to polygamy. But she was also
opposed to breast feeding, not just because it encouraged
polygamy but because she considered it immodest, unhygienic, and undernourishing. The African women waited
for their blue tickets so that they could come to the
dispensary for free medical care when they were ill, but
they were also given a supply of milk powder and contra-
ceptive pills. The pills were useless. Many of the women
forgot to take them, or took them all at once, or gave
them to their husbands. In some cases the fact that the
pills were taken for several cycles and then stopped meant
that the women's fertility positively increased. And the
milk powder was worse since the mothers fed it to their
children in unsterilized bottles, mixed with polluted water
and frequently in overdiluted proportions. By encouraging the mothers to abandon breast feeding and to live

monogamously, the Baptists were raising the birthrate beyond the point where the villagers could feed their children. By distributing milk powder, they were redressing the balance as effectively as the colonial system of overtaxation, forced labor, and consequent exhaustion had done. And on occasion the pills supplied were of a type (such as Depo-Provera) that were banned in America and Europe as being too dangerous.

During the drought of 1973, despite the state of the neighboring Sahelian countries, there was no famine in Gambia. There was a lower rainfall; but this did not result in shortages, and there was even enough surplus food to feed the "strange farmers," the refugees from the Sahel who entered the eastern part of the country from Senegal. But despite the adequate provisions of 1973, the United States Agency for International Development unshipped 7,000 tons of unrequested free food that year in Banjul docks. It was possible then to suppose that a mistake had been made. But three years later, when there had been no regional food shortage anywhere in West Africa, the United States supplied without charge 35,000 tons of sorghum and rice to Gambia. For a population of 400,000 people this represented nearly 100 kilograms of free food per head, two-thirds of each person's minimum annual need. It was almost as though the American government were intending to take over the responsibility for feeding the Gambian population.

There are four methods of reducing world hunger, according to the American government. Food production must be increased, poverty reduced, adequate storage capacity provided, and population growth retarded.[6] Flooding a self-sufficient country with surplus grain does not form part of any of these methods, but there was no protest from the Gambians when the grain arrived. Although it was surplus to requirements, it was not allowed to rot. Much of it was smuggled over the border to Senegal, where there is an annual food deficit. The rest

was put to use in the way that had been intended; it replaced food that would otherwise have been produced by
Gambian farmers.

The agency that distributed USAID's free grain was
Catholic Relief Services, an organization that has worked
with USAID in many parts of the world.[7] In Gambia it
uses the food as part of its "Food for Work" program,
under which farmers are encouraged to leave their fields
and work on various improving schemes, in return for
payment in food. The individual's incentive to grow food
is diminished, and the means to rearrange the country's
economy on lines that allow it to be reduced to dependency are implemented. As a way of reducing an independent and inattentive peasantry to servile obedience it beats
even taxation. Aid becomes not only the moral equivalent
but also the economic equivalent of war. Once dependency
has been established, a price can be demanded for the
food, and if it cannot be paid in cash, it can be funded in
loans at interest or tied to trade deals involving American
goods.[8]

By 1976 the process was well under way in Gambia.
Most of the food was being paid for by labor, but where
there were no projects on which farmers could be employed, some of the food was on sale for cash. Thus, one
family in a village received a CRS food parcel free, a
second received it after a specified period of labor, and a
third paid $5 for it. In each case the parcel was stamped
"CRS—Not for Sale," to the bewilderment both of the
villagers and of the Irish Catholic priests who ran the
village mission but who were unconnected with CRS.
Frequently, when the parcels were still superfluous to
local needs, they would end up in the marketplace for
resale at a higher price. It is impossible to replace a
healthy food supply system overnight. But CRS and
USAID used another method in Gambia that was even
more sophisticated than "Food for Work."

In a continent that has a very high infant-mortality

rate and millions of cases of infantile malnutrition, it takes an inventive mind to think up the "Well Baby Clinic." The number of babies in West Africa that are by American standards "well" is a minority. But CRS's medical resources were extensive enough to hold weekly clinics in various villages which sick children were forbidden to attend. The assumption behind this scheme was that all the children in the village were undernourished because their mothers had to work in the fields while still suckling their infants and that even this labor at a time when they should have been resting prevented them from providing enough nutritious food.

These clinics were a novelty, and they attracted the attention of Dr. Tufo, an ambitious politician.

Dr. Tufo had once been a fiery member of the opposition, so fiery that he had caught the eye of the president, who did not deport him or imprison him, as might have happened in a less civilized country, but instead offered him a parliamentary seat in the government interest. Dr. Tufo had always made a point of attacking the government on the grounds of its mistaken policies and ineffective programs; he never descended to personalities or courted cheap popularity. So he had to overcome some serious political differences before he could accept the president's offer. He did this with little delay, and he was offered the same constituency which he had formerly contested in the interest of the opposition. With an election coming up, Dr. Tufo began to renew his interest in his constituents, and one day he decided that he should visit the Well Baby Clinic.

The clinic was held in the morning in a central shelter which had been erected for meetings or gossip. Most of the mothers in the village who had young babies came. It was run by a conscientious Methodist missionary from England who was also a qualified nurse. First each baby was weighed, and the circumference of its upper arm was measured; then the figures were recorded on a chart with which the mother had been supplied. The chart, which was a standard design used by USAID all over the world, showed whether the baby was normal or underweight. Then the children were taken into the next hut to see the nurse. She examined the chart and prescribed pills for malaria, gripe, or coughs from which, she said, they suffered to such a universal extent that the symptoms did not disqualify them from the state of "wellness." After the pills had been dished out and each child's proportions set against those of its average American equivalent—and found more or less wanting—the nurse joined her clients in the shelter.

The mothers sat around the four sides of the shelter while the English nurse introduced her visitors. "This man has come all the way from London to write a book about the clinic. And this man is from America and gives us all the food. And this man is Dr. Tufo, whom you know." Then the real sermon began. The nurse, who had been studying the principles of nutrition from a do-it-yourself book, laid down the dietary principles that she had decided on. She spoke in a high, tense voice, and her words were translated into Wolof by one of the clinic's young assistants, a high school graduate who would never become a nurse despite her grades but who at least had a job. "Some of your children," the nurse began, "have not gained a pound in weight for ten months. That is bad. It's because you took them off the breast too soon. There, I've said it right in front of you." And she smiled. Happy laughter rang back.

"The best food," the nurse continued, "is mother's milk. But after four months it is not enough. Then you must give your child pap. But the pap is too thin. You must add to the pap. Fish with groundnuts or onions and tomatoes." In the center of the shelter there was an open fire, and above this a large black pot was suspended. Another high school graduate was stirring the contents of the pot, and a most delicious smell circulated around the gathering. As they endured the sermon, both mothers and babies kept a close eye on this pot. "Make sure the babies swallow the pap." The nurse's instructions rang out down the village street and drew some older children out of their huts. The nurse was concerned to make everything clear, and she repeated her points several times. Her last words were: "Give each child its own plate, or the strongest will eat it all." Then the sermon finished, and the rush for food began.

The story had changed. The mothers of West Africa, who had, for one hundred years or more, been instructed by missionaries that breast feeding was ignorant and backward, were now learning that it was the best method. Their husbands, who for the same period of time had been encouraged or ordered to stop growing food for themselves and grow cash crops instead, were now advised to provide more nourishing produce for their children. The stew in the pot was made of peanuts and vegetables. And at the end of the meal came the "blue ticket," a bottle of peanut oil and a bag of rice. None of the mothers had given up half a day's work in the fields to take a healthy child to see the doctor and be told that it was underweight. They came because they calculated that the value of CRS's free oil and rice exceeded the value of the attention they would otherwise be giving to their crops. When the clinic stopped distributing the oil and gave away just rice, attendance of mothers at the clinic dropped from forty to ten. Rice was a cereal, a food they could grow themselves. Oil had to be paid for, was highly nutritious, and, even if they made the journey to market, it was not always easy to obtain, since most of Gambia's peanut oil is exported to Europe.

No matter how hard she tried, the nurse never could persuade the mothers to feed their children eggs, "because," she was always told, "eggs make the children dumb." She regarded this as superstition, the sort of thing education could correct, but it was surely a myth with a purpose, like the myth of the mimosa tree. The village was only an hour away from Banjul, with its population of Northerners and its six tourist hotels. The tourists had no use for cassava or maize or any of the village's other crops, and the only peanuts they used were in saucers on the bar; but the hotels did demand large quantities of eggs. The eggs were a valuable source of cash for the villagers, cash which could even be used to buy peanut oil or clothes or a bicycle. The value of the eggs in cash far exceeded any other use the villagers might find for them. Food had become something one sold, or went to the doctor for.

At the end of Dr. Tufo's visit the reason for the nurse's nervousness was revealed. She had supposed that he was a doctor of medicine, possibly even a specialist in nutrition. This was not an impression Dr. Tufo felt bound to correct; but eventually she requested his professional opinion, and he was found out. His status was severely diminished. "Doctor of Political Science" did not carry the same weight at all. But it did enable Dr. Tufo to appreciate the advantages of the clinic, irrespective of any queries that might be raised about its ultimate medical effects. Before leaving, he addressed the well-fed mothers and babies about the policies of the government which had arranged for this excellent clinic. And he assured the mothers that if they elected him, he would arrange for other clinics to distribute food in their area. He was lunching that very day with the president and would mention it then. (CRS later refused to set up any more clinics because there were no more nurses to run them.)

An hour away in Banjul, the city where many eggs were consumed, the layers of complexity receded; it was possible to view Gambia as a country that needed more investment, or a change of political emphasis in favor of the rural areas, or as a place that lacked only advice.

There were offices in Banjul and charts, so everything was bound to look more orderly than it did from the village shelter.

"If only we had just one new river steamer," said the politicians, or "if only the tourists would go away," or "if only the roads could be surfaced, and we could spend more on agriculture." There were three opposition parties, two of them run by lawyers, and their criticisms of the president's mistakes were chorused in harmony. Although the leaders of the UP and the NLP and the NCP lived within a mile of one another, they did not meet but sent emissaries to discuss tactics. At the NLP the "intention was to form the next government." The UP "expected to win every seat." So did the NCP, which was nonetheless "prepared to consider an electoral alliance against the PPP," the president's party. "It will be a major African achievement when we have removed the government without violence," said the NLP. "It is discipline we need," said the NCP. "Not Swedish entrepreneurs undermining the nation's morality." And at the UP the leaders reposed their confidence in "the People. They won't stand for it any longer, when we give them the facts. You'll see."

On the roads out of the capital, the villages sometimes displayed the various flags of the rival parties, but the people's grasp of which flag represented which party could not be taken for granted. The messages and reports that excited Banjul's smoke-filled rooms did not extend beyond the city limits. Up and down the riverbanks, lost in the trees, gathered around their particular patchwork of fields, the electors of Gambia seemed scarcely aware that there was a ballot in prospect. It made no impression on the self-absorption of this chain of remote communities. It was something that happened in Banjul, wherever that was. For among the facts missing in Gambia is an available, detailed map.

Not all the politicians in Banjul were as adaptable as

Dr. Tufo. Some of the older ones still preferred opposition, even if they were offered safe seats. Mr. Njie was one of the old school. He was *métis,* or mulatto, as it was called in the English colony. P. S. Njie came from one of the oldest families in Banjul; he still preferred to call the town Bathurst, the name originally given to it by the English traders who had founded it. He identified with this local aristocracy, the community of mixed blood which grew from the trading links between England and Gambia and which was dying as these links were broken one by one. Those were his people, the traditional rulers of Gambia, possessors once of their own language, Creole, which they shared with the European merchants and with the French *métis* of Saint-Louis and the Portuguese Creoles of Cacheu and Jeba. Even the bush Africans from the interior had had to learn Creole if they wished to do business with the people of Bathurst. Mr. Njie was usually called by his nickname, P.S.

P.S. lived in one of the handsomest stone houses on the main street, which his family had owned for years. It had a courtyard at the back where his dependents lived, but it was in dilapidated condition now; there wasn't the money to keep it up in the way his father would have wished. He lived in the rooms which overlooked the main street, and from one of the windows he still hung his party flag because P.S. was still the leader of a political party and the house was the party headquarters. To reach his private rooms, one passed through the largest room in the house, once the library. The bookcases which lined the walls right up to the ceiling were still there, but they were almost empty now; the only volumes left were a leather-bound set of the *English Law Reports* up to 1960, the year when P.S. retired from his legal practice.

"I come from difficult parentage," he said, and one waited for a discussion of race and decolonialism. But he continued: "My father was very Victorian. He showed little affection. I started my schooling here, but I was called to the bar in London. At Lincoln's Inn. I had the largest practice in the Gambia for many years. You saw the books outside? I still like reading them. I can still find my way around. And I still have my gown."

He sat in a rocking chair, smoking a pipe. He wore a crumpled drill suit over his pajamas, and he had brown brogues on his feet, highly polished, but without socks. There was a fresh white handkerchief in his breast pocket.

"They've rigged all the elections here since 1962. Did you know that? We've had thirteen or fourteen elections, and they've all been rigged. They bought up half our seats; my chaps changed sides. But for that I should be president. In point of fact, constitutionally, I am still the prime minister if anybody is. I wouldn't take the oath of allegiance to this 'president,' so they slung me out. So now I'm a gentleman of private means."

Conversations with P.S. in his own home were constantly interrupted by people who came to ask him favors. They came from the other end of Gambia because his fame at the time of independence as one of the powerful men at the river mouth, one of the rulers of Bathurst, was still bright. Subsequent events—his defeat at the elections, his dismissal from Parliament, the collapse of his party—had failed to discourage them, particularly since he listened to the supplicants with all his old attention and was evidently no less or more effective in satisfying their demands than he had been before. "I am sorry about these tiresome interruptions," he said. "The price I have to pay for wanting to be popular." And he mocked himself with his feigned regret.

When people had gone and he had noted their requests in a pad on his lap, he resumed his political history. "The people in power are, I'm afraid, a collection of— brigands." He produced the antique word with a restrained force. "He calls himself Sir Dawda now, the president. I always knew him as *Mr.* David in the old days when he was the vet, but he changed his name when he changed his religion. There are a lot of Moslem votes in the Gambia. I suppose he was tempted, and he succumbed. There are simple people upriver who vote for him on a tribal basis. They don't understand the issues at all. I am a Catholic myself. The old sort. I knew Archbishop Lefebre when he was at Dakar. I had all the Tridentine tracts once, but I left them at the luggage place in Victoria Station when I was last in London."

Outside the window his party flag stirred in the evening breeze, and he shuffled over to admit more air, his suit and pajamas retaining their creases when he rose, emphasizing the courtesy of his uncustomary impulse. "Have you read about the race riots in London?" he said suddenly. "Very disturbing. It never used to happen in England. But I was interested to see that the troublemakers were not Africans but from the West Indies. Detribalized. They don't have the background. Communists.

"When I was eating my dinner, you know, for the bar, before I qualified, I used to do night work at the post office to pay for my Christmas presents. I was sorting letters at Mount Pleasant. It was the largest sorting office in the world, the hub of Empire, and a white man next to me said, 'What cell do you belong to?' I said, 'I am a law student at Lincoln's Inn.' He said, 'Aren't you a communist?' Then when I said, 'No,' he leaned over and said, 'I heard there was an African traitor here.' He was a ridiculous man. The next thing he said was: 'If I prick you, what would happen?' I suppose he was trying to quote *The Merchant of Venice.* I just said, 'I would jump, of course.' He didn't bother me again."

His granddaughters came in, and he started to talk of his plans to send the younger one to school in England. "I get on well with the expatriate population here. I still have many friends in England. Do you know B———? Used to be in the administration here. Tall. Good fellow.

Came to see me last year when he was out. Himself and the wife. As a rule I like a quiet life, but I always have time for visitors from U.K."

The younger girl sat on the arm of his chair. She had an intricate African hair style which amused him. He began to tease her about going to England. "But if you go there," he said, "you'll have to do your hair nicely, in the English way. They have nice things to put on the hair there." When the girls had gone, he said, "It's a pity about the schools here. They are starting to go down. It doesn't matter so much for the boys. They can manage. But the girls should have good schools." His last words were of the forthcoming elections. "We are fighting every seat. We should win them all. You'll see."

But they didn't win one. His party was another of the ideas which the world had forgotten.

In 1977, the year when P.S.'s party lost another election, a famine was declared in Gambia, and an appeal was made for international help. Even for USAID this was something of a record. To render drought and famine synonymous only four years after making the first grain donations, to a country which had survived the great Sahelian drought without exhausting its own resources, was an achievement. The other opposition parties had no more success. But Dr. Tufo was elected safely and was reported to be seeing new virtues in increased package tourism. Gambia apparently needed the foreign currency to pay for imported food.

NOTES

1. The ambassador justified this by saying that it was one of the conditions of the grant that 80 percent of the money should be spent in Britain.

2. See Richard West, *The White Tribes Revisited* (London: Deutsch, 1978).

3. A hundred years later, in 1895, Mary Kingsley noted in *Travels in West Africa* that the practice of long nursing and polygamy regulated the birthrate, but that the missionaries, who disapproved of polygamy, were encouraging bottle feeding, thus freeing the mothers for renewed copulation.

4. Margery Perham in *East African Journey, 1929-30* recorded that the Wambulu tribe of Tanganyika commonly indulged in promiscuous sexual relations before and after marriage but that the pregnancy of young girls was a serious and rare offense. It was not known how the Wambulu avoided it.

5. Geoffrey Gorer, *Africa Dances* (London: Faber, 1935).

6. Report by the Research Council of the National Academy of Sciences to the President, June 1977.

7. Catholic Relief Services is responsible for coordinating the overseas relief programs of the Catholic Church in America. In Vietnam CRS worked with USAID by setting up and running camps for peasant farmers who had been forced off their land in pacification operations. In return it accepted free housing and transport for its staff. CRS also supplied the American army with any information it received in the course of relief work. It saw its role as "being the Christ in Vietnam."

8. One American wheat company, Great Plains Wheat, Inc., estimated that between 1977 and 1981 imports of wheat in Senegal, Sierra Leone, Liberia, the Ivory Coast, Nigeria, Zaire, and Ghana would rise from 1.3 million tons to 2.1 million tons and would take a higher percentage of these countries' scarce foreign exchange. According to the U.S. Department of Agriculture, the growing popularity of imported wheat in West Africa is due to the growth of urban populations that were formerly employed in producing local staples and that regard bread as the food of the colonial masters and, therefore, as a status symbol. That this imaginative suggestion is not the whole story is well illustrated by another incident in 1975 in Zaire.

The government of Zaire owed the Continental Grain Company of New York $16 million for wheat. There was no sign of payment. At a well-chosen moment Continental diverted its monthly cargo of wheat to a different country. Almost at once the bakeries in Kinshasa began to run out of flour, and payments due from the government of Zaire to Continental were immediately resumed. None of the country's many other creditors was able to exercise similar pressure. A widespread shortage of staple food is the one situation which even a powerful and authoritarian government will do anything to avoid. The political possibilities are obvious.

PART 3

PARALLEL AFRICA

AN OMINOUS PATIENCE

I am not you—
but you will not
give me a chance
will not let me be *me* . . .

You are unfair, unwise,
foolish to think
that I can be you,
talk, act
and think like you.

God made me *me*
He made you *you*.
For God's sake
Let me be *me*.

> Roland Tombekai
> Dempster,
> *Africa's Plea*

CHAPTER 8

THE TIME MAP

Two decades later it is clear that the impact of the Interstate System on the national life [of America] has been immeasurable. It has extended the practical horizons of the everyday citizen by leagues and become the ultimate agent of his liberation from the bonds of geography. With Walt Whitman he can say, "I inhale great draughts of space, the East and the West are mine, and the North and the South are mine." Distance is now conceived in hours instead of miles.

Advertisement in the *New York Times,* 1976

There was a rocky valley between Buxton and Bakewell . . . you might have seen the gods there morning and evening, Apollo and the sweet Muses of the Light—You enterprised a railroad. . . . You blasted its rocks away. . . . And now, every fool in Buxton can be at Bakewell in half-an-hour, and every fool in Bakewell at Buxton.

John Ruskin, *Praeterita*

I landed in the desert to take my lunch in the shade of a wing. A caravan of Saharan nomads approached. I asked the leader of the caravan how long it would take him to reach Semara. He shrugged and said, "About three or four days." I laughed and said my plane would reach Semara in only two hours. "And what will you do with the extra hours?" he asked.

Recollections of a Spanish Foreign Legionnaire

In many independent African countries the city limits mark the effective borders of the state. Outside the city official life evaporates; within is the favored area, the place where all the money goes, the place where the entire educated community insists on living. It is the one lump of earth out of the whole inheritance which the fragile governments can make more than a pretense of governing.

The first means of linking the city to the state, the road, is also the first cause of the division between the two. Almost all the cars in Africa are to be found in or around African cities, and in Lagos the traffic jams last all day. For hours and hours every morning the traffic attempting to reach the center of the city sits motionless, festooned in delicate patterns across the marshes and townships and plains surrounding it, now looping over and back onto itself as it follows the filigree of six-lane highways which enterprising German engineers have sold to the government, but which lead eventually to the impassable alleyways of the colonial settlement. This is getting to work.

Later in the day there is going home. The same bus lines, but now in the heat and filth of the city afternoon. The same traffic jam, day after day.

The slowness of the traffic is so predictable that a sizable part of the city's commerce takes place by the side of the road, in just such a leisurely manner as was possible before cars were invented. All along the looping overpasses there are peddlers with full trays. One can buy car accessories, toys for bored children, immersion heaters, tool kits, toothpaste, patent medicine, clothing, cassettes, jewelry, oranges, or pornographic home movies. As one sits there in the back of a rusting twenty-year-old sedan, half-asphyxiated by the gas fumes, life takes on a dying pace which overwhelms the Northern sense of purpose. The signs on the grimy buildings seem less and less plausible, "Right Time Hotel—Barristers and Solicitors Within," "Motherless Babies Home," "School of Dental Hygiene," "Mukky Cuts—Butcher"; when the traffic does move, the car behind promptly rams the old sedan.

The passengers, still in their blue-fumed dream, do

not look around. The drivers clamber out and argue; an unwary policeman joins in and is at once the object of joint recrimination; he ends by justifying himself to anyone who will listen. The drivers are ready to forget the matter, but they cannot disengage their cars; there is no room; the jam is back. An army truck drives past, from its front window a steel-helmeted soldier leans out, holding a leather switch. As he passes the accident, he lashes one of the taxi drivers and shouts at him, his face distorted with fury. Only the soldiers move through the Lagos traffic jam. The military government has placed them in charge of sorting it out.

The former Nigerian head of state, General Mohammed, died as a result of his government's inability to solve the traffic problem. He was shot dead in his official car on his way to work. It was a simple matter to predict his movements. His car was stuck in the same place at eight each morning. As news of his death spread up and down the traffic jam that ringed the city, people began to run in panic. They dropped what they were carrying and ran away from the center of Lagos, looking for somewhere to hide. Their cars remained locked together and motionless for much of the day.

For most of the people who work in the city, the bus is the only means of transport, and the jams are not the only hazard. In Nairobi the bus crews work for rival companies, and they earn more money if they carry more passengers, so they race each other from one bus stop to the next. Sometimes rival buses, having raced side by side down a stretch of road, reach a crowd of passengers at the same time. The conductor and driver then fight each other, armed with crankshafts and wrenches and knives, to decide whose bus shall be filled to the point where any further passengers would fall off. In Kenya a single bus crash resulted in the death of ten passengers and the injuring of ninety-two others. After such a crash the police do not expect to interview the driver. If he is able to, he runs away and hides for some days. You have to wait to overcome the universal shock of a road accident before you realize that the survivors are not gathered around the injured people, assisting them, but are gathered around the driver (having left the bodies strewn all over the road) and are beating him to death. For Africans the business of travel is attended by much of its original horror.

One of the major obstacles to altering matters is expense. In Gambia 6 percent of the annual budget is spent on health, 9 percent on education, and 43 percent is spent on the telephone system and road, air, or waterborne transport. Yet the country's roads are as ill repaired as they were forty years ago, and the government is unable to afford to replace its one aging river steamer. In the remote areas of Ghana and Uganda it is increasingly difficult to obtain regular supplies of food or medicine, and news of these shortages takes longer to reach the depots in the capital. The war in a remote province of Zaire which was waged for more than two months in 1977 was barely reported for most of that time since there was no means of obtaining information locally and no means of sending it back to the capital of Kinshasa even if it was obtained. In Mozambique a flood was reported to have killed three hundred people; in Ghana there was said to be widespread famine. Days later both reports were officially denied. It was impossible to check on the historical truth in either case.

It is impossible to establish the truth partly because governments frequently object to the attempt and partly because it is increasingly difficult to travel through Africa. The continent's communications system is breaking up, and strangers are less welcome. A time map of Africa, locating places on the basis of the amount of time it took to reach them, would show the same string of coastal cities that were accessible in 1891, though now they are connected by air rather than by sea. In addition, there would be the capitals of the interior and the few towns or rural areas that had road or rail links with their capital. But these few favored places would stand out against a background whose increasing obscurity resembled the time map of the nineteenth century, a terrestrial black hole.

If it is difficult to travel, within city or state, it is equally difficult to communicate. The recent history of communications in Africa has been one of steady disintegration. Twenty years ago at the start of the era of independence the colonial system was at its peak. Then the original method of approach, by sea, was still flourishing; now, with rare exceptions, it has stopped. Then the air service was expanding and was reliable. Now it is contracting, and although the machines can move faster, the burden of maintenance means that flights are frequently abandoned. If war breaks out between Somalia and Ethiopia, road communications for the whole eastern side of Africa are cut. There is only one eastern route from Cairo to the Cape, just as there was fifty years ago. Someone wishing to drive from north to south on reliable roads would need first to cross the whole of North Africa and take the western road, the only other one in existence. Africa is not a place which anyone has ever needed to drive from one end to the other. The foot safari is dead; river navigation, always limited, is less frequent. The steamship lines which, until ten years ago, ran regular services from Europe and America around the continent have now closed all passenger routes. Off Lagos the vessels at anchor waiting to enter port are attacked by pirates in canoes. The attackers climb up the anchor cables and murder seamen who resist. They are so well informed of the ship's cargoes that it is assumed that this revival of an ancient craft has been organized by the Nigerian customs department. Just north of Dakar, off the westernmost point in Africa, Cape Verde, a Japanese freighter lies beached in the surf. Eight years ago it ran into trouble in a storm and radioed for help. The Senegalese navy responded by inquiring how much the owners of the ship would pay to have the crew taken off, so the captain ran his ship ashore to deny them both a fee and the salvage money. The freighter has lain on the beach ever since, intact but useless.

More and more of the observable life of Africa takes place within twenty miles of its three dozen international airports. Air travel is now almost the only way to move about the continent, and this, apart from the impossible expense it poses for most people in the world, is in itself one of the main reasons for the process of isolation which Africa is undergoing. Nothing reduces the internal communications of a remote country as quickly as an international airport. It limits the experience of most of those traveling there to two places, one of which, the airport, is designed to be as little unlike the place which the traveler departed from as it is possible to make it, and the other of which, the capital city, is continually attempting to resemble every other of its counterparts throughout the world. It prevents most of the people of the country from meeting most of those who travel to it; there is none of the experience of a road, none of the commerce of the towns and villages which would otherwise flourish. And it tends to gather the country's political, social, and commercial life around itself. Things that happen in parts of the country where there is no airport, like basket weaving in Mali, move to the airport if they can. If they are immovable, like the uranium mines of Niger, an airport opens beside them. In either case other more sociable methods of transport atrophy, and the places in that country which lack an airport become less important. Air travel closes the country down.

For the expatriate air traveler the plane itself is the place where he would prefer to spend most of his journey through Africa. It provides him with hot water, refreshments, a comfortable chair, a familiar newspaper; it is a refuge from the inconveniences of African life. The Africans who board it will usually conform to his standards of behavior; the natives will be prosperous and sanitized. The heat and odor of the world which he is supposed to be visiting will be repulsed. But even this tangential form of contact with Africa becomes less predictable. Several airlines flying over central Africa still carry specialist navigators because they distrust the air traffic control system and the land beneath is so large. It is the only inhabited landmass where this precaution is still advisable. The printed airline schedules are often abandoned. Political disagreements become more frequent. When the Kenya-Tanzania border was closed for six months in 1977, a forty-five-minute flight which covered the four hundred miles between the two capitals had to be replaced by a two-thousand-mile journey via Ethiopia, the Sudan, or Zambia which took nearly two days.

Even the airports which provide such a limited form of access to these countries sometimes provide too much access for the convenience of the government. At Burundi there is a smart new airport building which bears no name. Its most prominent notice forbids photography, but there is nothing to photograph. It is nonetheless welcoming after the effusive notices erected in Entebbe, the previous airport ("Welcome to You," "Welcome to Uganda"), which invoke a feeling of relief that is all the more unsettling when one realizes where one is and how quickly one has been reassured. The most striking thing about the airport in Burundi is its emptiness, its lack of identifying notices, and, finally, the grandeur of the organization which is responsible for selling its coffee. In Nairobi, which is one of the busiest airports in Africa, one buys coffee at the Simba Café, and it is cheap and drinkable. At Entebbe one buys worse coffee, more expensively, from Uganda Restaurants Ltd. But at Burundi, an airport that airlines overfly if there are fewer than six passengers booked to join the flight there, one usually cannot buy coffee at all, but one is informed on an enormous placard that, if one could, it would be supplied by l'Office des Cultures Industrielles de Burundi. To put the finishing touch to its national airport, the government of Burundi has ensured that apart from its being empty and without food or drink, apart from its being anonymous and frequently bypassed, the airport, for those unfortunate enough to land there, is impossible to leave. There is a splendid paved area outside the building for autos, but there are no buses to or from the airport and no taxis. It is necessary for the air traveler on arriving in this country either to hitch a lift or to walk. If one has arranged to be met, that is another matter, but the only people who usually do so are officials or businessmen, people with access to corporate cars.

The only sustained attempt to establish reliable communications throughout Africa was made by the colonial powers, but they devised a system to suit their own purposes. The interior was linked to the coast and the coast to the mother country. Even the more advanced means of communication, such as radio, telex, telephone, and telegram, were not linked to an African network but to Europe. This was a relatively efficient way of discovering and transmitting information about Africa, but to receive the results, it was necessary to go to Europe. Today this system remains the best available—so much less concerned are the independent governments with the discovery of information of any type.

The difficulties of subjecting a country to modern administration in these circumstances are never-ending. In Egypt a provincial governor who is 350 miles up the Nile is unable to make a telephone connection with Cairo in less than twenty-four hours. A letter takes ten days, if it is ever seen again. But in equatorial Africa it is impossible to make a telephone call from Abidjan to Monrovia, neighboring capitals which are 400 miles apart, without going through Paris, London, and New York. There is no telex connection from Abidjan to Accra, its neighbor on the other side, nor is there a road, although if there were, the journey would take only six hours. When Monrovia did establish a road connection with its other neighboring capital, Freetown, in the form of a road bridge over the Mana River, such euphoria broke out that Liberia and Sierra Leone declared a free tariff area. The only telephone connection that can be made to anywhere in the world from Fernando Po, the capital of Equatorial Guinea, is to Madrid. Lomé, the capital of Togo and the headquarters of the West African Economic Community, is only two miles from the border of its neighboring state, Ghana, a fellow Community member. But cables from one country to the other have to go via Paris and London and take forty-eight hours. In that time it is possible to walk from Lomé to Accra.

It is cheaper to fly from Nairobi in East Africa to Libreville in West Africa via London than direct, even though the journey is five thousand miles longer. Diplomats who cover Kinshasa and Brazzaville, which are separated by two miles and a river, sometimes have to make a two-thousand-mile round trip by air because the frontiers are closed. In an attempt to bypass such difficulties, the British government has stationed its embassy to Chad in London. It has embassies in Nigeria, Cameroon, the Sudan, and Libya, all neighboring states to Chad, but communications between each are more uncertain than the relatively simple problems of traveling to Paris and taking the weekly direct flight.

The most obvious beneficiaries of this lack of communication are the governments that preside over it. If ministers do not have to answer letters, if the telephone rarely works, if there is less traveling, fewer newspapers, less reported knowledge, whether correct or not, and fewer agreed facts, then less happens as less is known to happen, and the business of appearing to control events is considerably simplified. It is easier for any government to contain criticism if it is delivered in a remote part of the country, orally. There is a reduction in shared experience to the personal level, to an area bounded by the known community. In the absence of individual isolation, there is no need for the members of a close community to compensate for it, and while life within that community is enriched by the concentrated attention of its members, the great rush of messages and reports from distant places is no more than an unlamented potential distraction.

Where the means of communication are so poor, their control becomes more important, and they assume an influence out of all proportion to their significance in developed countries. It is notorious that the first objective of any military coup is the radio station, but on a less dramatic level the monopoly of commercial transport enjoyed by the "market queens" of Accra enables them to fix prices and control the food supply in the whole of southern Ghana. Because the means of communication and transport are so limited, access to them is much more rewarding.

The control of or suppression of the press is one of the first tasks of any independent African government. There are certain exceptions; Kenya, Nigeria, Senegal, and the Ivory Coast are among the countries that allow a certain degree of free speech, but the more typical African newspaper is well represented by the *Daily Times* of Malawi. This paper regularly devotes an entire page to the activities of the president of Malawi, Dr. Hastings "Conqueror, the Saviour" Banda. During a tour of the north of Malawi, Conqueror made speeches in three villages. The *Daily Times* did not report the speeches but recorded that at the end of the day £168.95 (about $338), 27 cows, 18 goats, 4 sheep, 4 chickens, 1 duck, 1,775 eggs, 36 bunches of bananas, 3 cabbages, 2¾ bags of peanuts,

2 bags of corncobs, one bag of rice, one bag of coffee, one chest of tea, one basket, one tablecloth, one table mat, and one toy hoe and sickle had been presented to the president. The names and addresses of all the donors were listed, and it had no doubt been a great day for numerous lobbies and interests as well as for Dr. Banda. The significance of the information circulated did not lie in the list of items so much as in the occasion and the association with it of those who had been named.

A more subtle technique sometimes employed is to make foreign news that can be reported serve for the news from home that cannot. "Heath is afraid of a subversive plot to destroy Britain" was the headline over a routine report of British trade union activity in one Kenyan newspaper. This story followed weeks of tension in Kenya caused by mysterious bomb explosions and the murder of a member of Parliament, and the way in which the British story was reported carried clear echoes of what was believed to be happening in Kenya. The chosen angle was exaggerated when applied to the country used to illustrate it, but true of the country the readers were thinking of—their own.

M'backé, a Senegalese journalist, was a good example of the dual function he was expected to fulfill. For part of the time he acted as a correspondent for foreign newspapers and circulated reports, passed on agency telexes, and wrote acute analytical articles about West Africa. He was good at his job, he wrote in both English and French, and there was nothing in his work to distinguish him from the expatriate staff of his Northern employers. But for the rest of the time M'backé earned a living as a journalist in Senegal. He ran his own magazine; but it carried no news that was discreditable to individuals, and its political criticism of the government was veiled in the most academic abstractions drawn from textbooks of political theory. To visiting journalists M'backé offered himself as a guide. He made introductions and took the visitors around, but he also reported on the reporters to the government and briefed officials who were about to be interviewed on the interests of their questioners. He saw nothing dishonorable or inconsistent about this. It was simply that in his country the journalist was expected to behave differently.

Other African countries deal with Northern reporters less gently. In Zaire, where the government information bureau is called the Ministry of National Orientation, reporters are expelled for such offenses as mentioning that a presidential rally is sparsely attended. Those who mistakenly reported government losses during the Zairean army's successful campaign against secessionist invaders in a distant province were flown seven hundred miles to see their mistakes for themselves and then put on television to "recant their lies." Others, whose reports of setbacks were accurate, were told that they too were lying but refused permission to make a personal inspection. When they did so anyway, they were arrested, imprisoned for some days in a remote part of the country, and finally expelled. Throughout, the Zairean government maintained that its own behavior was impeccably correct and that it was the journalists who were abusing their privileges.

Elsewhere it may not be necessary for the country to be at war. In Nigeria the Reuters office was closed down and its representative expelled after he had circulated an erroneous report that there was tribal unrest and fighting in the north of the country. This left one of the largest and wealthiest countries in Africa to be covered by just one resident agency reporter. The government also protested angrily at accurate reports in the Northern press about outbreaks of Lassa fever in remote parts of Nigeria. Following a normal scientific practice, Lassa fever is named after the place where it was first identified, which happens to be the Nigerian district of Lassa. But instead of taking this as, if anything, a form of distinction, the Nigerians have taken it as an insult and regard all mention of the dangers of Lassa fever as anti-Nigerian.

African governments do welcome journalists when they can make use of them, as in summoning assistance in time of war or famine. The news that will then be reported is easily foreseeable, and indeed, most of the stories are indistinguishable from each other since "disaster reporting" is usually based on the publicity handouts of the United Nations or the international charities. But as far as freedom of the press is concerned, African governments do not wish to strengthen their lines of communication with the rest of the world. They wish to weaken them. When Park traveled as a trader, he was made welcome, but when he began to gather information, he was suspected of being a spy who intended to acquire the knowledge necessary to cut out the coastal tribes and deal directly with the interior. Those from the North who wish to acquire information unrelated to approved commerce are increasingly regarded with the same suspicion today.

In contrast with the process whereby the old simple communications of Africa become increasingly decrepit, there is a superior process which depends on new areas of knowledge and new scales of wealth and resources and which is, therefore, as inaccessible to most people as the earliest radios were. Infrared photography from satellites now covers the entire continent. In Juba, in the southern Sudan, a new regional capital has been proposed. What is the order of priorities in setting about such a venture? First a Parliament, eleven ministries, and twenty-eight official residences. Then a color television station. Then telephones, telex, and radio. Then a theater and a supermarket. And then a satellite communications station. This city has no reliable gasoline supply, most of its inhabitants

live in mud huts, and the only road which leads to a new
dairy farm, eight miles away, is often impassable. Although there is a daily jet service between Juba and
Khartoum, the Sudanese capital, Juba's best link with the
world is via Mombasa, a port in Kenya which is the same
distance away in the opposite direction. And the only
chance of a road link is, again, through Kenya, since
Khartoum and the rest of the Sudan are on the other side
of an impenetrable swamp. The latest means of communication to be employed in the southern Sudan are
videotape films, which are used to record the gestures, expressions, and postures of the tribes that, anthropologists
believe, will be destroyed if the proposed road is ever
built or the swamp is drained. And the information obtained by remote infrared sensors and by videotape oper-
ators is all the time being stored in data banks and on
computer tapes for the leisurely inspection of armies of
expatriate eyes, apparently in innocence of the notion that
the activities of film crews can be as destructive as a new
road and that the acquisition of such information by the
North is in itself an acquisition of power over undisturbed
areas of the world which the North will eventually use.
Information about the food supply and the climatic conditions of the southern Sudan has a strategic application
as well as a humanitarian one, and it is unlikely that this
will pass unnoticed. But until the ending of the recent
secessionist war, this extension of Northern power over
the area would not have been possible. The war was the
southern Sudan's best protection against the impending
devastation of peace.

In 1956 it was estimated[1] that 20 percent of the employed population of the United States was directly or
indirectly employed in the operation or servicing of transport and communications facilities. An increasing number
of those facilities are deployed in Africa, but they are
not intended to interest or amuse Africans. The people

of the southern Sudan, of a different language, religion, and race even from the leaders of their own government, are as uninspired by the facilities of their new capital as if they had never been invented. Perhaps they suspect that the Parliament and the official residences are only formally intended for their welfare and that whatever information will be transmitted by the satellite, it will benefit them even less. There has seldom been such a division between the people and their rulers as is effected by color television or by remote sensing from a height of twenty-three thousand miles. The communications station has brought a new blanket of silence to the southern Sudan.[2]

But remote sensing is an exception to the general state of African communications, the overall disintegration of which suits the purposes of both the native governors and the expatriate controllers of Africa. The men who rule Kinshasa and claim to rule "Zaire," an area which is about 900,000 square miles in extent (it has never been exactly measured), do not wish to expose their pretensions to the world's gaze. So they multiply the regulations that govern entry and exit and justify their suppression of reporters' activities by reference to Northern domination of the news agencies. They saw nothing inequitable in meeting to make such announcements in Uganda,[3] although at that time President Amin had threatened broadcasters with death for using television film that (owing to a technical mistake) showed him shaking hands with his left hand.

The future of communication in Africa may be the satellite photograph, the data bank, the color telephone receiver, and the dial-a-disc service. Or it may be a continuation of the present reality, in which French mercenaries fly jets armed with heat-sensor rockets to little effect against men armed with poison darts who send messages by drum beats.[4] Or in which one African country, Lesotho,[5] hoaxes the United Nations Security Council for

several months into giving it emergency aid on the pretense that its borders have been sealed off by its neighbor,
the Republic of South Africa. Or in which, as in Benin,[6]
an unmarked airplane lands at Cotonou's elegant international airport and disembarks one hundred armed and
uniformed men, forty of them white. This party proceeds
to shoot up the city, attack the presidential palace, and
stroll about the streets, sipping lemonade, smoking
Gauloises, and shouting instructions to the citizens in
French. Six people are killed, including one patriotic
drunk armed with an ax who charges them on a bicycle;
after three hours they return to their vehicle and depart.
Despite the capture of one of these invaders and a United
Nations inquiry, nobody knows to this day who they were,
what they were doing, or whether they were employed
by the Martian government or Twentieth Century-Fox.
Nor did they show up on the satellite photographs.

For a day in the life of Cotonou the death of six men
violently in the street at the hands of strangers was unusual but not extraordinary. Benin has a long tradition
of resisting the arrival of foreigners. The handsome
wooden benches on sale to tourists at the airport are
modeled on the old royal throne, although the legs of
that were fashioned from human skulls. Today the
country is a sovereign state which spends one-third of its
budget on education and forbids its citizens to talk to
foreigners in public or to visit foreign embassies or to
consult the books available in foreign-controlled libraries.
The state radio, the only one *Beninois* are permitted to
listen to, must be played at all times, in all public places,
at full volume so that the programs of martial music,
national self-justification, and denunciations of "imperial-
ism, capitalism, colonialism, feudalism, and the middle
class" may be heard by all. This is the proper message for
a country with diminishing communications. No word is
received but the one sent yesterday, and away from the
loudspeakers normal life becomes simpler as communica-

tions become more difficult. In the poor, slow, secret places of Benin the needle has stuck; the fantastic invasions pass without explanation or notice.

NOTES

1. Blunden and Haggett, eds., *Fundamentals of Human Geography* (London: Harper & Row, 1978).
2. Even simple technologies of communication, such as radio, are sometimes beyond the experience of quite technically minded Africans. An attempted coup in Niger in 1976 failed partly because the insurgent troops believed that by cutting off the electricity supply to Niamey, the capital, they had also silenced the government radio station, which ran on its own generator.
3. November 1977.
4. Katanga, 1977.
5. January 1977.
6. January 1977.

CHAPTER 9

THE CHESSMEN

So Alice picked him up very gently, and lifted him across more slowly than she had lifted the Queen, that she mightn't take his breath away . . . she smoothed his hair and set him upon the table near the Queen. The King immediately fell flat on his back, and lay perfectly still.

Through the Looking Glass

Prince: I did never see such pitiful rascals.
Falstaff: . . . food for powder, food for powder; they'll fill a pit as well as better: tush, man, mortal men, mortal men.

Henry IV, Part I, Act IV, Scene II

By 1970, after fewer than ten years of independence, the United Nations estimated that there were in Africa one million refugees. By 1978 the number had risen to more than four and a half million, and an additional two million people were still unsettled after returning home. In twenty years since the start of decolonization African refugees have been accumulating at the rate of 200,000 people a year, and that is just the number of those who have sought United Nations assistance. In one country after another the result of independence was that thousands of the newly enfranchised citizens had to escape into a neighboring country. The language of international diplomacy proved up to the task. The terrible massacres of the minority Tutsi tribe in Rwanda, which forced 160,000 people to flee for their lives, were described in the United Nations as "a severe internal crisis"—as though there had been a drought or a run on the banks. What could not be said publicly was that the people of "Rwanda," thrown together by the imposed divisions of colonial Africa and now cast off as an ill-assorted crew in a very leaky boat, had taken to throwing each other overboard with such spirit that it was as though they all would rather drown than remain alive in the same craft.

African refugees have been presented as many things in this effort to avoid describing them as what they are. There is the refugee as "a problem," an inexplicable abstract demanding general compassion. This is only briefly satisfactory, and the refugee is a persistent presence, so next we have the refugee as an idealist. In the words of the All-Africa Conference of Churches, refugees are "people who somewhere, somehow, sometime had the courage to give up the feeling of belonging, which they possessed, rather than abandon the human freedom which they valued more highly." This kind of analysis, "somewhere, somehow, sometime," has a purpose: to prevent the exact consideration of particular refugees, here and now, and to forestall awkward questions as to "how."

Refugees are not just idealists; there is also the refugee as a sign of progress. "The refugee is a by-product of the development of Africa. Refugees are therefore one aspect of the growing pains that Africa has to suffer before she attains the maturity that is essential to ensure freedom and equality of all races, tribes, creeds and the expression of controversial political opinions."[1] This leads to the refugee as pioneer, not someone "to be pitied, far more people to be admired." And so, naturally, to the refugee as an opportunity, "assets of the economic and social balance of the countries' development."[2] In fact, as elsewhere in the world, the refugee is nothing to do with pioneering or continental maturity or national development. If he is a sign of anything, he is a sign of national sickness. The refugee is the awkward evidence of Africa's

inability and unwillingness to be reorganized into countries that have nothing to do with the real organization
of the people who live there.

Tribalism is the most delicate political issue in modern
Africa. The pretensions to government of so many African states amount to little, outside the cities, than a denial
of nominal control of the land to other equally illusory
kingdoms. Even that pretense is idle in the case of Chad,
part of whose land is governed by Libya, and idle in the
case of Ethiopia, which has lost territory to Somalia and
to secessionists in Eritrea, and idle in the case of Angola
and Zaire, both of which experience recurrent civil wars.
But the steps taken to enforce this pretense are often real
enough, infrequent though they be, for those people
against whom they are directed. And so independent
Africa presents the strange spectacle of free men who
have first suffered colonial conquest and its piecemeal attack on their tribal identities, and have overcome it, now
struggling to preserve those arbitrary boundaries which
were imposed on them at a whim and prepared to inflict
brutal sufferings on each other in this struggle. In the
last ten years tribal wars have taken place in Nigeria,
Chad, the Sudan, Zaire, Rwanda, Burundi, Uganda, and
Angola, and the same struggle can be seen in embryo in
Rhodesia before independence has even been achieved.

Yet the true nature of these wars is admitted only
when it becomes impossible to disguise it. The issue is so
sensitive that if the London *Times* prints a tribal map of
Africa, it leads to academic and diplomatic protests.
"Romantic Africa's old human subdivisions must conform
to progress or face extinction. Otherwise developing land
won't develop. Game, not man, can be preserved arti-
ficially," was one comment at the time. Tribes were
equated with herds; tribespeople, presumably, with
animals.

Zaire's continuing war with the Katangans is described
as "the trauma of birth," and the fact that the Zairean

province of Katanga, or Shaba, has fought under four flags and for almost every known conventional ideology is described as "bizarre"; that it is as long as observers are determined to ignore the obvious explanation—that the Katangans do not care which flag or ideology their struggle is associated with as long as it leads to autonomy for their region. The tribal maps and the national maps of Africa very rarely coincide, and the first loyalty of the overwhelming majority of Africans is not to nation but to tribe. Consequently members of tribes that are divided by national borders struggle with the national governments, and tribes that are thrown together within national units struggle with each other for supremacy.

Africa is perfectly capable of forming effective tribal confederations, as it has done in the past. But that does not mean that every part of Africa would be part of a state, and it does mean that for the nations that did emerge to be effective they would have to be formed according to contemporary imperatives rather than the incidental cease-fire lines of nineteenth-century colonial armies. The alternative to the present boundaries is always said to be "chaos" or "tribal warfare," but that is exactly the result of the attempt to maintain them. Until Africa has achieved self-determination and stepped out of the colonial shadow which was cast at the time of independence, the real nations of Africa will never have a chance to develop. Until they do, the pseudonations that exist today will remain under the control of the powers which set them up and of the native rulers who act as their proxies. And the strain this causes to African society will continue to be felt by the citizens of these states, the mortal men of Africa, who fill a pit at regular intervals.

On the tenth anniversary of its independence Kenya held a day of celebration. It was to be attended by great numbers of *wananchi*, "the people," and by three foreign heads of state, the Emperor Haile Selassie, General

Numeiri of the Sudan, and Field Marshal Amin. There
were also numerous visiting vice-presidents and the Aga
Khan. The highlight of the day was a two-hour speech
made by the late President Jomo Kenyatta, on one of his
very rare appearances outside the grounds of his palace.
It was a most instructive occasion, not always in the way
intended by the authorities.

The celebration took place in a field sandwiched between the game park and an army barracks, presumably
on grounds of security. There was a great deal of security,
and insecurity, to be considered. Emperor Haile Selassie
was not on speaking terms with the vice-president of
Somalia. Field Marshal Amin had to be kept away from
almost everyone, but in particular from the vice-president
of Tanzania, from General Numeiri, and from the Aga
Khan. Amin had just insulted Julius Nyerere, the president of Tanzania, by saying how much he would have
liked to marry him; he was of the same tribal group as
the people of southern Sudan who were still waging a
covert war against Numeiri's government, and he had
expelled all of the Aga Khan's Ismaelis from Uganda.
It was all right to let him talk to the vice-president of
Zaire, because Amin had had close ties with the Zairean
authorities ever since his gold-smuggling days when he
was second in command of the Ugandan army. Ethiopia,
Somalia, Uganda, and the Sudan were in visible apprehension of assassination, and the Kenyan police were also
worried about their own president. In all these circumstances it was unfortunate that the organizer of the jam-
boree should have seated the potentates in line on a raised
dais, facing directly into the setting sun.

The official program of marching and dancing did not
start till late afternoon, but all day long the tribal groups
swirled around the dusty field, practicing or playing for
fun, quite indifferent as to whether or not they had an
audience. There were fifty different bands of dancers and
musicians, all playing at once, oblivious to each other in

the noise and dust. All that was missing were the *wanan-chi*, the free citizens of free Kenya, the fascinated audi-ence of this glittering spectacle. On one side of the field stands had been erected; but they were filled with official guests, and the rest of the perimeter was sparsely en-closed by a crowd that stood only one deep. This lack of spontaneous joy had been emphasized by a clumsy direc-tive from the district commissioner of Nairobi, who had announced that any shop in the city which failed to dec-orate its premises would be closed on sight. The com-missioner explained that this was a perfectly reasonable decision because "ample notice and appeals to decorate premises had been made." He was now strutting around the parade ground in his colonial officer's solar topee and khaki uniform, occasionally attempting to direct the move-ments of the drummers with his steel-tipped cane. Be-tween his lips there was a silver whistle, and judging by the position of his cheeks, he was blowing on it. But any sound he made was lost in the din.

Also lost in the middle of the dancing was the only tribal group that had not brought a single instrument, the Masai. They wore red cloaks draped over one shoulder and carried spears. They were ranged in line, leaping al-ternately up and down, their spears held rigidly by their sides. If one stood close enough, one could hear that they were chanting as they jumped, the red ocher on their hair and shoulders seeming to tint the air about them. One wore a red and white Coca-Cola sun visor. The Masai boys were joined by a tall man in a business suit, starched white collar, and horn-rimmed spectacles, who, when he began to leap with them, became recognizable as a *moran* who had joined the government.

The commissioner was particularly agitated by the Masai. For some time he had been directing them to wear trousers. Now here they were in front of him, trouserless, flapping up and down in the dust and smiling contentedly, almost as though they were interested enough in him to have known who he was. It was too much for the commissioner. He rushed through the dancers toward the Masai and ordered them off, like a referee on a football field, his cheeks, bunched behind the little whistle, seemingly at bursting point. But they could neither see nor hear him. They continued rising very slowly to a great height and falling one by one at the same speed, their spear tips glinting in the haze, their chanting lost in the thunder of other people's drums. The commissioner also began to dance. He stamped his feet and waved his arms, out of time with the music, beating a tempo to the orders of a different drummer, the martinet of his frustrated rage.

When the official guests eventually arrived in their sparkling limousines, like a circus parade, for the real performance, most of the dancers were exhausted. The big black cars drew up at the empty podium with their hazard-warning lights flashing "hazard warning," and their national flags fluttering, to find that they all had been forestalled by Field Marshal Amin. He had arrived early, having had nothing else to do, and had spent some time leaping with the Masai, lightly covering his fawn suit and single-breasted waistcoat and pigskin shoes and striped silk tie with ocher and dust. Then he had donned the leopard-skin cap of a Kikuyu wizard and practiced some spear throwing. By the time the Aga Khan arrived Amin was back on the podium, his dark glasses concealing most of his face, waving and laughing at the small crowd who had gathered to look at him, sitting alone without his men. The Aga Khan, to all appearances a European gentleman, carefully picked his way between the crowd and selected a seat as far from the field marshal as he could manage.

The self-confidence of African leaders is a slender attribute. Kenyatta had long felt sufficiently safe to pardon many of those who opposed him before he became president. Even the man who was said to have given false evidence against him at his trial, which resulted in Kenyatta's detention for involvement with the Mau Mau, still lived at Gatundu, unworried and unhindered, only a mile or so from the presidential residence. On the other hand, after ten years of independence and unchallenged rule, Kenyatta was sufficiently insecure to lay down that no one in Kenya might call himself "president" of anything. So just before the celebrations a directive was sent to every association, whether it was the bowling club or the local orphanage, which read: "The existence of the title of 'president' amongst the posts of officers of societies, trade unions, and other associations can cause confusion with the title of His Excellency, the President of the Republic of Kenya. In the circumstances, the Government requires that the constitutions of such associations be changed to make fresh provision for the title of such posts."

On this occasion, possibly to increase the drama of his own arrival, Kenyatta seemed to have given each of his fellow heads of state a different time for the start of events. After Uganda came Sudan, who was able at least to have some conversation with the Aga Khan, this being the only conversation that took place. Ethiopia, a shrunken little figure with a gray uniform to match his skin, shambled out of his car and sat alone, looking slightly apprehensive and polishing his nails. Everyone stood up for his arrival except Uganda, who did not see him and was still preoccupied with scowling at an Englishwoman who had mounted the podium, leaned across him, and removed the chair beside his. Finally, Uganda also got to his feet, shoulders hunched, and, not knowing where to look, looked down, caught sight of his hands, held them up to see them better, then, wondering what to do next, shifted them around until they eventually found his pockets, into which they plunged as though they contained stolen fruit. Ethiopia also had something to conceal: news of the great famine that was killing thousands of his

people each day and which would shortly bring his reign
to an end. The calmest of them all was Sudan, who gave
an impression of kindliness that was commendable in a
man who had just (for the second time in four years)
given orders to suppress an attempted coup in an unnec-
essarily brutal manner. There had been ninety-eight secret
executions in Khartoum.

None of these men looked truly at ease as they sat in
a row in the cool of the evening, trying to avoid each
other's glances and the absent gaze of the crowd, which
pressed in empty curiosity right up to the platform, while
the sun sank directly into their eyes, causing their uniforms to twinkle and lighting up their blinded faces like
a row of bull's-eyes in a shooting booth.

And then the largest car of all came into view at the
end of the field. It was preceded by a V-shaped plow of
police motorcyclists. The thinly gathered crowd drew in
toward the car until it reached the line of policemen.
Some photographers happened to be standing in front of
the car. As Mr. Kenyatta alighted, twirling his fly whisk,
a police inspector, an Indian, turned to the photographers
and said in a quiet and desperate voice, "Get out of the
way of the car. I promise you that if you do not get out
of the way, I cannot stop the driver from running you
down." The adulation paid to the leader was also due to
his empty car. It would move forward in measured dignity, crushing anyone in its path at five miles per hour.

In the speech that followed, Kenyatta recalled the original independence day and the distant dream he had then
of "true independence," the economic freedom that Kenya
would one day achieve. He did not suggest any reasons
why so little progress had been made toward it; he did
not need to because as long as he ruled the country, it was
held together not by the events of the day, but by those
of the past. The achieving of independence which he
personally represented was achievement enough in itself.

The mere fact of the country still sufficed as his justifica-
tion; it did not matter what the country had done. But the
time will come, probably quite soon, when the memory
of the old struggle for independence will no longer be
enough to hold the various African nations together. And
without it many of them can be expected to break up. In
some cases this process has already begun.

In the Sudan a long war of secession in the south was
halted only with the granting of regional autonomy and
promises of future prosperity which it will be difficult to
fulfill. Ethiopia has been fighting a secessionist war in its
northern province of Eritrea, a war against a Somali
annexation in the south, and several armed uprisings in
the west of the country. Nigeria fought one of the most
terrible wars of recent times to prevent the secession of
Biafra and succeeded only with the assistance of Britain,
the former colonial power. Mauritania was threatened
with annexation or dissolution as a result of its own claims
over the western Sahara and the claims of its ally Mo-
rocco over itself. Zaire has fought several wars in dissident provinces in the south and east of the country—if
it is realistic to refer to an area of two hundred tribes
and seventy-five languages as one country. Kenya has used
force to suppress tribal uprisings in the north and west.
In Rwanda and in Burundi tribal wars have been waged
for most of the time since independence in 1962. Force
has been used against minority tribes in Uganda, Guinea,
Ghana, and the Congo. The nomadic minorities of the
Sahel have suffered violence from the governing tribal
groups of Niger, Upper Volta, and Mali. In Angola the
process has reached its most advanced stage, with the
colonial war for freedom overlapping with the subsequent
war of tribal secession, disguised, as usual, under the
cloak of ideological disagreement and encouraged by
competing Northern interests. In Rhodesia the leaders of
rival liberation movements, each with different tribal
backing, were in correspondence by letter bomb for some

years before independence could even be seen on the horizon. In Namibia the same pattern is ready to emerge. But it is Chad which can so far be counted as the most progressive country in this respect.

Within two years of Chad's independence in 1960 its three tribal groups had started to quarrel with the central administration. The civil servants, in fear of their lives, retreated into the scattered fortified townships; crops were burned, machinery was destroyed, and tax collectors were murdered. The country split into five different regions, each officially in a state of civil war with the central government but each "war" remaining quite a peaceful affair with little fighting taking place for long periods. Along the enormous stretch of Chad's borders with Libya, the Sudan, and the Central African Empire, the territory was in the hands of the rebels or of the Libyan regular army, who simply occupied northern Chad, and still do. Although the administration in the capital remained in nominal control of Chad, it was a city without real authority. The national flag flew there, but it was never raised in three-quarters of the rest of the country.

The rhetoric of the various dissidents was in no important way distinguishable from that of other African liberation movements—even though they were opposing their own native rulers rather than a colonial government. There was the Chad Liberation Front, which quickly split into northern and southern groups with different tribal loyalties. And there were "the Armed Forces of the Northern Command," and there were the followers of "General" Bagahalani. Each faction was utterly dedicated to a united Chad, and each by its existence ensured the further disunity of the nation. For a time 3,600 French troops helped successive presidents of Chad to maintain the appearance of control, but they were expelled after a French scholar, Mme. Claustre, was captured by one of the rebel groups, and the French government negotiated for her release over the head of the central government, even offering arms as an exchange.

When Mme. Claustre was finally released, it was neither through the efforts of the Chad government nor through those of France. Instead, after three years of her captivity, it was the Libyan government, the de facto rulers of the part of Chad in which she was held, who arranged it. And official opinion throughout Africa was critical of France for giving even that much recognition to Libyan authority in Chad. The truth, that the nation of Chad was dissolving into its separate components, was too disturbing to contemplate.[3]

Under pressure of these events the president of Chad, Ngarta Tombalbaye, was eventually overthrown and killed. His political prisoners were released, among them the new president—General Félix Malloum, who immediately announced that no political activity would be tolerated. There would be no political parties and no legislative assembly. For African leaders like General Malloum the moment of regaining their own freedom and the act of restricting the freedom of others are simultaneous. Those who are released do not dissolve the political police force; they command it. One man's liberty is his enemies' captivity; the two are inseparable and equally fragile. On April 13, 1976, the first anniversary of the glorious coup, Malloum arranged an open-air ceremony on the racecourse at which he planned to arrive by parachute. His Cabinet ministers were instructed to jump with him. The ministers duly arrived by parachute, but Malloum did not. Standing by the aircraft door, on the point of jumping out, he noticed that his parachute had been tampered with. When he did get to the racecourse, he survived a grenade attack. On the second anniversary of his glorious coup, General Malloum's palace was attacked by troops drawn from the nomadic northern tribes. They were garrisoned just across Independence Square, at Camp April

13. The president survived again[4] and later in the day departed the country on an official visit to the Congo. The purpose of the visit was to attend a memorial service for the president of the Congo, who had himself been slain in a coup a few days earlier. It was a Friday, so in Ndjamena General Malloum left the population preparing for the compulsory task of each weekend. All men, women, and children of whatever rank had to clean the public buildings and streets of their capital.

In the People's Republic of the Congo the president had been murdered by members of his own bodyguard. Shortly before he died, the president had met the archbishop of Brazzaville, Cardinal Biayenda. Within a week the cardinal too had been murdered, by fellow tribesmen of the dead president, some of whom were Christians. The obligations of African tribalism are honorable, and they are constantly honored. They are an extension of the obligations of the family, and they are supported by customs and language to an extent that simply does not exist on a national scale. They have survived colonialism and independence and all the high hopes of an Africa of sovereign states. For Africans to deny tribal feeling or to indulge it covertly is for them to compromise their fundamental identity, that which they know intuitively, which governs much of their daily behavior, and which unites people across the continent. The fact that Africans are thoroughly organized in one way, a fact which is unacknowledged, and have to pretend to be organized in another, a fact that is strange and uncomfortable to them, can itself account for much of the chaos which attends political and social organization. Tribal loyalties are strong enough to destroy conflicting ties, even to such well-rooted Northern institutions as the Catholic Church.[5] If there was a choice to be made between the stability of the tribal family and the moral demands of the Christian religion, the Congolese Catholics who assassinated Cardinal Biayenda did not hesitate to make it.

The leaders who have to unite different tribes in one nation tend to exaggerate the traditional aspects of leadership. Mungo Park discovered the symbolic importance of this leadership in watching the public manners of a royal court. "The usual place of rendezvous for the indolent," he wrote, "is the king's tent, where great liberty of speech seems to be exercised by the company towards each other, while in speaking of their chief they express but one opinion. In praise of their sovereign they are unanimous. Songs are composed in his honour, which the company frequently sings in concert; but they are so loaded with gross adulation that no man but a Moorish despot could hear them without blushing." Today in Gabon the country's leading pop singer, Alain Bongo, whose father, Bernard, is the president, greets the president of France with a rock song which is played everywhere for days. The lines, "Giscard is Bongo's friend, Bongo is Giscard's friend, and France is Gabon's friend," are repeated throughout, and references are made to President Bongo and President Giscard as great men who are uniting their nations in the fight against tribalism and carrying them forward into a glorious reformed future. And in Kenya, in a letter to a newspaper, criticism of the country's MPs was expressed as follows: "All constituencies can agree with me that most of these men, the ones we voted for, have done little or nothing to benefit us. Every voter has eyes to see. . . ." Then comes the ritual invocation, which would safeguard the writer from any unpleasant repercussion: "Mzee Kenyatta is 100 per cent right in his occasional speeches that some MP's go to parliament to measure their happiness by the size of their bellies." The headline to this letter, whose subject is that of a corrupt and self-serving legislature, was: "Mzee is 100 p.c. right."

The position of the leader as father of the nation and as uniter of a house that would otherwise be divided does not, obviously, admit of a system of government that is based on criticism and eventual rejection of the leadership—except in moments of extreme crisis. There can be dissent, and there must be debate; but this must take place in private, or, if it takes place in public, the criticism must not include the leader personally. This personal immunity can be abused, and defense of it is sometimes tinged with hypocrisy;[6] but the native respect for the person of the leader is genuine, and the leader draws strength from it. When President Idi Amin instructed his Foreign Service to discover the height of Margaret Thatcher, then the leader of the British opposition, he was not only playing the fool but inquiring about a matter that could be as important in Africa as Richard Nixon's television makeup was in America. Nor is it mere vanity that leads Bernard Bongo of Gabon, who is four feet ten inches tall, to wear thick elevator heels and forbid his people to use the word *pygmy*. The person of the leader must exercise visible authority, and where nature has omitted to assist him to do so he may have to take precautions.

There are two fundamental weaknesses in the practice of traditional personal leadership in national Africa. The first is that it is very difficult to arrange an orderly transfer of power from one living individual to his successor. Since some of the potency of personality survives loss of office, the undisgraced existence of old leaders casts doubt on the status of new ones. The fallen leader has to be killed, exiled, or at least imprisoned.[7] Only the most ruthless challenge to the leadership can be expected to succeed, which explains why so few African governments—once independence is established—have entered or left office by constitutional means and why on so many occasions the army coup has proved to be the only way in which a change of government can be effected.[8]

In toppling the leader, those who initiate the coup usually inherit his mantle; only the army represents a force in the African nation which is psychologically independent of the leadership. It is a national institution, it has a monopoly of organized force, it is self-sufficient, and it is largely outside the theoretical democratic process. It is the natural dispatcher of weak rulers and thus fulfills the function of certain powerful courtiers in the old kingdoms who were counted on to kill old kings.

The old chief who had power of life and death, but who could not himself rise from his stool without stumbling, weakened the respect of his people—on which his power was based. Why should the will of an old and feeble man direct the lives of so many young and vigorous ones? This question threw into doubt the order of an entire society which, like a wheel, circled the absolute power of its chief. If the hub cracked, the spokes would splinter.

That this conception of leadership and society continues today is shown by events in Kenya in 1975, when a popular and critical young opposition legislator, J. M. Kariuki, was found brutally murdered in a forest near Nairobi. An official inquiry established that President Kenyatta's bodyguard was implicated in the crime, but the president made no direct comment on the affair. Instead, at the height of the crisis he attended a huge loyalist rally and said, "Nothing is dearer than human blood, and we shed it as a sacrifice for the attainment of our independence. Our veins have not dried up." The vice-president then said, apropos of nothing in particular, "The son who is jealous and ambitious to sit on his father's throne dies young and leaves his father still kicking hard." From Kenyatta's point of view an attempt to usurp him had failed; the just price had been paid. Order was restored. But he appeared in public less and less; in the last three years of his reign he became almost invisible. And a year before he eventually died, the strain of containing speculation became so great that the attorney general of Kenya had to announce that any public discussion of the succession amounted to treason and could be punished with the death penalty.

The second great failing of the present style of leadership is that it depends on the exercise of absolute power; but little real power can be exercised, and this encourages tyranny. The leaders cannot really unite the divided tribes or bring the improvements in material conditions which they constantly promise. They are not in truth the fathers they would wish to be because their resources are so overstretched. The progress of their governments has been away from the imposed practices of colonialism and toward the genuine authority that existed before the colonial interlude. Were it not for the support of the former colonial powers, the pretenses of many of the independent leaderships to government would have been long since abandoned. The choice before the leaders was plainly summarized by President Félix Houphouët-Boigny, whose Ivory Coast is one of the most prosperous and most dependent states in Africa. On being reproached, at a conference of heads of state, with the close ties between his country and France, he replied, "It is true, dear colleagues, that there are 40,000 Frenchmen in my country and that this is more than there were before independence. But in ten years I hope the position will be different. I hope that then there will be 100,000 Frenchmen here. And I would like at that time for us all to meet again and compare the economic strength of your countries with mine. But I fear, dear colleagues, that few of you will be in a position to attend." Were such a conference ever to be called, many of those rulers who did attend it, and who had maintained an economic distance between their countries and the North, would be there only by reason of their ability as tyrants.

* * *

The Eastern and Western factions of the North, struggling with each other across the world for areas of influence and for strategic advantage, prefer to have Africa pegged out on a mutually agreed map. If the nations were to dissolve into their natural components, the game would be more difficult to control. As it is, East and West respect each other's attempts to maintain the colonial borders, and by their control of the administration of each country's capital city, radio station, airport, and port it is possible for the Northern powers to run invisible empires across the African continent. It is as the local representatives of these expatriate forces that the leaders of independent Africa can feel most secure. But it is of the first importance to the African leaders that their complicity in this deal is not acknowledged. To see how this is arranged, the trail of French diplomatic initiatives in Africa in 1977 is helpful.

In March 1977 France airlifted military supplies and Moroccan troops to Zaire to assist President Mobutu fight and win a secessionist war in the country's copper region. In April the French president, Valéry Giscard d'Estaing, announced his support for the general limitation of arms sales in Africa. The president of the Ivory Coast welcomed this and said, "I am convinced that the Europeans intend to act in our best interests. I ask my African brothers to work hand in hand with our European allies so that Africa may remain in African hands." In May, France and the Sudan expressed their conviction that African countries should settle their problems by peaceful means and without foreign intervention. The same month the Sudan took delivery of a first consignment of new military equipment from America, and the French announced their participation in a new Sudanese sugar project, one of the largest in the world. In July France announced that it had reentered the secessionist struggle in Chad by sending military assistance to the Chad government of President Malloum (who had succeeded Mr. Tombalbaye partly because of the latter's overdependence on the French military). In August France announced a new policy in Africa: "special ties with all." France felt it important that following the communist victory in the Angolan civil war, its former colonies such as Senegal and the Ivory Coast should not "feel endangered." According to French thinking, independent Africa was vulnerable in its dealings with the world since it was armed only with the old colonial system of states. It was, therefore, French policy to support this system at every opportunity.

Later that month the French foreign minister, Louis de Guiringaud, embarked on a tour of fragile states: Kenya, Zambia, Mozambique, Nigeria, the Ivory Coast, Ghana, and Cameroon. His last call was on Tanzania, where the ideas of modern democracy were sufficiently well implanted for him to be greeted with a peaceful but critical student demonstration. He left the country at once, without fulfilling a single engagement and complaining of an insult to France. In November French fighter-bombers were flown to Mauritania to assist the government against secessionist guerrillas and were in action within a month. Congratulating himself at the end of the year, the French president, at a meeting with President Carter, said that he believed France had saved both Zaire and Mauritania from collapse during the course of the year.

Distracted by the innumerable problems of internal dissension, many of the leaders are in no position to oppose those whose support is their best hope of maintaining power. The process starts early, in some cases before a country is stabilized under one government—as when the British multinational investment company Lonrho put a Lear jet at the disposal of the UNITA guerrillas during the Angolan civil war.[9] And it continues well into nationhood. Zaire (formerly the Belgian Congo) owes the essential forms of its independent life to the U.S. Central Intelligence Agency. The first president of Zaire was Patrice Lumumba, who died by an act of treachery before his rule over the least accessible African country could be firmly established. The CIA has since admitted complicity in his death. The man it selected to replace the highly educated Lumumba was a populist faction leader in the mutinous Zairean army, Sergeant Joseph Mobutu. Mobutu was also an educated man, a journalist, one of the very few members of this trade to have become a head of state. But his great advantage, as the CIA imagined, was that he was not a socialist, unlike Lumumba, whose chosen rhetoric had been that of the left. Joseph Désiré Mobutu has long since illegalized the use of Christian names among his people, he himself becoming Mobutu Sese Seko Kuku Ngbendu Wa Za Banga, which is sometimes translated as "the all-powerful warrior who because of his endurance and inflexible will to win goes from conquest to conquest leaving fire in his wake" and at other times as "the cock that leaves no hen alone." As an antisocialist Mobutu is impeccable, but as a capitalist he is less impressive.[10] Within ten years of Mobutu's coming to power Zaire had accumulated $800 million of debts to commercial banks, debts incurred only on the security of CIA backing, and for eighteen months the country was unable to meet its repayments. At the center of this typhoon of insolvency was one of the most flamboyant leaders of all Africa, a man who revived animism as a semiestablished religion, who deliberately fostered bribery as a quasi-official financial instrument, and whose picture was the only one allowed on public display. This was not necessarily what the CIA had in mind, any more than the accumulation, under the agency's guidance, of unrepayable debts. But the relationship with Mobutu is nonetheless considered a partial success by the CIA because the banks Mobutu cannot repay are American, not Russian.

* * *

"No known existing governmental system works in Africa," one Nigerian political observer has concluded in desperation, and it is not difficult to see why this should be said. Since independence the Ivory Coast, Kenya, Nigeria, and possibly Gabon have, whatever their other problems, at least become more prosperous. Guinea, the Congo Republic, Uganda, Equatorial Guinea, and the Central African Empire have virtually withdrawn from the world economic community. Ghana, Zaire, and Equatorial Guinea are near economic collapse, as are Mauritania, Niger, and Chad. Senegal, Rwanda, and Zambia are appreciably poorer than at independence. And of the thirty-three countries of equatorial Africa only Gambia, Senegal, the Ivory Coast, and Malawi do not suffer from serious, active tribal dissension.

Deprived of the real power to govern which would win them the respect of their people, the leaders of Africa take refuge in poses. President Kenneth Kaunda of Zambia on successive days in November 1977 first urged his people to replace copper mining with subsistence agriculture as the country's economic basis and then urged the Organization of African Unity's Atomic Energy Conference to establish a uranium enrichment plant for the use of industrialized African countries. International conferences are the only forum where such statements can be made without echoing hollowly in their speaker's ears. When a leader with real power, such as Indira Gandhi, chose—at the height of the compulsory sterilization campaign which was to lead to her own downfall in the forthcoming Indian elections—to spend four days in Zambia, where she was invested as a Grand Commander into the Order of the Grand Companions of Freedom, first division, did she go there merely to discuss mutual interests and world affairs? Or did she go with something of the spirit of Florence Nightingale and comfort herself with that experience of patronage which was once enjoyed by the British *memsahibs* in India?

A leader at an international occasion has merely to look like a leader, he has little to do, and that, for a man who can do little, is the ideal condition. Even Emperor Bokassa, the perfect twentieth-century chess king, with his tall crown and Napoleonic robes and a broad dais to prevent him falling flat on his back, was able to attract the president of Mauritius, the premier of Cameroon, and the first lady of Mauritania to observe his coronation and to witness the military procession of the Union of Pygmy Women. For the chess piece, the game is the thing. Even real leaders have to spend days and weeks at international conferences, displaying themselves in a daydream of crisp shirts and snappy ties. Even if the reception is for a leader who has been assassinated and one has oneself been nearly assassinated that morning (Malloum), even if one's absence from one's palace is to result in one's own deposition (Obote, Gowon, Nkrumah), it is better to be there with other leaders, some of them people of real power, sharing at least that one experience, knowing that were one to be a real leader, one would have to be doing exactly the same thing.

Sitting on the dais in Nairobi, when night had fallen, surrounded by the lurching shadows of the people, first watching the exhausted dancers and then listening to Kenyatta's exhaustive summary of the nation's progress over the past ten years, delivered in three languages, by far the longest version being in Kikuyu— which none of them understood—the row of leaders appeared at last to have found some peace of mind. This was their element. Numeiri *was* Sudan; when one looked at Kenyatta, one saw "Kenya." As one listened to his interminable recollections of the victories over colonialism, one heard the history of the only events which had given him or any of his colleagues a reason to be up there. Ethiopia was deep in thought, his eyes closed, his mouth open, his head to one side. Uganda still wore his dark glasses and directed them watchfully out into the blackness, where the flicker of a dancing shade might still be glimpsed beyond the gesturing fly whisk. As a man who has said that he knows how he will die he must have known what to watch for. But even he savored the air of contentment and of stillness, as though the real competitors had adjourned the game and replaced the pieces in their box.

NOTES

1. Canon Burgess Carr, general secretary of the All-Africa Conference of Churches.
2. UN high commissioner for refugees.
3. Subsequently 2,500 French troops returned to Chad to assist in the secessionist war in the northeastern part of the country. And the rebel leader who kidnapped Mme. Claustre was appointed prime minister of Chad. But half the country remained beyond central government control.
4. General Malloum was eventually overthrown in March 1979. At the subsequent constitutional conference held in Lagos in August the number of armed factions demanding representation had risen to eleven. Libya continued in control of the north of the country.
5. According to Bishop Henry Okullu of Kenya, tribalism divides the Christian Church in East Africa from top to bottom: *Church and Politics in East Africa*.
6. When General Gnassingbe Eyadema, president of Togo, was criticized in the London *Times* for staging "spontaneous" demonstrations at international conferences, where political dancers chanted in adulation as though they were at Nuremberg in the thirties, he replied, "Everyone knows, particularly those who are familiar with our African folklore and culture, that when an orator at a meeting says something good, we don't applaud him but we sing a little to acknowledge his

wit or his insight. This might not please certain strangers, but it is a way of life that we intend to safeguard."

7. Even exile is not always sufficient disgrace. When the BBC broadcast radio interviews with General Yakubu Gowon, the former Nigerian head of state, who went into exile in Britain, and with General Odumegwu Ojukwu, the former Biafran leader who went into exile in the Ivory Coast, the Nigerian government described it as: "A carefully orchestrated strategy by the British mass media to shake the confidence of Nigerians in their Government and leaders." Ojukwu had been in exile for seven years at the time, and Gowon for two years, but the treatment of the two men with normal courtesy and respect, indeed with anything other than revulsion, was enough to arouse memories of their former power and the insecurity of their successors.

8. The practical importance of the coup is shown by the fact that at the time of writing only three out of thirty-three independent African countries (Gambia, the Ivory Coast, and Guinea-Bissau) have not yet experienced at least an attempted coup.

9. UNITA lost to the rival tribal group, the MPLA, backed by Cuba, but is still in control of a large area of Angola.

10. To be fair to Mobutu, he is an extremely impressive capitalist in his personal capacity. In 1978 he was estimated by the Belgian magazine *Choc* to be the second wealthiest ruler in the world, after the shah of Iran, and before the queen of England. Mobutu's wealth included real estate in Belgium, France, Italy, and Spain worth £12.5 million ($25 million) and a Swiss bank account containing £70 million ($140 million). On one occasion in 1978 he was even generous enough to allow the Zairean treasury to borrow money from his private account to pay some urgent bills.

CHAPTER 10

EXILES

The general record of former British colonies since achieving independence has been reactionary almost everywhere and cannot fail to cause dismay. In Africa . . . the fact must be faced that colonialism has been widely followed by a retreat to nationalism backed by military dictatorships. . . . Most of the free parliaments, independent courts and uncorrupted civil services bequeathed by the British have been abandoned.

> Lord Caradon, former governor of Nigeria, giving the Maitland Lecture to the Institution of Structural Engineers, 1976

In the books she had read, love was something that went with parties and costume balls, weekends in the country and trips in automobiles . . . and the fall showings at the great *couturiers*. Real life was there; not here, in this wretched corner, where she was confronted with beggars and cripples at every turning. When N'Deye came out of a theatre where she had seen visions of mountain chalets deep in snow, of beaches where the great of the world lay in the sun, of cities where the nights flashed with many-coloured lights, and walked from this world back into her own, she would be seized with a kind of nausea, a mixture of rage.

> Sembene Ousmane, *God's Bits of Wood*

Zaire's got to be great. I've never seen so many Mercedes.

> Muhammad Ali

There were 23 eyeshadows (stick, powder and water-mixable), mascara, blusher, eyebrow pencils and false eyelashes, all in several shades (before Barbara took over the Boots cosmetic range). "I don't know what happened to the old stuff," she says wryly. "It was either thrown away or shipped to Africa."

> *Daily Telegraph Magazine*, 1977

If one climbed to the top of the tallest building in Lagos on a clear day in 1976 and looked out over the Gulf of Guinea for as far as the eye could see, there were lines of ships at anchor, four hundred or five hundred of them, waiting for berths in a port that was already blocked, with more ships arriving by the hour to join the serpentine line. Each of the ships was loaded with cement. It was one of the most extraordinary moments in the development of Africa, this great fleet of ships, carrying the means to construct half a dozen modern cities, inching their way solemnly toward the quay—while the closer they approached it, the more unusable their cargo became. For after a number of months cement becomes unreliable, and the structures it supports are liable to sudden collapse.

Struggling to participate in this profitable calamity were all the cement suppliers of the Northern world, equipped with the leakiest vessels and the most watertight contracts they could obtain. Any boat would do, as long as it could survive the single voyage to Apapa, where, in waiting fees, it would earn a daily fortune. Some suppliers did not even bother to load up with cement; they just undertook to deliver it and then sent an empty boat to wait outside the port. Who in this involved deceit, the purchasers or the vendors of this cement, were the more corrupt? Whatever the answer, in international law there was no doubt who was in the right. And when the Nigerian government itself had collapsed (partly brought down by its overenthusiasm in ordering eighteen million tons of cement all at once) and its successors attempted to break the contract, the most respectable Northern suppliers enforced it to the letter, and the new government duly paid up. The rules of international law were properly observed.

Nigeria is one of the few African countries that is rich. It is an oil producer, and the export managers of the North are drawn to it like sharks to blood. Few sales are

made without a "dash," or bribe, usually amounting to
10 percent of the value of the sale. Since these payments
are officially illegal, they have to be concealed. One of the
commonest ways of doing this is by double invoicing.
Mr. Walters, the representative of an American multinational pharmaceutical company who had just arrived
for his first visit to Lagos and had signed a $150,000
order on the day of his arrival, explained how this
worked. His company would receive only $135,000. The
balance would be paid into the Nigerian purchaser's bank
account in Zurich. The Nigerian health administration
would record a $150,000 purchase. Mr. Walters would
mark it as a $135,000 sale. Nobody at the head office in
the States need ever know it had happened. It was a very
simple trick and also a very old one.

It is exactly the same trick as that which travelers to
West Africa reported in 1795. At the time the people of
the interior employed an agent from one of the coastal
tribes to sell their produce to Europeans. The agent
spoke English, struck the bargain, and received a part of
the payment, which he immediately handed over to his
African principal who had arrived with the goods. When
the principal had departed upriver, the agent returned to
the conniving European trader and received the balance
of the payment, which was called the cheating money.

Whoever instituted and christened this system, it is
possible that the seller was well aware of the second payment, but like the laborer in the parable, he had received
a fair price for his goods; anything that happened subsequently between agent and European was a matter of
indifference to him. He lacked the sense of theoretical
fairness which was the European's subconscious and
demon ideal. He was not necessarily a dupe, any more
than the agent was a cheat. Both concepts were European
and stemmed from an assumption of the worst motives
in native behavior. The fact that "dash" outrages the
sensibilities of Northern individuals does not compel dis-

honesty or disorder. It is not the traditional African commercial conventions which challenge the good order of
Africa. As long as they are well understood and acceptable to all parties, they support order rather than destroy
it. What does destroy it is the conflict between the instinctive behavior of African society and the demands of
Northern custom that have been imposed on it.

Sometimes these conventions are more strictly imposed
in Africa than they are in the North. In 1976, after the
cement scandal, the new Nigerian government dismissed
seven thousand civil servants for dishonesty, and the
death penalty was introduced for serious and less serious
corruption offenses. At the same time in the Netherlands
Prince Bernhard, who one year previously had been publicly accused of soliciting bribes of $5 million in rela-
tion to aircraft purchases, received the annual award for
sales promotion of the Netherlands Export Association.
A spokesman said, "Everything he did was for Holland."

In the departure lounge of Lagos Airport a gorgeous
middle-aged figure, a fat chieftain in flowing robes
trimmed with lace, the whole effect topped off by the silk
braiding on his floppy velvet hat, stalks up behind an unsuspecting young policewoman. Before she knows it, he
has seized her hand. Startled, she turns and recognizes
him and is surprised into smiling—whereupon she is lost.
The large man tells her that he is taking her into custody
at the airport bar and transfers his affectionate grip to
her arm. The policewoman in her starched green uniform
is dragged across the departure lounge by his awkward
embrace, protesting, giggling, clutching her cap to her
head, and looking embarrassed. An hour later she is still
seated beside him on a low sofa, and the small table in
front of them bears a number of empty beer bottles and
two full glasses. She has placed her cap on her knees, and
every now and then the chief thrusts his hand into his
robes and pulls out a leather pouch which jingles when he

waves it at the waiter. Each time a tray of beer arrives
the policewoman giggles again and says that she has to
go, but she drinks up obediently nonetheless.

Then a cloud appears in the sky for this wealthy, generous, frivolous, corrupt-looking, charming man—in the
shape of one of his relatives. A younger man, about the
same age as the policewoman, but of gloomier habit, sits
down on the wealthy one's other side and proceeds to
unfold a most detailed and distressing story of his misad-
ventures at work. He is employed by the post office, and
he has been dismissed for theft. It's a trumped-up charge,
it will disgrace him, it will shame his mother, and he
would have this ample figure's intervention. The ample
man is sympathetic but is not at all inclined to interrupt
his delightful conversation with the policewoman. He
considers that the purchase of beer for the young man
will discharge his obligations quite satisfactorily until he
returns from his journey. But the young man is persistent.
He has traveled out to the airport especially to interview
his mentor. He wants his attention now. He does not
drink the beer but continues to plead fiercely in the big
man's ear. "Why should you let them do this to me?" he
says over and over again. The chief still seems disinclined
to intervene, but the young man becomes fiercer, not
against his companion but against his own enemies. He
touches the chief's knees with his downturned palms; he
murmurs on and on. Occasionally the chief is forced to
make some response to this agitation on his left; he has
to abandon his conversation with the girl and sit back and
glance at the young man and allow an expression of concern to pass across his face; then he turns back to the
beer and the jokes on his right. But eventually the young
man starts to prevail. The policewoman sits very quietly;
she too begins to look absently to the front with a deep-
ening appearance of melancholy; the life of the party
slowly seeps away.

The chief would prefer to renew his attention toward

her but is more and more distracted by the supplicant postman. Sometimes the chief turns back to her and pours her more beer, which she always drinks. It is as though she has been trained never to abandon a half-full glass. Eventually in his distraction the chief turns and pours the beer over her knees, reassuring her at the same time that this is not serious. Until this moment the policewoman had appeared to be indeed under arrest, incapable, despite the chief's preoccupation, of making a move. But with the beer running down her legs and staining her short cotton socks the spell is broken. While the chief's back is turned, searching once again for the waiter, she replaces her cap on her head and is no longer a girl. She has been transformed back into a policewoman. "Excuse me, I must go now," she says, and the chief turns to find that she is on her feet. She has escaped. They do not smile at each other; instead, both look rather pained at the abrupt end to the distraction. The policewoman makes her uncertain way back to the departure lounge, and the chief once more begins to hear the angry pleas in his ear. For him there is no escape.

The chief in the airport lounge was torn by opposing loyalties. As one of the governing class of his country he owed allegiance to a system of public appointment by merit.[1] But the demands of the young man who came to the chief and asked him to exercise his influence in the post office could not be ignored either. There is a greeting card on sale in Lagos which is sent to children who are about to take examinations. It reads: "He who climbs well deserves a push." The chief had climbed well and been given many a push. He was a leading member of an extended family, and he was in debt to its other members. If they came to him and asked for his help, he could hardly refuse. And the only way he could afford to meet their demands was from the money he received in "dash."

The public officials who use this money to assist their

relatives or to purchase Mercedes-Benz have been accorded the derisive mock-tribal name of WaBenzi by their more idealistic or less well-connected countrymen.

In Kenya, the WaBenzi are famous for their official motorcades. When the provincial commissioner drives to open a new cattle dip, his car may be followed by others bearing the veterinary officer, the livestock officer, the district officer, the educational officer, the medical officer, the chief game warden, and the district engineer. Each of these officers has a quarterly gasoline allocation, much of which is exhausted by these trips to ceremonies that have nothing to do with their own duties. Each of them is supposed to have a full day's work to complete, but they seize every opportunity, instead, to attend these convivial functions. As the motorcade comes over the hill, with its misleading air of purpose, there is a feeling of fulfillment among those whom it carries along. Here at least all is correct; the flags, the cars, the uniforms, the salutes, the whitened gaiters, and polished heels, these are all just as they were when there was both a conscious plan and a subconscious pattern to all these administerings. Sitting in the motorcade, the official is free at last from that nagging doubt about the fundamental good sense of his job. And there are other compensations for undertaking these long-winded and dusty ceremonies. As one livestock officer pointed out, the district's entire annual allocation of funds for chemicals to be used in the new cattle dip had been exhausted by the refreshment costs at the dip's opening ceremony.

But the men who undertake these journeys also enjoy real power, of a sort that is no more compatible with good administration than the official motorcade. The cattle dip had been built for the government in record speed by an Indian contractor, and the district commissioner seemed very gratified by the event. When the party was over, he visited a nearby grocery store which was owned by the builder's brother.

"Are you running this business down?" he asked as he came in. "There seems to be less on the shelves than there was." The grocer denied it, with reason—it was by far the best-stocked shop in town, and the penalty for running a business down was confiscation. The district commissioner strolled around for a while, then, without purchasing anything, went up to the grocer again and invited him to contribute to "the DC's charity walk." Some traders he said had given as much as £50 ($100). What was it for? asked the grocer. It was for various charities, all excellent. It was for children. The district commissioner had the names somewhere, back in the office. He drummed his fingers on the till. Who would be walking? asked the grocer. The district commissioner himself would be walking. He was in training already and had walked a mile that morning. But there was no need to pledge so much per mile. Lump sums were quite acceptable. The grocer gave £20 ($40) and tried to smile with his teeth. "Oh, well," he muttered when the DC had driven away. "Another twenty quid down the drain." Later he explained that although he was a Kenyan citizen, he had lost his trading license earlier in the year, and it had cost him much time and money to get it back.

The WaBenzi, however odious their methods, still receive support from unexpected quarters. "I am an African socialist," said one young man, who was a student and was prepared to defend the supplicant postman. "An African socialist has more responsibilities than a European socialist. I work hard. But there are not many people in this country who can work at all. Those who do work all the time. Because, you can count on it, for every man at work in this place there are twenty mouths at home waiting to be fed. It does not matter at what time of day or night my friends come to my house—they are fed. My family arrive from the country; even in the middle of the night they are invited in and given a meal. And then they can stay. For as long as they like. How would your European socialists like that? Of course, I can do the same to them. But I do not. Because I have no need to go to their village, while they all want to come to the city. And that is my socialism. It is very practical. It helps people directly, only people within the family group, perhaps, but everyone is in a family group. It is not like that in Europe, but what you call socialism would not be thought very admirable here. Anyone who refused to help his relatives here would be treated as an outcast and an affliction to his entire family. That is African socialism. I call myself a revolutionary socialist, but my own father works for the government medical service and supplements his income with £200 ($400) a month in bribes, and I do not judge him. How else could I continue with my studies at the university? Or how could my younger brothers and sisters continue at school? My father could never support us without the bribes. And he knows that one day we will support him. I think Europeans invented what they call socialism to make up for the lack of what we have here."

For those members of the administrative class who are responsible for making things work under these perplexing conditions, there are certain refuges. One refuge is the theory of backwardness, the commonly held opinion that Africa is a "backward" area which is "progressing" (as opposed to a different society which is being forced to conform) and that African society is accomplishing in half a century—as it moves from tribalism to nationalism —what it took Europe a thousand years to achieve. But can any society achieve any such thing?

The theory of backwardness is also comforting to the WaBenzi because it justifies the role they play. Without the myth of backwardness, but possessing their Northern education and swollen expectations, they might almost be latter-day slaves, slaves of the intellect, who have been brainwashed and manumitted back to their country to represent the interests of those who captured them and to flourish in the service of the North against the interests of their own people. Because they are neither tribal potentates nor soldiers, the WaBenzi's best chance of advancement is as able and corrupt functionaries of an ostensibly democratic system. Without the theory of backwardness, the confusion that follows independence begins to resemble a deliberate reduction of orderly, traditional communities to a condition in which only an alienated elite can govern them. This is the despotism of the elite, as in Senegal, rather than the tyranny of Life President Nguema of Equatorial Guinea. It is the steady growth of food dependency, rather than atrocities in jail, not the cathedral litany in praise of the tyrant, but the publication of another slim volume of President Senghor's verse (evoking autumn in Normandy) at the height of student riots against Senegalese unemployment; it is the regular orders for Vichy water to Bamako, *moules marinières* to Kinshasa, and "gentleman's relish" to Nairobi.

Another refuge from turbulent national reality is the ideal of "a united Africa." For the people who know the hopeless situation of their single countries, the goal of "one continent with one language" is a comfort. It gives political importance to their shared experience of alienation, despair, and distracted rhetoric. "One Africa" as it exists at international gatherings, and in the endless resolutions of grandiose and impotent committees, is exactly what they have in common. It unites them far more than membership of their own nations can. To drive the white man away, the leaders of Africa had to become as white men themselves. They triumphed, and they were left in possession of a white machine, the nation-state, which did not work. Only in the cities, where the leaders of Africa live, can this machine even appear operable. For the WaBenzi the cities are islands of plausibility in a sea of incertitude and they cling to these islands, aware of their duty to build the nation but aware also that if they leave

them, though the life of the nation is likely to be enriched, they themselves will certainly be drowned. They
grow loyal to their fellow castaways and disloyal to their
nominal countrymen. When in September 1975, after the
Sahelian drought, gangs of Tuareg beggars from Niger
roamed the streets of Nigeria, the ambassador of Niger
agreed to accept responsibility for them and to arrange
for their repatriation. He said that he did this because
the beggars held Niger identity cards but added that they
were "mainly light-skinned Tuareg from the north of
Niger" and pointed out that many Niger nationals who
were of the same stock as Nigerians[2] had been easily absorbed into the Nigerian community. The sense of fellowship evident in this announcement did not tend to unite
the holders of Niger nationality.

The WaBenzi owe their allegiance to the newest tribe
in Africa, the continental tribe of exiles who govern it.
This is a complete reversal of their previous position.
When their colonial predecessors were still the administrators, the educated Africans who pressed for independence could afford to develop their indigenous identity and
use it as an exclusive badge. On the Gold Coast in 1934
the native leaders who were beginning to grow dissatis-
fied with their status in the colony were, in the words of
Geoffrey Gorer, "conscientiously reviving negro customs
and dances in the spirit of English morris dancers: the
Gold Coast Independent announces that 'the Olum Festi-
val of Akyem Abuakwa will be celebrated on Tuesday 3rd
of July next, after which Yams will be brought to town
for consumption.' "[3] But whereas then traditional culture
served its purpose, today it is frequently seen as a threat
to the progress of the independent states which have inherited it. In 1977 a government commission suggested
that Ghana should adopt a new constitution that would
reflect popular support for the abolition of political parties and national elections and replace these with a system
of elected delegates from villages to districts to regions,

more closely resembling the traditional councils of chiefs
(which are still very influential in Ghana). The idea was
most hotly resisted in Accra by the country's professional
leaders who have most to gain from the reinstitution of
the pseudodemocratic political parties. They, who once
used the society of the bush as a form of rebellion against
the colony, have now compromised their status in bush
society because of their need to become urban individuals
on the Northern model. And they have replaced their
previous enthusiasm for their cultural roots with
contempt.

It is (as an instance of such contempt) not unusual for
the World Health Organization to receive official denials
of serious outbreaks of notifiable disease (such as cholera) from African countries because the damage such an
admission would cause to the national economy or to the
self-esteem of the government involved is thought to be
more serious than the unreported sufferings of untreated
cholera victims—few of whom would be educated men.
The most extreme example of this sort of contempt occurred in Ethiopia in 1973, when a famine which may
have resulted in the deaths of more than 100,000 people
was concealed for seven months by the Ethiopian administration, with the assistance of the white WaBenzi, the
international community of relief agencies, development
organizations, and Northern embassies. One of the most
serious sources of potential embarrassment to the Ethi-
opians was the possibility that the assembled delegates of
the Organization of African Unity, who were meeting in
Addis Ababa, might notice the crisis, and so columns of
peasants who marched to the capital begging for food
were turned away by the police.

But the conflict between the demands of an educated
self-esteem and those of hunger is not restricted to
times of famine. Schooling is incompatible with subsistence farming, and the child of a subsistence farmer who

returns to the fields will have to regard either his education or his life as a failure. The cash-crop plantations which have been established on much of the most fertile land in Africa nurture the country's WaBenzi; if these plantations were to be replaced by maize plots, national food production would increase and the peasants would be better fed, but the country's leaders would lose many of their lucrative jobs, regulating or servicing the cash-crop industry. In many African countries "higher" education is a process by which a small and able group is encouraged to spend its working life in activities that interfere with the means whereby the majority of its countrymen are able to eat. The cities live off the peasant hinterland and slowly drain it of its vitality. If the nation-states achieve nothing else, they do at least achieve a Northern standard of living for their privileged classes, but it is an achievement which is directly related to the growing impoverishment of the rest of the people.

The conflict between the people of Africa and their own educated elite is clearly reflected in the general failure of African governments to persuade qualified men and women to leave the city and live in the bush, where they can do the jobs they have been trained to do and where they are supposedly most needed. By staying in the city, doctors, for instance, can build up private practices and acquire second homes, and their families can engage in related business deals—the burden of personal obligation can be discharged. In Zambia, President Kaunda has attempted to oppose this tendency by confiscating second homes, penalizing private medical practice, and nationalizing the ownership of land. In the war between Zambia's urban middle class and its uneducated peasants the president has been forced to change sides because Zambia can no longer afford to import or subsidize the food needed to feed its urban population. It is a far cry from the days when Kaunda launched a training scheme for Zambian astronauts in the belief that it was "outrageous that only one nation in the world could put a man on the moon." For the WaBenzi, moon shots are a symbol of national virility, and the United Nations will know no peace until an African spaceman has blundered around with the rest of them. But for the time being the Zambian scheme, which partly involved packing the trainee astronauts into empty beer barrels and rolling them down a hill (to familiarize them with the experience of weightlessness), has been postponed; if the intensive agricultural development of Zambia continues at its present pace, Kaunda's people will not need special training to accustom them to lunar conditions.

Apart from the material disadvantages there is another reason why the WaBenzi hesitate to leave the city. They know, all too well, the life of the bush and the difficulty of reconciling it with the life they have come to prefer, and they are afraid. They fear the isolation which will be imposed on them if they return to the interior and the strain this will throw on their newly acquired personalities. Their individuality has deprived them of membership of that small segment of the continental community into which they were born. It is the reverse of the fear that the Northerner feels when confronted with the overwhelming power of the African forest, the mass of life which permits only life in the mass and which emphasizes in the African context the obliterating unimportance of the individual. For the African professionals, if they are to remain individuals, must remain out of Africa—in the city—and true to their new identities.

In the traditional African community there is no such thing as "a man and his wife and children alone against the world,"[4] the assumption of the individual on which the society of the city is based. The urban African individual has before him a choice of exiles. He has resigned his membership in the interdependent group into which he was born and has accustomed himself to the terrible individualism of the North, which divides clans and causes

men to abandon even those who reared them and to for-
sake those they should have reared. When the Northerner
Park threw himself on the goodness of the poor villagers,
who nursed him back from serious illness to health, the
women sang to him: "The winds roared and the rains
fell. The poor, white man, faint and weary, came and
sat under our tree. He has no mother to bring him milk,
no wife to grind his corn." And then, in chorus: "Let us
pity the white man; no mother has he. . . ." It is the
black individual, exiled in his own capital city, who may
feel that he has no mother now. And if he returns to the
bush and the enveloping community that knew him before,
he fears that he will lose his new self. It is this dilemma
which can lead him into a contempt for his own heritage
and, eventually, into a hatred of every influence which
challenges it.

Faced with this conflict, many of the most able men in
Africa have chosen the literal exile of Europe or America.
The director of Nigeria's External Broadcasting Service,
the novelist Chinua Achebe, was imprisoned in Lagos
during the Biafran war and later went to teach in
America, where he remains. The director of Ghana's film
industry, Kofi Awoonor, left the country after the downfall of Nkrumah and went to work for the State University of New York. He returned to Ghana in 1975 and
within a year had been arrested, tried for subversion, and
imprisoned. A young man who gets a good first-class degree at Cambridge, a Ghanaian, is spoken of as "having
a brilliant future." In Ghana?

"In England."

There is a lack of knowledge as to who, in ten years'
time, the African individual will be called upon to be.
Several African states have found it necessary to pass
laws that make it a criminal offense to "insult an African." How fragile must be this sense of self that it needs
such defenses against verbal insult. What strength is im-
puted to tribalism that, in general conversation, one never

even mentions its name? What is it that impedes the
growth of a national identity if it is not the same force
that obstructed and finally expelled the foreign bodies of
colonialism? The African individual feels this force opposed to himself every day. Though it may be suppressed,
he fears that it will not be destroyed until he too has
changed or been driven out of Africa.

The effects of a growing isolation can be seen in the inherited institutions of Africa as much as in those who
attempt to serve them. And there is no institution of the
African state that is so crippled by the distractions of
custom as the system of law. Sometimes it is discredited
by partiality, as in Ghana, where in 1977 two generals on
the ruling council were dismissed for illegally importing
Mercedes-Benz, while a rival car import company, which
was owned by the head of state's wife, was not investi-
gated. Sometimes it is distorted by overenthusiasm as in
Liberia, where 15,000 citizens packed the football stadium to watch 15 pickpockets being whipped on the
president's orders. Outside, another 15,000 disappointed
fans jammed the streets for hours. In Nigeria they order
these things better, and public executions are held on a
fashionable beach near Lagos so that all those who have
been ordered to attend can do so. At the last count 608
Nigerians were in prison awaiting execution.

But the exotic adornments of African legalism are best
illustrated by events in Zanzibar. In 1973 seventy-two
people were charged with treason and with the assassination of the island's previous president. The only lawyer
in court (it was "a People's Court") was the state prosecutor, a barrister trained in London called Wolfgang
Dourado. The defendants were not allowed their own
lawyers despite their allegations that torture had been
used to extract confessions. But this apparent disregard
for due process of law proved misleading. In the first
place, despite the absence of defense counsel, the trial was

not a hurried affair. It lasted for more than three years. And the absence of defense lawyers was remedied when Mr. Dourado, the prosecutor, offered to undertake the defense brief as well. On some days he would argue for the state of Zanzibar, and the defendants would be plunged into gloom by his appearance in court. On other days he would represent the defense, and his speeches would be warmly applauded by the mob in the dock. After one year Mr. Dourado the defender secured the acquittal of twenty-four of his clients, and Mr. Dourado the attorney general of Zanzibar was rewarded with death sentences on forty-three of the accused. The remaining five were sentenced to prison. All those convicted were advised to appeal.

Zanzibar is small, but it has a complicated appeals structure. After a year for the preparation of the case, the High Court heard the appeals, and Mr. Dourado managed to get ten of his death sentences quashed. He also succeeded in getting the other thirty-three upheld. Again he advised those who had been convicted to appeal, and again it took a year for the matter to be reopened, this time before the Supreme Court of Zanzibar. Mr. Dourado still appeared for both sides, but this time, as attorney general, he announced that he had "changed his mind" about capital punishment. The situation now was that not even the prosecution was asking for any of the thirty-three death sentences. Nonetheless, after a further year of argument the Supreme Court decided that it would commute only twenty-six of them. That left seven of the accused still under sentence of death, although only three of them were in any real danger since the remaining four had never attended the court. They were living in prison in the capital of mainland Tanzania, seventy miles away. Tanzania and Zanzibar form one state, but the central authorities, while strongly disapproving the rebellion that formed the basis of the trial, had declined to return the missing defendants to the island because of the absence of independent defense counsel. The request for their return had been forcefully made by Attorney General Dourado, while the four fugitives had been strongly advised to remain on the mainland, by Mr. Dourado, their lawyer.

The three men who did face execution were advised to plead for clemency to the president of Zanzibar, who is, ex officio, the vice-president of Tanzania and who would naturally take Mr. Dourado's advice—on both sides of the question. Mr. Dourado was of the opinion that whichever one of his advices was more persuasive, it was a near certainty that nobody would be executed, since the president was a devout Moslem. He had spent nearly four years urging a penalty that he knew would never be imposed.[5] The story of the Zanzibar treason trial does not support the view that independent Africa has a contempt for the processes of the law. But neither does it support the view that African states will continue indefinitely to find in their inherited legal systems a sensible way of administering justice.

All over Africa the legal machine of the cities is grinding down. In Gambia, a country of less than half a million people, the Supreme Court under its supreme judge, an Englishman, dispenses a mixture of customary and colonial law. There have been some interesting legal points dealt with on the usual basis of statute or precedent, but the judges and their clerks and the honorable members of the Gambian bar have their work cut out with the case law, for Gambia has no law reports. On the other hand, there is no death penalty either, and justice is dispensed from a cool stone room with simple wooden furniture that is more modest in appearance than the average magistrate's court in England. Furthermore, the prison service is said to be a model of enlightenment.

In Ghana, where the people took to the common law like cradle litigants, all sorts of refinements have been imported. Such seventeenth-century offenses as sedi-

tion and criminal libel are lovingly preserved, and when
the British send out a judge from the House of Lords to
celebrate one hundred years of legal association, he can
be greeted by a judge advocate general, a fearsome
creature recalling the days of Cromwell, who is kept busy
imprisoning argumentative leaders of the Ghanaian community, after trials in military courts which are held *in
camera*. It is a comforting historical touch. In Nairobi the
East African Court of Appeal, presided over by an Englishman, quashes a death sentence after an African High
Court judge has tried a man for manslaughter and convicted him of murder.

Outside the courtroom a shoeless man in ragged
trousers bursts from the doorway of Woolworth's and
runs down the crowded street with the vigorous concentration of one who is interested in preserving his life. A
leg is stuck out; the running man with both feet in the
air is tripped; his equilibrium is lost; his head moves
forward as though struck from behind; the rhythm of his
pace is broken; first one foot, then the other claws at the
ground; both fail to bear his weight; he stumbles; his
knees give; in an instant he sprawls on the pavement.
. . . Before he can recover his breath, the man who
tripped him has kicked him in the face. The man on the
ground, it is now clear, is wearing a white T-shirt and a
pair of salmon pink trousers. In one hand he holds two
dozen yellow ball-points removed from Woolworth's and
bound together with a rubber band. While the crowd by
the stamp booth is still uncertain what has happened,
perhaps beginning to wonder how a man without shoes
ever got into Woolworth's, another man, a third African,
has joined in, and side by side, taking turns, these two
men are kicking the man on the ground in the salmon
pink jeans and plastic belt—another detail floating up to
the stamp booth, that transparent sort of plastic which at
once solves the mystery of the shoeless shopper, since it

suggests the sort of plastic slippers worn by half the
Woolworth's shop assistants and which this customer
must have slipped off when he decided to make a run
for it.

By this time another pedestrian has joined in, but he is
not kicking. He is carrying a lump of concrete, normally
used to anchor a street sign, and as the man in salmon
trousers twists around on the pavement, he is trying to
batter his head. Perhaps in the lynch mob there is something of the reaction of people who are constantly thinking of turning to theft themselves, but who lack the
courage or the desperation to do so and are all the more
determined to ensure that no one else shall profit from
the possession of a quality that they themselves lack. But
theories aside, it is unusual to see half a dozen wretched
young men beating a wretched seventh, a stranger, to
death. Whatever else they were, they were certainly not
outraged representatives of the property-owning class.
By the time the uniformed Woolworth's security force
had arrived, and the police had fought their way through
to the body in salmon pink, he was a dead man. The ball-
points were returned to Woolworth's, their elastic band
intact.

The regular and irregular proceed hand in hand.[6] The
Kenyan attorney general takes it upon himself to rebuke
judges for drunkenness on the bench at the opening ceremony of a new court building. The English chief justice
looks silently on, himself, naturally, as sober as a judge.
The Kenyan courts retain the independent power to direct
that ministers be dismissed from Parliament for threatening to kill their opponents on election day, as happened
to the burly minister for local government, a former
Mau Mau terrorist. The minister proceeded to Parliament anyway, but as a special member nominated by the
president. And when an opposition member of Parliament is taken away from the Hilton Hotel in the center

of Nairobi by the head of the security police and brutally
murdered a few hours later, the Kenyan courts cannot
ensure that anyone is brought for trial.

A parliamentary select committee is set up. It discovers
who murdered the critical MP and how. It names the
minister responsible for running the office of the president
as being among those culpable. The report is published
and made widely available through the newspapers. The
attorney general objects to the lack of "evidence" in the
report (which consists of nothing else), and then it is
forgotten. A subsequent parliamentary committee on
ministerial corruption is disbanded. A few months later
members of these two parliamentary committees are arrested and detained without trial. Again this is a legal
act, an act made so by laws posted under the former
colonial regime and once used by the British against the
man who was to become the president. Just because a
tyranny is embryonic does not make it parvenu.

In the eighteenth century King Damel of the Wolofs
captured (after a fierce battle) his neighbor King Abdulkader, who had invaded his country on a Moslem
jihad and who had announced his intention, for the glory
of God, of slitting King Damel's throat. By tradition the
victorious Damel should have placed his foot on Abdulkader's neck and stabbed him with a spear. Instead,
Damel asked Abdulkader what *he* would have done had
he been the victor. Abdulkader gave the traditional account of behavior and said that he expected the same
treatment, and make it snappy. Damel declined, saying
that if he made his spear any redder, it would not build
up his town or bring to life the thousands who had fallen
in the woods. Instead, he kept King Abdulkader as his
slave for three months and then, at the request of the
king's subjects, released him. This story was cited all over
Senegambia as an example of wisdom and justice. Doubt-
less King Damel's merciful behavior was exceptional, but
it reveals that the indigenous African sense of justice had

no need to be bolstered by the Northern legalism that has
supplanted it.

Beneath the façade of legalism the equally dreary
hierarchies of the North are seeping in: the promotion
of long service and short expectations; the cultivation of
intimidated loyalty in the minds of a million free men.
For the junior WaBenzi, the clerks of Africa, the ritual
continues for a lifetime, and clerk is knitted to clerk, entire armies of them, three employed to do the work of
one Northerner at one-tenth of the wages, spending their
conscious hours in the caverns of Victorian tropical commerce, their final task being to supervise the booklet
which lists their years of service.

High tea and an illuminated scroll recording the appreciation of their firm. "Outline of Programme—1 Introduction of Chairman, by Personnel Manager (Managing Director standing in for Chairman). 2 Chairman's
opening speech, read by Managing Director (Chairman
unavoidably absent in U.K.). 3 Presentation of Awards.
4 Vote of thanks by senior pensioner among those present
who have toiled for twenty-five years in the service of
ABC Ltd. Please be seated half-an-hour early. Refreshments will"—eventually, dear God—"be served."

One sunny Sunday in Lagos an Italian building contractor
called Agnelli carried out a site inspection with his engineers. The site was on a reclaimed swamp, and the
contract was for an enormous new government complex.
Earlier that week a three-story block of flats had collapsed
in the course of construction on a neighboring site. It was
common knowledge in the expatriate building fraternity
that the collapse had been caused by incompetent work;
supports had been removed before a wall had been built,
and half the structure had gone down like a pack of cards,
killing one man and burying another. That contractor
had been so eager to conceal his mistake that he had
ordered a bulldozer to knock down the other half of the

building at once. No check was made to see if the work-
man who had been buried was alive, there were no protests from the other laborers, and the collapse was not
reported in the press. Even after the accident the Nigerian
authorities continued to make payments to the contractors.
Not one of the penalties that operate in the North was
exacted in Lagos. Sgr. Agnelli, once the urgent circumstances were explained, had lent his bulldozer for the
job; it did not seem to cast a shadow over his own site
inspection.

Since the Agnelli site was on a swamp, the question of
drains was of some importance. The Italian was fortunate in having an engineer who had designed an entirely
new system of drains which would do the job perfectly.
It was just a question of deciding how far the drains
should run. For most of the morning Agnelli and his
team tramped around the site under the sun, deciding not
on the best way to drain the swamp but on how they
could extract the maximum amount of money from the
agreement they had reached. The engineer was pleased
with his drainage system and wanted to demonstrate its
efficiency. Agnelli just wanted to know what holes there
were in the contract which would allow them to do the
same work several times over at greatly increased profits.
To get to grips with the matter, they eventually had to
leave the site and walk out across the leveled mud banks
toward the deepwater sea channel at its edge which is
used by ships to approach Apapa Harbor. There was no
cover out on the flats; the sand bounced the light up into
their eyes, making it more difficult for them to avoid
stepping in the little piles of human ordure that were
dotted everywhere. Sgr. Agnelli provided no latrines on
the site for his employees, but although he was entirely
responsible for the results, he managed to convey an impression of fastidious disdain as he stepped over the
compositions and noted wittily, with his artist's eye, how
very neatly they were spaced. By the end of the morning

the Italian had his way. Every time the engineer explained how the drains should be arranged Agnelli wanted to know if they could not be done another way. Every time he was told what it would cost he wanted to know if it would be possible to justify a higher price. "If you do it that way," said the engineer finally, "there will be a flood."

"Yes," said Sgr. Agnelli. "Then they will need more drains. It's their fault really for not giving us a tighter contract."

As they left the site, they had to cross a shallow sewer which led from the city to the sea. There were three Africans crouched beside it, absorbed by something they had seen in a pool which was fringed with grass. Now and again one of them reached quickly into the water; sometimes he pulled out a small fish. After some hours they would have a bucketful and a feast and a day well spent.

Nobody supervised Sgr. Agnelli because nobody cared. The WaBenz who employed him merely had to ensure that a likely-looking tower block was erected on the designated patch of swamp and that his Swiss bank account received the agreed amount of money. Similarly Mr. Walters's customer, the health administrator, felt no responsibility for the effective distribution of the American drugs.

Although wealthy Lagos seems to have become independent of the influences that dominate life elsewhere, it is in reality as much under the control of the North as its poorer neighbors. The chaos of the place conceals this; the wealth and ostentation of its governing class make a show of sovereignty. But the roads and buildings that are being erected at such great profit to the expatriate firms are far removed from the needs of the Nigerian people. And polite, excited Mr. Walters was of just as much benefit to Lagos as Sgr. Agnelli and his disconnected drainage system. The drugs Mr. Walters sold were overpriced and took up a disproportionate amount of Nigeria's health budget. They were powerful agents needing skillful use, and the doctors (or more usually pharmacists) who had to prescribe them were given inadequate information about their limitations and side effects. Although they were paid for and delivered, the drugs were frequently undistributed until their effective life was over. When the patient did obtain them, even if they were still effective, it was frequently in the wrong quantities so that he either poisoned himself or failed to affect his condition at all. Despite Mr. Walters's commodities, the city's infant mortality rate (of reported deaths alone) would remain at 40 percent. The population would continue to be infested with worms and to suffer endemic malaria, polio, pneumonia, dysentery, tetanus, measles, anemia, meningitis, and bronchitis.

Before he left Lagos, Mr. Walters obtained a little souvenir. It was a crudely printed handbill advertising the extraordinary properties of Almaro, a locally produced medicine: "Almaro cures Pile, Dysentery, Roundworm, Tapeworm, Rheumatism, if person is suffering from Gonorrhear for more than ten years, and Burantasi (if man prik no work well) this medicine can cure, and Qack ache, also Malaria. Not recommoded for Pregnant woman (it can spoil pregnant). Works like magic. To be taken with Tea, Coffee, Beer or Stout. If your belly is strong take content of the packet at once but if not divide it into two." Unfortunately for most Nigerian patients, Mr. Walters's specifics were going to be as effective as Almaro's magical potion. The Burantasi might be bad. But it was the Qack ache that got you in the end.

There are, however, a few left of the old school: porpoises that can paddle away from the feeding frenzy, stand on their tails, and get an overview. The old colonial governor sniffs the wind and detects something amiss. The inheritors of these countries are not exercising the necessary will. They are not advancing. Instead, positions have been abandoned; nations are retreating into nationalism. It leads His Excellency to experience what he can only describe as "a sense of dismay." Hear the trumpet note of measured reproof, a dismayed old governor, tracing out the overview to a rapt audience—the members of the Institute of Structural Engineers—men who know a bit about exports and about the watertight contracts which buoy them up, as well as the many uses of a bulldozer. And throughout that memorable evening, while the old governor reflected on his independent Africa and reproved the WaBenzi (the only fruit of his lifelong altruism), the cement ships were accumulating outside Apapa.

NOTES

1. This demand is not taken lightly by the Nigerian government. In an effort to reduce bribery, an order was made in 1978 to make it pointless by reducing the range of luxury goods that could be purchased. Forty-eight thousand bottles of imported champagne were seized from wine merchants in Lagos, and many other imported goods such as air conditioners, spaghetti, cheroots, and jewelry could be imported only with special permission.
2. That is, fellow members of the Hausa tribe.
3. Geoffrey Gorer, *Africa Dances* (London: Faber, 1935).
4. E. M. Thomas, *Warrior Herdsmen* (London: Secker, 1966).
5. In March 1978 the president duly commuted these three death sentences to life imprisonment, and on the mainland the four men who had been sentenced to death *in absentia* were released.
6. Kenya, unlike Gambia, has not abolished the death sentence, which is frequently imposed for robbery with violence. One resident magistrate in Samburu, when asked to justify the frequent executions, explained that they were carried out to reassure the tourists that their property would not be stolen and that, if it was stolen, those who had taken it would be punished.

CHAPTER 11

BLOOD AND GOD

These days we do not have competent witchdoctors. We have charlatans. May the God of Black Africa, and the spirits of our forefathers, pour down in torrents Wrath upon these bloody witchdoctors! I call upon both literate and illiterate witchdoctors, wizards, astrologers and others of that profession living in this country to form a Kenya African Witchcraft Union, with a view to healing in the African traditional way. . . .

Letter to a Nairobi newspaper, 1975

If you say you are a doctor, people will believe anything.

Eric Ambler, *The Light of Day*

On the extensive lawns surrounding the headquarters of a prosperous Italian mission in East Africa, two boys are sitting down. It is late afternoon. The older of these boys starts to move across the lawn slowly, on his bottom and backward. His legs extend behind him. The other, his brother, walks beside him step by step, carrying the older one's boots. The larger boy cannot walk because he has broken his leg. He broke it in the morning when the dew was still on the grass and he was practicing the long jump. His foot slipped on landing, and apart from removing his boots, he has made little progress during the day. It is a Sunday, and there are not many people about. His younger brother had failed to secure any assistance for eight hours. Eventually the boy with a broken leg is lifted into a truck and driven to a hospital.

The hospital is an imposing building which is defended from the outside world by tall iron railings. Since it is

Sunday, the gates are locked. Eventually a man is persuaded to open them, and the truck reaches the doors of
the emergency room, from which a young man emerges
dressed in a white jacket which bears picturesque red
stains. Relying on this costume for authority, he orders
the truck to be moved. "This place," he says, "is for the
doctors only." When he has been assured that the truck
will be moved as soon as the patient has been admitted,
he takes his first look at the boy with a broken leg. "Get
out," he says. Again he is told that the patient has a
broken leg. "How do you know?" he asks suspiciously.
"Try walking," he says to the boy. After some warm
discussion a stretcher arrives, and the boy is placed on it
and wheeled inside to join the line for treatment.

Inside the hospital there is a tangle of benches on
which three more men in white coats appear to be asleep.
Eventually one of them sits up and agrees to complete the
formalities for admission. The boy is then instructed to
join a long line of patients who are being examined by
the medical attendant for preliminary inspection. An hour
later he is in his third line, this time for X-ray results,
sitting in a room whose walls and floor have been violently
splashed with a purple dye, as though the mental patients
had been celebrating the end of the term. Outside in the
central hall there are lines at every corner, only one of
which is moving at all. Inquiry shows that this leads not
to a doctor but to the mortuary. "It is the dead house, in
there," one of the patients explained. "They have brought
in a young girl who hanged herself. I am going to see her.
She was very pretty. But they have had to cut her neck to
get the rope off." Shortly before midnight the boy with
the broken leg was told that the X ray would have to be
done again, and he should go home until the morning.
There was no transport provided. He had still not seen
either doctor or nurse.

Bonesetting is one of the outstanding skills of traditional African medicine, but there are few native bone-

setters at work in the cities. Instead, the people naturally turn to the practitioners of modern medicine and to the large, modern hospitals which have been erected to safeguard their health. The ability of these institutions to carry out this task has never been less confidently asserted than it is today. In Zambia in 1977 the government had to institute an inquiry after twenty-five patients in one ward of the university teaching hospital died in one day. Five days later twenty-seven patients died in the same ward. Many of the deaths were caused by a shortage of simple supplies—disinfectant, bandages, painkillers—which was well known to both doctors and administrators.

In Lagos the state governor paid a surprise visit to the city's General Hospital. Of the eight doctors who should have been on duty, only one was present. There were no doctors in the emergency room. The staff was publicly rebuked, but a week later an American woman, who drove her watchman to hospital with a strangulated hernia and in a state of shock, failed to get a doctor to examine him from seven in the morning until seven at night. The only doctor who visited the hospital that day declined to see the patient, preferring to spend the time in a private room with his girl friend. He sent out a note stating that if the watchman were left in the emergency room, he would be "kept under observation." The watchman eventually died. At a children's hospital in central Lagos a child of two and a half died ten hours after falling ill and in front of a doctor who had spent the previous half hour unsuccessfully searching for a vein in which to insert a drip. The doctor said the child died because "he had no blood."

Since independence the quality of scientific medicine in Africa has fallen steadily. This is not because of a lack of qualified doctors or of a lack of funds. It seems chiefly because of a lack of interest. A Northern medical administrator with years of experience in Africa noted the fact that as sophisticated African health services have become more independent, they have become less reliable. It is partly a matter of administrative failures, but there is also a failure of will among the most capable and experienced medical staff. In Nigeria, for example, the West African Institute of Trypanosomiasis has steadily run down over ten years. The universities keep quite a high standard, but the specialist establishments have declined. Achievement at the highest level seems unattainable, and the staffs become increasingly isolated. Where so many of the routine tasks become more and more difficult, the more difficult ones quickly become impossible. Where vaccine is available, as for measles, it perishes through inadequate refrigeration—a result foreseeable by pharmaceutical salesmen and medical administrators alike. Nigeria recently staged a £1 million ($2 million) malaria control program, which failed because the drugs that were purchased were improperly stored. With many other drugs knowledge of their side effects is suppressed, and even their correct application remains a mystery.[1] When highly qualified African doctors have returned to their own country, they frequently seem to lose all commitment to their work. And as the general hospitals fall to pieces, the expatriate diplomats and advisers, their last discriminating customers, naturally avoid them, thereby accelerating their decline. In Banjul, the Royal Victoria Hospital, the only one in the country, stands conveniently close to the British High Commission, but none of the British attend it. "It wouldn't be fair on the Gambians, you see," explains the man from the embassy. "We don't want to occupy beds in the government hospital when we can afford to pay for private treatment at the clinic. Do we?" And there is indeed a private clinic just outside Banjul, owned and run by a Gambian-European partnership, where reliable treatment can be obtained. "Of

course, we don't send the serious cases there," added the
diplomat. "We fly them home." So the process of separa-
tion becomes complete.

The most effective scientific hospitals in Africa are the
least ambitious. The three commonest diseases in Tanzania are malaria, bilharzia, and hookworm. One thousand medical aides have now been given six months'
training to enable them to diagnose these diseases. All
other cases are sent to rural health centers, where medical
aides who have had three years' training deal with 85 percent of the cases referred. The remainder go to one of
sixty-five district hospitals which are supervised by qualified doctors. At independence Tanzania's hospitals took
90 percent of the health budget but could serve only the
urban 3 percent of the population. Now nearly everyone
in the country should be within reach of a village health
worker, and the hospitals take only 50 percent of the
budget—which may still be too high. At this level—the
level of the family, the village, the clan—African scientific
medicine works. But few African countries have been
able to impose this simplification on their reluctant medical professions, the members of which find the notion of
"a barefoot doctor" a contradiction in terms. For the
village children of Africa the point of becoming a doctor
might be to acquire a dozen pairs of handmade calfskin
shoes, preferably from Lobbs of St. James's. At the age
of twenty-five, after he has spent twenty years training, the typical African doctor does not intend to return
to the solitude of the village to practice his art, although
a few idealists have tried.

One who did try finally gave up when he foresaw a
serious outbreak of cholera and sent urgently to the capital for vaccine. It reached him more than two months
later and in sufficient quantities to immunize three people.
On his return to civilization he opened a private clinic

and built up a prosperous urban business. But he also
treated poor people for whatever they could afford to
give him. The fame of his clinic spread back up the river
to the village where he had once worked. People traveled
for days to reach him. Since they came from so far, he
could not decline to treat them, but if they had malaria,
he could not dose them with an effective drug either. If he
did, they would be unable to maintain the dose, and a
partial treatment would destroy their natural immunity.
So he gave them aspirin, and after a few days they returned home, feeling better for the time being and loud
in the praises of the scientific medicine which had diag-
nosed their condition, found it treatable, and been quite
unable to treat it.

It is not only in the case of malaria that scientific medicine has failed to make an impact on African health.
Mungo Park noted the suddenness of death from fever,
and 140 years later Geoffrey Gorer, in *Africa Dances,*
noted the frequency of death among Africans of the
French colonies from imported diseases, such as tuberculosis and syphilis, under urban conditions that resulted in
infectious epidemics, and from the increased malnutrition
consequent on the tax system. Death still came suddenly
as well: ". . . It is not from any recognisable causes that
the young people die. I do not know how many times
Benga asked after a schoolfellow and was told that he
had died some time ago; and on every occasion when the
cause of his or her death was asked we were told, 'He
just died; in the morning he seemed quite all right and he
was dead by nightfall.' " And in 1976 a European hotel-
keeper in Gambia said, "Many of the people in the city
die quite unexpectedly. Especially the young people. In
the morning one of the boys working here will say he has
a headache or something. He seems all right, but you let
him go home. And the next day he is dead." The most
that Northern doctors can suggest about such cases is

that they succumb to a state of perpetual triple infection from malaria, polio, and worms. The theory has never been proved.

The great victories of scientific medicine in Africa have been against the infectious diseases such as yaws, cholera, measles, and smallpox.[2] Just down the road from the hotel where the waiters kept dropping dead stands one of the world's largest centers for the study of tropical disease. Here the Medical Research Council of London has taken over what was once a vast military camp and established a small hospital and a number of laboratories. The site is still surrounded by a wire fence and approached through a gatehouse, where smartly uniformed guards sign each visitor in and out. Inside the enclosure the research center's herd of experimental cattle is almost lost to view across the hazy meadows of the old camp. It is a self-sufficient community which produces its own food and keeps itself at arm's length from the continent in which it is situated.

Such, in Africa, are the necessary conditions for the highest levels of scientific research. The people of Gambia are admitted to the research hospital only if their illness is likely to further research, the chief purpose of which is to develop a vaccine against malaria. The present lines of inquiry have been given a further two years to run before they are exhausted.

The ruthless nature of the choice between therapy and research is well illustrated by another of the center's projects. For the last twenty-five years it has conducted a survey in four villages in the Gambian interior where the health of the villagers was constantly monitored by a team of doctors. But since the purpose of the project was to discover a possible connection between chromosomes and disease, the villagers received very little medical treatment. If they had been properly treated, the experiment would have failed. Their health was not harmed, but the doctors did decline to treat, over twenty-five years, numerous conditions that were easily curable, in an attempt to place the future priorities of health care on a more scientific basis. Such an experiment would be impossible to conduct in Europe or America.

It was possible to conduct it in Africa for three reasons. The first was urgency. The quality of medical knowledge latent in the research center was grotesquely out of proportion to the needs of the population it had been placed among. If some such project could not have been devised, the center would have been withdrawn altogether. Second, there was no pressure among the people of Gambia to prevent it. There was no public demand that Gambian children should be cured rather than used as subjects in an experiment. And third, these two factors combined to produce an attitude of mind in the luminaries of the research center which enabled them to look on the native people of Gambia as highly suitable cases for experiment. These doctors were prepared to do things, and omit to do other things, to Gambian children which they were certainly not prepared to do to their own children and to behave in a way in which they would never have been authorized to behave in the North. The results of the experiment, when published, should prove interesting, though they may also recall that West Africa was the original range of the guinea pig.

The story of the center's attempts to understand and overcome malaria illustrates some of the inherent unsuitability of Northern medicine to Africa. Malaria is believed to cause one million deaths annually (which is only a 1 percent mortality rate of all cases). After the advances resulting from the need to protect troops during the Second World War, the World Health Organization believed that it would be able to eradicate the disease—until 1967, when this hope was abandoned in favor of an attempt simply to control it. But the number of reported cases still increases each year. This is partly because the mosquitoes have become immune to insecticides, partly because less insecticide has been purchased as its price has risen, partly because drug prices have also risen, and also because some of the drugs have become less effective as the malaria parasite develops a resistance to them. Furthermore, there has been a decline in the competence of rural medical services to distribute the drugs and to explain their use. If a vaccine that will need to be administered only once or twice during a person's lifetime can be produced, it will avoid the problem associated with the distribution and consumption of regular pills. Until such time the best suggestion that medical science can make is that "people's living habits might be improved."

In the case of another African disease, leprosy, the only cure, which is medically simple, takes ten years to complete. It is very difficult to achieve such prolonged treatment in Africa, and so the number of cases remains constant at seven million, with seventy thousand new sufferers each year. Sleeping sickness, which has been well understood for many years, is actually increasing again and reaching areas of Africa where it has never appeared before, the result of the spread of the tsetse fly, which now flourishes and extends from parts of Ethiopia, Somalia, Rhodesia, and Angola where warfare has interrupted chemical spraying. Warfare also resulted in the reestablishment of tuberculosis on an extensive scale in eastern Nigeria. Four years after the end of the Biafran War, twenty thousand active cases were thought to need treatment in the neighborhood of Enugu alone.

At the same time as medical advances are made, new and baffling fevers are discovered. Africa may be riddled with undiscovered fevers, cases of which have formerly been put down to known diseases with similar symptoms, particularly to malaria, which is everywhere and which has so many symptoms. In the last ten years alone three new fevers have been discovered in central Africa: Lassa fever, the Ebola virus, and green monkey fever. There is no cure for any of them, they have a 50 to 90 percent death rate, and not even the process of infection is understood.[3]

For a new disease to be discovered it is usually necessary for a Northerner to be infected with it in a situation where he can be treated by a sufficiently interested and skillful doctor. When the disease is identified in this way as a threat to Northerners, urgent action may suddenly be taken. The World Health Organization may even mount a special operation if there seems to be any danger of the disease's spreading out of Africa.

But for the Africans who have to risk these conditions of life every day the application of scientific technology is largely unknown. They are underdeveloped, and it is underdevelopment that saves their lives. Their main hope of surviving malaria is to become infected by it and to acquire an immunity by surviving the infection. However brutal, however imperfect, it is their best chance of life. If they fail to contract a natural immunity, all but the tiny privileged minority, who have access to drugs, will die. The power of an epidemic begins to falter only when the great mass of a community has succumbed to it. Disease is the best defense against disease. No form of medical immunization in Africa (smallpox excepted) offers such effective protection as experience of the disease itself. By destroying natural immunity to malaria among Africans, Northern medicine substitutes dependence on its own pills and vaccines. If that dependence were ever to become widespread, and natural immunity to be destroyed, the people of Africa would be incapable of withstanding even the threat of withdrawal of the medicine, unless they were prepared to risk a calamity that would far outweigh the slave trade in its destructive effects on their society.

Faced with the failure of Northern medicine in caring for the health of the majority of African people, the World Health Organization steeled itself into making an astonishing about-face in 1976. It announced that "village healers" would in the future be encouraged to integrate themselves into rural health services. "Witch doctors," of course, were not to be encouraged, and the use of "spells and superstition" was to be replaced by sound principles. The WHO thought that it could draw a distinction between African midwifery, bonesetting, and herbal cures (which have long been offered a grudging respect by science) and "primitive superstition." (In a few cases the North was even prepared to concede that the traditional African treatment was superior. Scientific medicine, for instance, is able to control diabetes with the use of insulin, but witch doctors in Sierra Leone, Ghana, and Nigeria all recognize the symptoms of diabetes and are not only able to control the disease but can frequently cure it.) But the process of acknowledgment, once started, had to go much further. Within a year the World Health Organization, admitting defeat, had issued a much more radical statement which implied a complete redefinition of its theory of medicine. Since 90 percent of Africa's rural population still primarily relied on "witch doctors" for the care of their health, these would in future be given the same status as scientifically trained practitioners. Otherwise, said the director general of the WHO, "the target of achieving health care for all by the end of the century could not be attained."

And so by a magical stroke of the pen in 1977, 90 percent of the African population suddenly found that they were benefiting from competent medical attention, just as they had always suspected. In Zambia witch doctors were given professional status. In Lagos there was to be a joint teaching hospital for witch doctors and M.D.'s. The decisive factor, according to the WHO, had been the refusal of Africa's own medical scientists to practice their profession in their own countries. Modern medicine had expelled itself.

The usual explanation for the failure of scientific medicine in Africa today is a social one. All would be well, it

is said, if there were only new drains or better training
in hygiene.

But an important part of the reason for this failure
must lie in the strength of the rival systems, which are
based on the surviving power of traditional African
spirituality. For a demonstration of this power among
the most sophisticated and the least sophisticated people,
it is only necessary to attend the weekly wrestling
match in Dakar. The arena is a small enclosure shaded
by the high wall of the soccer stadium. From the marks
on the ground one can see that it is usually intended for
basketball, but a large sandpit has been poured into the
middle of the concrete pitch to convert it into a wrestling
ground. As one approaches the arena, there is the sound
of drumming, and when one takes a seat on the concrete
benches, the drumming rattles around the enclosure and
rebounds off the basketball scoreboard. It is so hard
and high that it passes through the concrete benches and
around one's head and shivers out through the more sensitive edges of the teeth. For a Northerner the drumming
has an urgency which is immediately captivating. But for
the African audience of devotees—men and women, cool
and chiefly aware of the minor details of each other's
appearance, the Gauloise at just that angle in the corner
of the mouth, the ash growing longer and longer, the
smoke wisping back along the paper and up into the eyes,
the complete determination not to handle the cigarette—
the drumming seems to be no more than taped music in
a supermarket, something one has to make a conscious
effort to hear. There is nothing studied about this torpor;
the audience must listen to a vast amount of drumming
before they are moved by it. And as the drummers prance
back and forth on the edge of the crowd and the preliminary events are prepared, the point of popular stimu-
lation seems to be some way off.

The first events are between boy wrestlers or light-
weights. For an hour, while the seats fill up, the wrestlers

stalk backward and forward past the drummers. The more prominent are accompanied in their pacing by one or two companions, who keep step in a casual and unmilitary manner. The most noticeable thing about the wrestlers is the number of charms they wear. They have strips of cloth bound to their heads and little pouches on strings attached to the neck or wrist. Up and down they go in the sun, the sweat turning their track suits blotchy, and each time they turn the wrestler and his companions do it in rhythm, ducking their heads and twisting from side to side, like racing swimmers at the end of a length. Slowly the drumming increases in strength and speed, and so, slowly, does the response to it. Near the drummers a man, apparently wearing a pair of white woolen pajama trousers, is leaping up and down. For nearly a minute he manages to spend more time off the ground than on it, or gives the impression of this feat by his conspicuous activity in flight and the way he distracts attention from his occasional landings. When the performance is complete, he flexes his biceps and chassés daintily around. Then he climbs back into his mohair suit and rejoins the appreciative crowd.

He was not part of the official program.

As the time approaches for the show, the smaller wrestlers fall back and leave the edge of the arena to the four main participants. One of them, a tall, slim boy, sweats through his hair, the impression being one of foaming snow. The chief wrestler of the day avoids this exhibitionism by pouring beer over his head and shoulders while on the march. To get the maximum benefit, he fizzes it up with his thumb over the bottle before directing the explosion straight onto his thrown-back face. The parties of wrestlers and supporters have continually to cross each other's paths, but even their order of priority is part of a ritual. They never obstruct each other or even break step to avoid doing so.

The champion's opponent, the man with the foaming

hair, gives the strongest impression of faith. He carries
a long, twisted animal horn and holds a very long twig
in his mouth to chew. He also has the longest charm
ribbons, which stream behind him in his march. Once or
twice, when he thinks he can catch his opponent's eye, he
pauses and points the horn at the larger man, crouching
behind it and muttering. Then he has to hurry on to
catch up with his companions, who, despite their subordinate status, do not check their progress in the interests of his dignity. This they maintain most effectively
by ignoring the incident, holding the pace, stepping out,
as though he were still between them, in their Wee Willie
Winkie nightcaps and knitted woolen sweaters, through
the prostrating heat of late afternoon.

The wrestling, when it commences, is almost per-
functory. The two men circle in the middle of the sand,
facing each other in a half crouch and flapping their
hands in front of them with limp wrists. Then they rush
at each other and lock into a grip. They push for a
while, one sometimes tries to trip the other, and then
with a twist they collapse onto the ground, and the man
lying on top is the winner. When they get up, the loser
is covered in sand, which is caked onto his moist back,
while the winner is appropriately unmarked.

But the real sense of struggle comes before the fight
begins. As the time approaches for a bout, there is much
discussion between the striding wrestlers and their witches,
the personal spiritual advisers who sit cross-legged at the
front of the crowd. These men send out the bottles of
beer for pouring over the head and the amulets and
beads for stringing from the body, and they do the
important business with the sandals and the sand. The
seconds carry scoopfuls of sand from the arena to
the witches and return with a pair of sandals, which are
sometimes exchanged for those the wrestlers are wearing.
Then, when the wrestler steps into the pit, it is a matter
of great thought as to when he will step out of his

sandals and what pattern the second will describe with them on the sandpit before running backward to the witch, dragging the sandals along the ground. Sometimes in a difficult case the second will even approach the opposing wrestler and run rings around him with the sandals or clap the soles together in his sight, adopting an insolent and provocative pose to do so. After these spiritual duels the fight itself appears almost incidental. Nobody watching the feverish consultations between wrestler and witch could doubt the power of belief in the strength of the charms or query the practical uses of magic. By watching the activities of the seconds and the relative preoccupation of the two wrestlers, one can even see which of them is the more spooked by the prospect of battle. Invariably the more anxious man loses. Possibly, as the wrestlers become more skillful, the value of magic recedes and is replaced by an individual self-confidence; but even between champions, in a closely matched contest the psychological aspect is important, and it is the responsibility of the witches, through the manipulation of charms and spells, to manage this to their clients' best advantage.

In the main match of that particular afternoon the magical preliminaries were extended, and the challenger for some time refused even to leave the ringside until the liturgy of sandals and sand had been repeated several times. He was a defeated man from then on, and the fact that the champion was much bigger than he seemed of little importance beside the challenger's inability to trust to the powers of his witch. For a short time, after the contest began, he struggled, and several times, showing superior skill, he managed to slip past the champion's defense and hook one leg behind his opponent's knee. Even then, he was too light to twist the champion off-balance, and the matter was eventually settled when the champion simply moved forward and fell on him head to toe, to lie there for an ungenerous period of time.

This event was celebrated without restraint by the crowd. The champion was mobbed, the drumming reached a new crescendo, the victorious seconds were loaded with favors, the challenger was mocked on his way home, and in the crowd's release the magic, too, was dispersed.

Whether in healing or wrestling or any other aspect of life, evidence of the surviving strength of magic is presented every day all over Africa. The papers report such events as the stoning of an old man's hut by spirits, without mockery or skepticism. In an industrial town in Nigeria in 1975 an animist procession was held to appease the gods. Some soldiers tried to push their way through, a scuffle broke out, and one of the masked dancers was unmasked. For this offense those following the masquerade put a spell on the offender, who collapsed. His comrades believed him dead, and the whole military garrison went on a rampage. The town's market was set on fire, forty houses were destroyed, and the population began to flee. Eventually the bewitched man recovered, and order could be restored.

In northern Nigeria a rumor started that a secret society was at work which was determined to afflict its victims with impotence, worked by a simple touch on the shoulder or the hand. Within two weeks fourteen people had been beaten to death in public, each one a stranger in a crowded place who had brushed against someone in the crowd. To stop the panic from spreading, the Nigerian army was ordered to shoot on sight any people threatening to take the law into their own hands, and there was a booming trade in antidotes to the touch of the brotherhood.

Animism grew in the rain forests, and it survives just as the forests do. But belief in the religion of spirits is not confined to the people who live in the forest or even to the unsophisticated or uneducated townspeople. Chief Beyioku is a prominent Nigerian trade union leader and a former senator of the federation. He has always practiced an animist religion, that of Ifa, the oracle god. "It is sad that many Africans have allowed the religion of other races to outshine their own," he says. "If we embrace the religion of our forebears in full and without hypocrisy, things will be better for us. A man who is not true to himself is like a body without a soul. We practice Christianity and Islam in public, but we don't believe in them absolutely. The moment we experience any setback, we fall back on our own ancient religions in secret." The chief recently had a leg amputated after a spell had been put on him by his political enemies in Lagos State. He considers that if he had been less lax about his religious observance, this would not have happened.

The fiercest opposition to animism was provided by the Christian churches, but they no longer approach the subject with the uniform disapproval of old. Instead, under African leadership, the churches have become more responsive to African influence.

In Ghana Anglicans became concerned that too many orthodox Christians were being seduced by the freewheeling "spiritualist" sects and that there was a consequent need to Africanize the Anglican liturgy. Cultural advice is accordingly being taken on how to incorporate song, dance, and drums into the Book of Common Prayer.[4] The elaborate funeral services of West Africa, which incorporate both Christian and pagan rites, represent virtually a fused religion. And in the pagan need to replenish the graves of the dead until the individuality of the African soul is lost amid the ancestors there is a shadow of Christian belief.

Against this gathering darkness the Christian churches can offer only a dimmer light. All along the west coast the colonial stones are crumbling. The bells still ring in the church tower; the doors still lock; the furnishings and candles remain undisturbed. But the face of the wooden statue to Saint Teresa of Lisieux has becomed pitted beneath the veil, transforming the Norman maiden into a black girl. And in the old French church on the slave island of Gorée, the steel money boxes set into stone pillars, "For the Holy Virgin," "For the Poor," "For the Suffering Souls in Purgatory"—even that one—are empty. In an ecumenical age the mission fathers whose main task is to secure conversions seem tired and lost. "We gave up another village last month," said one Holy Ghost father, who had become embarrassed even by the name of his order. "I don't know why really. None of us much wanted to go there. And in fifty years we had made little progress. I hear they've all gone back to animism since we left, even the verger. And there are juju shrines in the clearing where we built the church. They sacrifice animals there now, and the pregnant girls won't sit under the trees in case their child be born misshapen."

Meanwhile, Bishop Peter Sarpong, the Catholic bishop of Kumasi in Ghana, has pointed out that Africans can see no meaning in the preacher's stole, which conveys no impression of authority. The appropriate symbol which he suggests for the African Catholic priest would be the sword. "In Africa," said the bishop, "when a chief sends a message without holding a sword, he does not have to be obeyed."

The emphasis on temporal power is appropriate. Animism is not hindered by any theological distinctions between Caesar and God. Freed from the restraints imposed by the colonial administrations, traditional religious beliefs are able to resume their overt political role. President Mobutu of Zaire first banished the head of the Catholic Church and made it an offense for his people to use each other's Christian names. Then he invited the cardinal back and honored him with the Order of the Leopard, the country's highest award. The cardinal could hardly refuse it, despite its conscious reference to the animist secret society of that name which the president was believed to have joined and to which he too would now, by most of his flock, be thought to belong. For those Zairean converts the Christian invasion will have passed on. The church has succumbed to patience, and its beliefs have been assimilated by the older spirituality.

For better or worse, magic has won, and in the case of both religion and medicine the African practices that flourished before the colonial period now seem to have prevailed. Whether they have been opposed by Northern dogmatism, as in the case of medicine, or by Northern flexibility, as in the case of Christianity, it has made no difference. African tradition has proved too strong for Northern thought. If one were to look for a simple reason why this should be so, the real failure in both religion and medicine may be that both lack the contagious drama of their African equivalents. Reflecting on the imposition of modern knowledge on Africans, Karen Blixen wrote: "For they had our civilisation presented to them piecemeal, like incoherent parts of a mechanism which they had never seen functioning, and the functioning of which they could not on their own imagine. We had been transforming, to them, Rite into Routine. What by now most of all they feared from our hands was boredom, and on being taken into hospital they may well have felt that they were in good earnest being taken in to die from boredom." And die they did; on being threatened with the hospital, Karen Blixen's Kikuyu workers "died before my eyes, as Africans will."[5]

In view of that, it might be that the disorderly and unhygienic interior of the urban hospital is even an improvement on the original scheme since it has a markedly therapeutic effect on its African patients, who can there dispose themselves and their families as comfortably as though they were in the marketplace and then deploy those imaginative powers which are demanded by their traditional healing methods and which might refuse to function altogether in the clinical sterility of a Northern place of healing.

If this is so, it may be enough to account for the peculiar loss of concentration which affects so many African physicians who have to work under these conditions and who have to reconcile the intuitive methods of their people with the reasoned dogma of the scientific approach. The healing process in Africa manifestly contains numerous elements which fly in the face of scientific teachings, but what is merely manifest in experience cannot always be accommodated by the North's revealed truth.

When the disciples of this revelation, the representatives of the multinational baby milk companies, dress up their salesgirls as nurses and market their powder, knowing that many of those who buy it will mix it too weakly and with polluted water, the failings of the Northern doctrine become obvious. But there is no evidence that this lethal higher quackery is being overcome or that the arrogance is leaving the assumptions of medical scientists when they are faced with Africa. For an example, they might recall an earlier disciple who was discredited: Albert Schweitzer—the doctor whose efforts in the Congo for lepers and those suffering from sleeping sickness were ridiculed after sixty years by certain investigators who thought that they perceived a number of irregularities in the medical arrangements he had made at his mission hospital.

Since Schweitzer's death in 1965 his hospital has been pulled down and rebuilt because it lacked electricity and was considered unhygienic. The fact that Schweitzer, after a lifetime of working in Africa, had chosen these conditions was regarded as less important than the fact that his hospital differed somewhat from such an installation in Europe. The direct effect of the "exposure" of Schweitzer as an eccentric or poseur was that the government of Gabon, which had earlier given him the minimal support, mainly lack of interference, which he needed, became embarrassed by him, and as a result, his hospital very nearly had to close. Finally, with considerable help from America and Switzerland, it managed to stay open, but only at the price of being completely overhauled so that it resembled every other development hospital in Africa, with teams of visiting doctors and a stock of twenty million refrigerated pharmaceuticals, each item certainly approved by the International Federation of Pharmaceutical Manufacturers.

Two exceptions have been made to the familiar modern pattern. The hospital's leper colony still grows cassava for all the patients. For some years now cassava has been known to have little nutritional value, and it is appropriate that those who believe that they have so improved on the old doctor's achievement should have chosen to preserve a detail which, in the light of more recent knowledge, might have been altered.

Also, accommodation is still provided for one relative of each patient, the condition Schweitzer found essential if his hospital was to have any patients at all. Otherwise, Schweitzer's principle of "reverence for life," an intuitive preview of recent ecological arguments, has been diluted until it is indistinguishable from routine professional concern.

All that is left of Schweitzer are his room—now a museum, with his spectacles and letters neatly preserved in the position he left them—and, of course, his face, which continues to dwell at Lambaréné, adorning the head of the French administrator who succeeded him and who has cultivated an appearance strikingly resembling that of his mentor. But the mind is different, and the familiar features are as empty of Schweitzer's inspiration as his old spectacles are of their original eyes.

And so the work of one remarkable man who was prepared to leave a prominent career in Europe as a musician and theologian and go to Africa, and learn from it, is drowned in the conventional superiority of licensed scientific wisdom. The anonymous young doctors at Lambaréné today have climbed back onto the sterilized plinth which the old doctor had the vision to vacate. The only sustained attempt ever made to reconcile the medical skill of the North with the needs of Africa can be said to have failed.

NOTES

1. In October 1977 the World Health Organization drew up a short list of two hundred drugs that were effective, indispensable, and cheap. The list was intended to assist those poor countries which found that they could no longer afford to spend up to 40 percent of their health budget on imported pharmaceuticals. The International Federation of Pharmaceutical Manufacturers opposed the circulation of this list on the grounds that "the concept is unacceptable."

2. Although in the last case it is interesting to remember that Mungo Park recorded "that the Negroes on the Gambia practise inoculation" against it. In 1976 the World Health Organization believed that it was on the verge of eradicating smallpox throughout the world. The last area where it was reported was in the area of the Ethiopian-Somali border, and for seven months no new cases were found. Then in Mogadishu one man caught the disease. Before he could be stopped, he had set out toward Ethiopia in a family group of eleven. When health officials traced the group and isolated them in two small huts in a remote part of Ethiopia, the man himself had disappeared, but four of his children had caught smallpox. Behind him he left a trail of cases, more than one thousand, in the nomadic areas of Kenya, Somalia, and Ethiopia. The health authorities still believed that they could eradicate the disease within six months; they had made many false claims to have done so in the past, but they were confident that this would be the last. In August, one month before their deadline, the Ethiopia-Somali war broke out, and all efforts had to be abandoned. In October 1977 further deaths from smallpox were reported from southern Somalia, and in August 1978 additional cases were reported among Ethiopian refugees fleeing to the Sudan from the war in Eritrea. The WHO continued to claim that "smallpox had been eradicated," although this

claim ignored the evidence that a variant of monkeypox, known as whitepox, could infect humans with fatal results.

3. A fourth unidentified virus fever was reported from Lake Baringo in central Kenya in October 1977.

4. Some Ghanaian Christians are aware of the humorous aspects of this development. In Accra the mammy wagons, the small buses that bring people into town, carry painted slogans. Part of the message is on the front of the vehicle, and part on the back, for example: "No Woman"—"No Sorrow." One teasing driver has written "Monotheism?" on the front; the back of his car says "Maybe."

5. *Shadows on the Grass.*

CONCLUSION

YOU STILL EXIST!

So Geographers in *Afric*-Maps
With Savage-Pictures fill their Gaps;
And o'er unhabitable Downs
Place Elephants for want of Towns.

Jonathan Swift, *On Poetry*

Happy is the country that has no geography.

Saki, *The Unbearable Bassington*

Every night in the compound you hear them raising the
hue and cry, and you know they're beating someone to
death outside. . . . You should either stay away, or you
should go among them with a whip in your hand. Anything in between is ridiculous.

V. S. Naipaul, *In a Free State*

When the exiles of Kampala were reunited in the streets
of the city after the fall of the Amin regime, they greeted
each other in their delight with the phrase "You still exist!"
Under Amin's rule so many of the educated people of
Uganda had disappeared that those who had not seen
each other for some time simply presumed the other's
death. In eight years one of the most developed societies
in Africa had been dispersed, and the pattern of a
century had unraveled.

The city to which the exiles returned was a sad sight.
Glass from the shop windows was ankle-deep in the roadway. Offices, shops, and factories were wrecked. Documents and equipment lay scattered through the streets.
This damage had not been caused by the battle for

Kampala; very little fighting had taken place there. But when the Tanzanian soldiers entered the deserted capital, they were surprised to find that, contrary to reports, it was stocked with valuable goods. Liberators and liberated united at once, and within three days the city had been thoroughly plundered. The City Provisions Mart on Main Street lost £20,000 ($40,000) in food and household goods within a few hours. The New Singo Drapery was looted of £250,000 ($500,000) worth of clothing. All over the city, premises were stripped of furniture and telephones and typewriters and electrical goods and liquor. The government warehouses were found to contain coffee, rice, salt, and vegetable oils. In one day soldiers and Kampalans carried away thirty thousand sacks of sugar weighing 125 pounds each. The Ugandan economy had not, after all, collapsed under Amin's rule; instead, it had been diverted. Barter had replaced the devalued coinage of the national bank. Hoarding, which is practiced all over Africa, had flourished. And although imported goods had become scarce, they had not disappeared completely; indeed, they were more generally available than was the case in such countries as Guinea or Mali or most of Zaire.

Whatever had been happening to Uganda under Amin was different from what the world had been led to believe. "What Amin failed to destroy in eight years the people of Kampala accomplished in three days," said one shopkeeper. Another man, watching people greeting the Tanzanian army, remembered that the crowds had been bigger and had cheered louder when Major General Amin overthrew Dr. Milton Obote.

When Amin came to power in January 1971, there was widespread rejoicing in Kampala. Obote had become highly unpopular. At the time everyone seemed happy. A reporter in Kenya who tried to telephone Amin on the night of the coup was told by a voice on the end of the line, "The boss is out. Celebrating." And in the background he could hear the chink of ice and laughter. Amin brought with him an air of returning normality after the oppression and corruption of the previous regime. The day after he came to power he released the political prisoners. One of them, an army captain, gave details of how he had been tortured by the police. He sat beside the head of the plainclothes squad at a press conference, and turning to Inspector Hassan, who had been responsible for his mistreatment, he looked at him and said, "I wish I could be allowed to call Hassan a devil, but I cannot . . . I am a Christian." This spirit of forgiveness was widely extolled. There were to be no vendettas.

Shortly afterward Amin announced that he would arrange a state funeral for the late kabaka of Buganda, the hereditary leader of the people who live in and around Kampala. The kabaka—or King Freddie, or Sir Edward Mutesa—the first president of modern Uganda, was remembered as a slight, elegant figure, perfectly suited in appearance to his youthful role as a second lieutenant in the Grenadier Guards. But he had died an exile from the Obote regime, in the East End slums of London, aged forty. The verdict at the inquest was "death by alcoholic poisoning," and the Bagandan people believed that he had been slipped neat alcohol while entertaining a beautiful witch who was on a secret mission from Uganda. The state funeral made Amin very popular with the Bagandans. They hawked calendars bearing the kabaka's picture around the streets, and the peddlers sitting on the sidewalks made little shrines around his image and increased the sale of their matches and shoelaces. But the hereditary tribal kingships were not restored, and the kabaka's heir went to England for his education; under the Amin regime the royal palace, where King Freddie had been reburied, became a tourist attraction. As such, amid all the disturbances and turmoil that were to follow, it remained one of the quietest places in Kampala.

To reach the palace, one drove through a pleasant suburb of the city and then to the top of a hill where an enormous stockade surrounded several lofty huts. Despite the scale of these buildings, they were constructed entirely from vegetation. When the first European explorer, John Hanning Speke, penetrated the kingdom of Buganda in 1860 in his search for the source of the Nile, he depended for his life on the friendship of Kabaka Mutesa I, great-grandfather of the chic guards officer. Speke was taken to the stockade and was relieved to find that in the center of Africa there was an organized and cultivated society. He offered gifts to the kabaka, and after some months he was given permission to proceed with his journey. Speke's gifts still stand in the palace, in the same hut where the kabakas lie buried. The small brass cannon is mildewed now, and the writing desk and two flimsy chairs are falling to pieces as irretrievably as the stuffed leopard which was once a royal pet. But unlike the kingdom of Buganda, and the British colony that was a consequence of Speke's journey, and the first republic of independent Uganda, and Amin's second republic, the gifts still stand—beneath the shelter of the vegetable roof.

In Amin's time the tomb was attended by seven old ladies who described themselves as the widows of various former kings. They squatted morosely at the side of the largest hut, unobserved for a while by the occasional visitors who came in blinking from the heat of the deserted compound. Sometimes a party of Bulgarian technicians passed through, or a group of North Korean gym instructors, stragglers from the never-ending tea party of international friendship. There was a tattered visitors' book containing one name, "Stokely Carmichael of Conakry, Guinea," which stirred somewhere in the memory. The old ladies were the only people who were allowed to pass behind the bark-cloth curtain that concealed the remains of the kings. They spent the time plaiting rush mats, and when visitors came, they pushed forward wooden bowls, indicating that they would accept any coins that were thrown in. The oldest widow had given up making mats. She lay flat on the floor with her head twisted back in such a way that her bright eyes could observe everything from above her eyebrows and her tight gray curls. She cackled at the awkwardness of the people trying to kneel by King Freddie's grave. But her amusement did not disturb her visitors. There was no triumph in it. The stockade remained a refuge from the disquiet outside.

The silence of the royal palace was largely accounted for by the collapse of the Ugandan tourist industry. The original Amin, the cheerful, no-nonsense army officer, was a British invention. But as the years passed and the business of running a modern state in Africa became steadily more difficult for Amin and his colleagues, there was no visible sign of British or any other Northern influence.[1] Little that the government did had the intended effect. In 1974 an attempt was made to revive tourism as a useful source of foreign currency. A large party of East African travel agents were flown to Kampala from Nairobi. As they were ushered into the airport's VIP lounge for an official welcome, they met the head of the Ugandan Tourist Office being marched under armed escort to the plane which they had just left. He had come to the airport to greet them but had found, instead, that he was being deported. Amin had just discovered that an Englishman was running the tourist office. Uganda's tourist revival ended abruptly.[2]

Outside Kampala, life went on for much of the time as usual. The dispensaries ran out of supplies, the schools deteriorated, but subsistence agriculture continued to provide enough food for everyone. The organized tribal massacres of the early years were succeeded by a more casual terrorism. The extent of this persecution was difficult to judge at the time. Northern observers, like Swift's geographers, filled their gaps not only with elephants but with several karkadans, and many of their atrocity stories turned out to be untrue. A massacre of hundreds of students on the university campus in 1976 which was reported all over the world never took place at all.[3] Seven judges supposedly arrested in July 1977 never left their work. A Ugandan Olympic runner was reported to have been abducted and tortured. He had spent the day in question training on the Kampala golf course. "Eyewitnesses" claimed to have seen a British engineer hammered to death in September 1977. He was later released from prison and decided to stay on in the country.

Sometimes the Northern press just invented news from Uganda. When the foreign minister, Princess Elizabeth of Toro, was dismissed and in fear of her life, one British newspaper printed a nude picture of her and speculated on her chances of survival. Since Amin's disapproval of her had been based on a (completely false) charge of public immorality, the publication of the photograph was unlikely to assist her plight. Fortunately she escaped from Uganda and successfully sued the paper in question.[4] The photograph had been of someone else. The economic estimates were equally unreliable. In February 1977, when the British press reported that Uganda was on the verge of bankruptcy as a result of problems in the coffee industry, the United States was buying one-third of the crop for $150 million, and twice as much was raised in sales to other parts of the world. The year 1977 was a good year for Ugandan coffee, not one of bankruptcy.

In retrospect, what seems to have happened was that the members of the ruling Defense Council divided the country up into fiefs, which they plundered as their need arose. For the villagers taxes were replaced by "extortion," or taxes, trade became known as "smuggling," or trade, and the rule of central government was succeeded by the tranquillity of being for the most part forgotten in the unmapped interior. Sometimes the people were even able to resist the demands that were made. Members of the secret police were several times reported to have been beaten or speared to death when attempting to rob the supposedly fatalistic villagers.

The deterioration of the "State" was mainly confined to the towns and, in particular, to Kampala. But even here life proceeded for much of the time as normal. Outside the Grand Hotel a monument inscribed "In memory of the glorious reign of His Majesty King George V, 1910–1936" stood intact in the park. Amin changed the name of the Grand Hotel because "it sounded too British." But he renamed it the Imperial. When a military policeman vaulted over a bank counter to take away a teller at gunpoint, everyone tried to look as if a legal arrest had been made. There was still a small expatriate community, mainly diplomats and businessmen who were immune from the growing deprivation. At first glance many shop windows looked as if they were full of genuine goods. Then, after a while, one noticed that some of them were just packed with cardboard replicas, which were gathering dust like props on a disused film set. A gun shop displayed a faded sign stating that it was an authorized Winchester dealer, with a painting of a galloping cowboy in chaps. Inside, it could supply a .375 rifle at once, but "there is no ammo. It is coming." On the wall behind the counter the shopkeeper had pasted up a yellowing newspaper clipping. It urged members of the public to report any suspicious-looking soldiers to the Public Safety Unit and gave a phone number. The shopkeeper was unlikely to use this number whatever he saw. The Public Safety Unit consisted of the people who would return the bodies of men who had been murdered to their families, on payments of up to $1,000.

The minor irritations of this life were accepted philosophically by most visitors, who were frequently reminded that for many of the city's population the Amin regime could be even more disagreeable. At the hotel, people asked each other about a commotion in the night and two piercing screams in the garden. The manager, when consulted, said that it was "just skylarking." But he lacked conviction. He was a tall, gentle man, a Muganda, who expressed an equal distress at everything: the lack of bread, the discourtesies of his staff (some of whom also worked for Amin's secret police), or a scream in the night.

One day there was another drama. In the middle of the afternoon a young man lying on his face in the hotel pool started to drown. His friends drew back, and the crowd of swimmers cleared a little, leaving the muscular body to bob around, unattended, in the middle. On the edge of the pool people chattered and played more quietly than before. No one looked at the body, face down on the surface. The pool waiter was the only man with a certificate in first aid, and he was not present. No one liked to disturb the foreigners asleep on couches or preoccupied under striped umbrellas. A number of diplomats from the Yugoslav Embassy had started a card school. A group of Koreans were sucking warm Coke (the hotel refrigerator had broken down again). Two telecommunication engineers from Japan were reading *Beano* and rubbing each other attentively with sun oil. Eventually, when only the rippling of the water could be heard, the silence attracted the attention of one of the diplomats.

Immediately he leaped into the pool, followed by the card school, and they dragged the dying man to the side. The friends of the casualty gathered in an interested circle, while four Yugoslavs, one on each limb, waggled the motionless body to and fro according to a system of their own invention. The pool waiter arrived and, seeing that these efforts were having no visible effect, diffidently suggested the kiss of life. The suggestion was brushed aside, and the waiter resumed the status of an African— that is, of a bystander. A number of people agreed to fetch an ambulance. One man began to entertain the crowd with a graphic imitation of his friend's attempts to breathe.

Unexpectedly the corpse sat up, and the Yugoslavs sent the waiter to fetch a brandy. "But who will pay for it? But is it to be a single or a double?" The waiter reluctantly left. Then two burly men in sky blue trousers and white vests and gleaming army boots walked in. They were not the ambulance crew; they were the fire brigade. A misunderstanding. The revived corpse collapsed again. After five minutes the waiter returned to say that as it was not yet 5:00 P.M., under General Amin's new Moslem licensing laws the bar was still closed, and no brandy could be purchased. The chief Yugoslav, by now on the point of nervous crisis, threw up his arms, dropped the unconscious man's leg with a thump, and returned to his game of cards. Once more the corpse revived. The pool filled up with children in rubber rings; the firemen departed. Slowly the friends of the survivor approached him. They seemed surprised, as though they were greeting someone who had been far away and was no longer familiar. They had successfully prepared themselves to accept the fact of his death.

In the corridor leading to the pool the hotel manager repeated his concern. There would be a brandy on the house. He was most grateful to the Yugoslavs. There was to be no more fuss. Nothing to attract attention. Only the day before, one of his professional colleagues, the manager of a rival hotel which was owned by a member of the Defense Council, had been taken away by a party of soldiers. He would not be seen again. In the face of all this uncertainty the manager tried to keep the hotel going. He instructed his staff to be as helpful as possible. The telephone operator interpreted this with exceptional vigor. After forgetting to make a morning call to one of the guests, he apologized. "It will not happen again," he said. "If it happens again, you may beat me completely."

"All right," the guest replied. "I will."

"Yes, yes," said the telephonist, "you can."

There may have been no bread in Kampala, but there was still a band. Its presence ensured the hotel's popularity in the evenings. It was very popular with Amin's "intelligence officers," the men from the Public Safety Unit, or "the Economic Intelligence Unit," or the "Bureau of State Research." They danced decorously to the quickstep or fox-trot with their subdued companions. They looked like a party of businessmen taking their secretaries out for a spree. In the modern state, mass murder also has to be organized from an office. The band was led by a singer who stood very straight, her hands folded in front of her in the placid posture of a chorister. She wore a printed frock with a high embroidered bodice and puffed-out epaulets that could have been designed only by the wife of a Christian missionary. The singer delivered "Blue Moon" and "Where Have All the Flowers Gone?" in a strong, clear voice. In the second song the line "Where have all the soldiers gone?" was well received. "In this country," said a Tanzanian visitor, "what a question! Sing it again." And the "intelligence men" at the next table, few of whom spoke much English, were roused to the same enthusiasm. Later the singer came and sat beside the Tanzanian, and they tried not to talk about Uganda. She wore a rosary around her wrist, and her hair was twisted into a shiny coronet. "Are you a Catholic?" she asked the Tanzanian.

"Of course not," he said. "I am a parasitologist."

She sighed. "It is so hard to be good, even for me. I try so hard. I always go to church. But I am tempted. There are so many temptations."

The parasitologist became more cheerful. He had heard on the East African medical grapevine that "the

Big Man" had venereal disease and was suffering from
general paralysis of the insane. This diagnosis was a great
comfort to him. If it was correct, the president might not
have very long to live. Furthermore, he was no longer
such an embarrassment to everybody; he was merely an
aberration. If Amin was a lunatic, there was hope for the
rest of us.[5] Encouraged by his mood, the singer also
brightened up; maybe things would improve; maybe she
could leave the country and go to work for Miriam
Makeba. It had been different in the old days. Her father
had been influential before the white men left. "He was a
police officer," she said. "And the white men liked him
very much." She chattered on without a thought for the
listening intelligence squad at the next table. She was protected by the memory of her old happiness. It was the
dejected group of burly eavesdroppers that seemed in
need of a sympathetic word.

While his reign lasted, the man who presided over this
shambles was not abominated by the rest of Africa, as
Northern observers would have liked to report. When
Amin attended meetings of African leaders, he was feted.
There was a perverse pride in his reputation. Even a
tyrant, if he is notorious enough, can be a source of pride
on a continent with so long an experience of dependency.
Amin did not have to spend years of his life out of the
country, lecturing through damp London winters to tiny
socialist audiences who had never been nearer to Africa
than the London Zoo. He was never associated with the
colonial elite and rose no higher than *effendi* or master
sergeant in a British colonial regiment. He always seemed
too much like the typical Ugandan to be qualified to rule
Uganda. When he came to power, this was his great
advantage. And as his reputation as an irresponsible international citizen grew, so did his popularity. An irresponsible African leader causes the North much public embarrassment, and Africans admired and even respected him
for this, particularly if they did not have to deal with his

brutal regime. The more the North tried to persuade more malleable African leaders to denounce Amin in public, the more obvious it became that the motives behind such pressure were chiefly self-serving. When *Tass,* which never reported the atrocities of Amin's Russian-trained army, criticized America for trying to intimidate Amin, it was being no more hypocritical than the British newspapers, which grew frantic for a week over the murder of an elderly English lady, Mrs. Dora Bloch— but devoted one paragraph to the murder of Jimmy Parma, the Ugandan press photographer who lost his life in reporting the discovery of Mrs. Bloch's body. The double standard did not pass unnoticed in Africa.

The same point was underlined when Amin took a British hostage, a teacher called Dennis Hills, on a trumped-up charge as a way of reopening negotiations with Britain for the sale of arms and the resumption of trade. To the people of Kampala who had suffered the disappearance or death of thousands of their fellows, the arrival of the British foreign secretary on his mercy mission to free Mr. Hills was not an edifying moment. But the British had to respond to Amin's threats in order to avoid the public loss of face which would have followed the execution of Mr. Hills. The French did the same for Mme. Claustre in Chad. The North regards each of its citizens in Africa as a potential hostage because the loss of even one of them challenges the Northern assumption of control.

By issuing such a challenge, Amin became an African hero. He was the representative of a tradition of leadership which, in symbolic terms at least, was thoroughly African. The worst the North could say about the flamboyant coronation of a similar leader, Emperor Bokassa, was expressed by an official of the World Bank, who feared that it would "discourage the industrialized nations from developing Africa." Bokassa made the World Bank's job more difficult. For many Africans that was the most satisfactory thing about him. By rejecting Northern values and standards, Africa could also begin to reject the daily process of Northern direction. It found a refuge in our disapproval.

In Kampala, when Amin arrived at a meeting, the numberless possibilities of what he might say induced an atmosphere of fantasy. He was a very large man with a soft voice. People strained to see what he was wearing. If it was camouflage or a grotesquely bemedaled military uniform, there might be reason for apprehension. But if he had chosen the suit from Savile Row, with club tie and dove gray silk shirt, he was likely to be feeling more self-confident and good-humored. His most threatening effects occurred when he offered reassurance. Amin ended one speech to the terrified elders of the Acholi tribe by saying, "Let those who are in hiding come back. You should not fear at all, but you must be cooperative. Stay well, enjoy yourselves completely. Thank you very much." Within a week, killings had started among the people of that area. Waiting for this treacherous note of reassurance helped dispel the boredom induced by most of his remarks.

If he was addressing an educated audience, there was a particular tension apparent. Amin was very frightened of educated men. He was frightened of looking like a fool in front of them. As he listened to their fluent sentences, he twisted his hands together, and his eyes widened, and he began to sweat. Once he himself spoke he felt better. But it was a brief recovery. If he ended his speech by saying, in his gentlest voice, "There is no fear in Uganda," the whole audience shivered, and leader and people, gazing at each other in fascinated horror, shared a moment of intimacy.

This fear was also shared by members of the ruling Defense Council, such as Lieutenant Colonel Juma Oris. Like Amin, Oris was a Kakwa and a Moslem, and for some years Amin treated him as a favorite son. He called

Amin Effendi, his old military nickname, and he was sometimes singled out to lead the "suicide missions" against
the shadowy hostile armies that crowded his leader's
world. Among the permanent staff in his ministry Oris, in
his turn, inspired great fear. It was dispiriting to see men
who were old enough to be his father, and who regarded
the minister as little more than an illiterate, sitting on
stools outside his office, waiting to be summoned inside to
be abused, if they were fortunate, or dismissed and subsequently hunted to death, if they were not. But Oris too
lived in fear. His clipped manner and polished briefcase
and starched uniform could not keep an ingratiating note
from his laughter when he was talking to someone he
could not bully. And his uneasiness became blatant when
he lifted the phone and held it between his fingertips and
hesitated, before asking to speak to "Effendi."

The chief disadvantage of a reign of terror as a political method is that it is so indiscriminate. At the time
when Colonel Wilson Oryema was murdered in 1977 he
had been one of Amin's longest-serving supporters. On
the day Amin came to power Oryema was inspector general of police, and his approval was so important to Amin
that they were photographed together shaking hands on
the first day of the coup. Oryema became a minister, and
his younger son was sent to West Germany for training
as a military pilot. On the day the boy returned to join
the Ugandan air force he was abducted and shot dead.
But Oryema did not resign. For three more years he
carried on, presiding over the chaos of the Ministry for
Water Resources, until his influence was exhausted. Then
he too was shot. In the police force his place was taken
by Ali Towili, the man who was originally in charge of
the Public Safety Unit. Towili's behavior in public was
more relaxed than that of most other leaders, even
though he found it difficult to get anyone to talk to him. At
a diplomatic reception on meeting a foreign journalist he
once confided that he was very frightened of journalists.

Oh, yes, the idea amused him so much that he had to stop gabbling, take off his glasses, and wipe his eyes. His voice rose to a happy squeak and he clapped his hands and jumped up and down. Then he seized the arm of Colonel Oryema, who was standing beside him, and repeated his joke. "Very frightened! Of journalists!" Everyone laughed loudly. Then Oryema edged away.

The only Ugandan who behaved normally throughout the Amin regime was the Anglican archbishop, a lonely figure with the mannerisms and outlook of an English country parson. His loneliness was understandable. All his life he had followed the religion of England. Now all the Englishmen had left, and he remained, administering a faith that was unknown to the people of his country only a hundred years before.

The Anglican archbishop, when he was able to talk freely, had a tendency to interview his interviewer. "Which denomination do you belong to? Are you not a Christian? Do you not believe in the existence of God? Then I feel sorry for you. Not having a faith to lean on when you are pressed. This must be a trouble to you." His catechism was insistent only in its meaning; its manner was almost humorous.

He would not answer particular questions about politics. Instead, he emphasized the isolation of his church. "You taught us that Christianity is not a parochial thing. It unites people and tribes and nations. That is what we remember when we hear all this talk of 'Africanization.' We need the support of the people in your country more than ever now. We owe much to your country. We need you, and not just your knowledge; we need your fellowship. Most people here know this. What we have become, you made us." There was a degree of diffidence in his statement, as if he, one of those most at risk from the tyranny, still felt the need to apologize for its existence.

* * *

The archbishop's flock, the Christian majority of Uganda,
unrefreshed for the most part by their brethren overseas,
kept up their spirits as best they could. Passing down the
unlit streets of the city at night, one might be surprised
by a motionless group in the shadows. A choir of children
was rehearsing to the waving arms of an expressionless
choirmaster. They sang in a murmur, standing in an unlit
doorway:

> *"Rock of ages, cleft for me,*
> *Let me hide myself in thee."*

From above their heads a neon light had been removed
and the wires dangled onto the paving. There seemed no
reason why they should be doing this on the street and
in the dark. In other doorways men lurked carrying clubs,
guarding empty shops. Nearby two separately wrecked
cars had mounted the pavement. They were valuable, but
they remained unguarded and unmolested. Water bubbled
up from a broken hydrant. The few people around
avoided each other, until a visiting American woman in a
trouser suit was approached by two Ugandan girls of
about fifteen. "Hello," they called, "how are you?" Then
without warning their voices grew loud and shrill. "You.
Trousers are not allowed. We can arrest you. You must
disappear. Now! We can arrest you." They were refer-
ring to a proclamation from Amin about the appearance
of women. Trousers had been banned on the grounds of
Moslem decency. So had Afro wigs. "The President has
learnt from reliable sources that the wigs craved by unsuspecting Ugandan customers were made by the callous
imperialists from human hair mainly collected from the
unfortunate victims of the miserable Vietnam war, thus
turning human tragedy into lucrative commercial enter-
prises. On the home front, wigs have generated a number
of ills. Seldom cleaned, harbouring articles injurious to
life from lice to lizards, Afro-wigs promote health hazards besides making our women look un-African and

artificial." As time passed, and no help came, more and more Ugandan Christians agreed to convert to the relative safety of the Moslem religion.

The archbishop realized what was happening, his church was being dismembered piece by piece, but at first he declined to make a public protest. Then as more and more of his priests were abducted he made his only possible move. In 1977 he signed a statement of protest against "the brutality and murders and the law of the gun." Within a week the archbishop too had been arrested and shot in the mouth in Amin's headquarters. Two years later the Tanzanian army reached Kampala.

After the liberation of Kampala a service of thanksgiving was held in the Anglican cathedral. It was just a hundred years since Christianity had reached Uganda, and the founders of the movement were commemorated on the cathedral walls. There were plaques to "Frederick Jackson, first governor of Uganda . . . much loved," and to "Margaret Wrong . . . servant of God, friend of Africa." Another tablet quoted from the letter of the American explorer Henry Stanley to the *London Daily Telegraph* of November 15, 1875: "Oh that some pious, practical missionary would come here. What a field and harvest ripe for the sickle of civilisation. . . . You need not fear to spend money on such a mission."

Farther upcountry the Tanzanian army had met its first popular resistance. As they entered the northern province, several Tanzanian soldiers died from eating poisoned bananas which they had been given by women of Amin's Kakwa tribe. Ahead of the liberating army there were reports of 100,000 refugees. In its wake there were massacres, as Acholi warriors started to take their revenge on the Kakwa.

Back in Kampala the people who "still existed" had produced a preliminary estimate of the country's needs. According to the new Christian government of Dr. Yusufu Lule (who had gone into exile not under Amin, but under Dr. Obote) $2 billion of aid would be required. In justifying this enormous sum, the new government explained that "everything was much worse than it looked." Fortunately the World Bank was back in town. Within two months Dr. Lule had himself been overthrown by his new colleagues, and the demand for emergency aid had dropped to $100 million. Kampala was once again on the verge of civil war, and the chairman of the Ugandan Law Society said that the situation was "worse than under Amin." He and various other critics were then detained without trial. Several hundred people were murdered by troops, including doctors, teachers, and a religious leader. The foreign embassies started to withdraw again, and all political activity was banned for two years.

There is room for another memorial plaque on the cathedral walls. It might bear the archbishop's reproach: "What we have become, you made us."

NOTES

1. In fact, despite its attempts at independence, the Amin regime relied on Northern assistance from beginning to end. The British government, according to Rolf Steiner in *The Last Adventurer* (London: Weidenfeld, 1978), helped to arrange the coup that brought Amin to power. The British and Israeli governments both offered considerable aid to Amin in the early days of his regime when some of the worst tribal massacres were taking place. After Amin had expelled the British Asians (and the Israelis), he continued to receive regular economic and military assistance from British, American, French, and Kenyan private companies. He also received military and police assistance from the Palestine Liberation Organization and (when it suited them) from the Libyan, Russian, East German, Yugoslav, and Pakistani governments. Without this assistance from both of the Northern ideological

camps his "reign of terror," which is usually depicted as an exercise in African barbarism, would have been very much less effective.

2. This occasion even tempted the London *Times* into carrying a four-page advertising supplement on behalf of the Ugandan government drawing attention to "the Pleasures of Tourism in Uganda." It made no mention of the various government murder bureaus. Sadly the *Times* had still not received payment for this supplement several years later.

3. Henry Kyemba, *State of Blood* (Corgi, 1977).

4. The London *Sun* (owned by Mr. Rupert Murdoch).

5. This rumor also turned out to be untrue. No mention of syphilis was found in Amin's medical records after the liberation of Kampala.